To Katie,
with

"EVERLASTING LOVE" AND LOVE AFFAIR

from Patricia x

[signature]

EVERLASTING LOVE AND LOVE AFFAIR

*A Pop Idol's Life and Secret Romance
in the Swinging 60s*

PATRICIA JACKSON

FONTHILL

Certain names have been altered for the sake of privacy.

www.fonthillmedia.com
office@fonthillmedia.com

First published in the United Kingdom
and the United States of America 2022

British Library Cataloguing in Publication Data:
A catalogue record for this book is available from the British Library

Typeset in 10.5pt on13pt Sabon
Printed and bound in England

MIX
Paper from
responsible sources
FSC® C013056

Prologue

I think your writing style's quite good Patricia, a little bit like Bill Bryson's, but what's really good, are the bits about me.

Mick Jackson bass guitarist in the Love Affair, 1966–1971

Mick's comment, upon first hearing a snippet from this book, will ensure that I never get big headed. Note that I said hearing, not reading, I don't think he will ever bother to actually read it. When I happened to mention, that practically all of this book has been written in the dark, either early in the morning or late at night, he simply replied, 'Well, that explains a lot.' Those cheeky, humorous observations are some of the reasons why I've continued loving him since we met in 1966 when I was a bespeckled, shy, fourteen-year-old who thought that exciting lives only belonged to other people. It is also the year he told me that he thought the newly released 'Here there and Everywhere' by the Beatles should be 'our song'. He has, however, gone one step further, and although his compliments are rare, I think you'll agree, they don't come much bigger or lovelier than this song he has written especially for me—as long as you ignore that it is actually a blues song!

SIXTH FORM LOVESICK BLUES
Written, sung and recorded by Mick Jackson. 2017

I was Killing time
Just searching for a line
My friend said you were alone
And I thought could I walk her home
She slew me, looked through me
We were still at school
I guess breaking all the rules
You were so pristine
And I felt kind a mean
You thrill me, you kill me
We were drinking coke
I did, you didn't smoke
We walked down the street
And I said maybe we should meet
And you said maybe, maybe

We walked hand in hand
I said I was in a band
I had to go away
But I wanted you to stay
With me forever
So that's the 6th form lovesick blues
And one more time.
And if I really had to choose
I tell you now, I'd do it all over again
Yes, I would
All over again and again
I'd do it all over again
And again, and again and again
And again, and again …

My birth wouldn't have occurred had I not been a replacement for a brother I never knew. Barry heartbreakingly died, aged eight weeks, in a former workhouse known locally as Bradford Children's Fever Hospital. I became the hopeful twinkle in my Dad's eyes, and was so eager to please, that I popped into the world, exactly one year after the tragedy.

Thanks to a fortuitous win on the football pools, just before my birth, Mum and Dad had enough money to pay for a private nursing home, impressively called Mornington Villas. It was their attempt to make sure that history did not repeat itself, so you could say I was born 'posh' even though we, as a typical Yorkshire, working-class family, were anything but. The contradiction, in terms of my arrival 'status', has benefited me throughout Mick and my fifty years of married life as I've felt at home with people from all walks of life. Position, money, or power don't impress me one iota, but kindness does.

We've experienced our own ups and downs like most people and there have been many, but that is a different story. The one you are about to read is about the ordinary and 'extraordinary' years we spent together, before finally getting married. Mick and I are like chalk and cheese, different in every way, but it works. I'm calm, he isn't. I'm always right, he's not. Oh, I've just contradicted myself already, he's like me sometimes, he must be, because he's forever saying, 'I'm always right' too.

It is said that if two people agreed all the time, then one of them isn't necessary, that must be why, because we're diametrically opposite in almost every way, Mick and I have been such a good marital team. Happily, the one thing we both agree on is:

> I tell you now, I'd do it all over again
> Yes, I would
> All over again and again
> I'd do it all over again
> And again, and again and again
> And again, and again …

Contents

	Prologue	5
1	What Was Below His Waist?	11
2	The Beatles	21
3	Butlins Beckons	26
4	A Cockney Curse and Liverpudlian Elvis Presley	34
5	The Marquee	44
6	Dedicated Follower of Fashion	55
7	Jailed for Climbing Eros	61
8	Belfast	68
9	I Move to London	77
10	Her Majesty's Mini-skirted Tax Officer	83
11	Düsseldorf—Battle of the Beans	87
12	Home Alone at Christmas	92
13	Passively Smoking Pot	98
14	Mick Exposes the Pop Industry's Biggest Cover-up	102
15	Ronnie Scott and 'Igginbottom	111
16	A Terrifying Night Near Elstree Studio	119
17	No Minister	126
18	Frankenstein's Mother-in-law	129
19	Carnaby Street	136
20	Please Do *Not* Keep this Secret to Yourself	139
21	Anyone Can Disappear for a Grand	145
22	Hanging Out with the Who	147

23   A Tragic Encounter   154
24   The Love Affair Were Not Easy on Scott Walker   159
25   Shoulder to Shoulder with Steve Marriot   163
26   My Girlfriend's Not My Girlfriend   166
27   An American Dream Shattered   171
28   Our Wedding   183

Appendix: The Love Affair's Discography   190

1

What Was Below His Waist?

Little did I know when I married the bass player of the Love Affair, the youngest group ever to make it to the top of the UK charts with 'Everlasting Love', that the title would be so prophetic for us, and fifty years later we'd celebrate our golden wedding—but we have. Mick, along with Steve Ellis (one of the most iconic, English singers of the '60s), Lynton Guest and Morgan Fisher (who later joined Mott the Hoople and played keyboard for Queen), Mo Bacon (drummer), and Rex Brayley (lead guitar), were all members of a group that was almost as popular here and the rest of Europe as the Beatles. When the Love Affair first appeared on *Top of the Pops*, they were achieving their boyhood ambitions that they shared with almost every other wannabe youth on the planet. They couldn't have dreamt that one day, their song would not only become a classic, but would be played at thousands of weddings, used in scores of television programmes including a currently very popular British one, called *First Dates*, and accompany Bridget Jones in *The Edge of Reason*.

Not only did Coca-Cola and McDonalds jump on that bandwagon when they chose it for their advertising, the very latest passenger is Sir Kenneth Branagh for his highly acclaimed new film *Belfast*.

Mick is one of the rare '60s pop stars to have had such a long-lasting marriage and maybe even unique, in that he and I were together before he was in a famous group and are still living happily together now. There were many highlights for Mick during those heady days, which now seem like another lifetime ago, but he's never forgotten the thrill that even the most famous of stars must feel whenever they are before an audience. One such occasion was when the group were playing at a concert in Constance, a small valley town, on the border of Italy, Germany, and France. It was a twenty-four-hour, non-stop festival and there were many bands appearing, but of course in true '60s style, because he really was there, Mick doesn't remember every group that played, other than the Small Faces, Free, and the Edgar Broughton Band. However, he does vividly recall being ushered by roadies, from backstage where the air was heavy with the smell of hash, patchouli oil, and Brut aftershave, onto the huge, wooden stage that throbbed beneath his favourite, comfy, desert boots.

His ear drums vibrated in unison with the floor as they were assaulted by the electrical buzz coming from nearby stacks of amplifiers and speaker cabinets. The immense heat and smell that poured from them, created a great feeling of anticipation in his stomach, and the sweat that only trickled down his face at first, ended up like a torrential river that cascaded down his neck and back, drenching his T-shirt.

His fingers automatically placed themselves in the correct position on his guitar in readiness of playing the bass riff of 'Everlasting Love', one of the most memorable, instantly recognisable, that there has ever been. It was such a relief to Mick that his fingers knew what they were doing, as any conscious effort from him was impossible because he was overwhelmed by the onslaught of pleasurable feelings to each of his five senses. Almost as if someone else was playing them, Mick describes how those first nine notes sent shock waves throughout his body, just as effectively as any explosion. He says that even the loudest jet engine would struggle to exert a more intense pressure, than that, hitting his back during those first few seconds. At that precise moment, the gigantic rumble of thousands of people filled the open air as they screamed, applauded and whistled. The group could not only sense, but almost taste the euphoria, that was simultaneously experienced by their audience. The love emanating from the crowd was as near perfect as the then, popular mantra, 'Peace brother, peace.'

I'm afraid I've jumped the gun, I should really have begun at the beginning of our story, so I will retrace my steps and do just that.

1966 may have been the year that England won the World Cup, but as I'm not the least bit interested in football, for me it's memorable solely as the year that Mick and I met. However, it wasn't the chance meeting I thought it was—from his point of view, it was a blind date. I was fourteen and he'd just turned seventeen. I was in the Continental coffee bar, in the centre of Bradford, with my friend Linda—she'd recently split up with her boyfriend Geoff, who was in the same form as Mick, at Hanson Grammar School. During that morning's assembly, Geoff confided to Mick that he wanted to get back together with Linda—there was, however, one big gooseberry problem: me. Geoff knew that Linda and I would be there, so in order that he could win her back, he asked Mick if he would talk to me, suggesting that maybe we could become an item too. Mick agreed, but not before checking out if 'Pat' was worth getting to know. I am flattered to report that he received a positive reply, as apparently, I was.

I was a pupil at Bolling Grammar School, educational home to 700 girls and I was therefore unused to the opposite sex, apart from my brother Brian, and a platonic friendship with a boy who'd asked me out, three months previously. Truth be known, that had the loveable children's book character, Worzel Gummidge, got in first and offered me a date, I think I would have accepted—even though he was a scarecrow. I was simply desperate to find out if I was pretty enough to be someone's, anyone's girlfriend. Most of my peers had already started dating, at least they said they had, and I was beginning to think that I might be left on the shelf.

By the time Linda and I entered the Continental, Mick was sitting at a table talking to Geoff. I instantly liked him and had no idea that the two of them had been plotting earlier. My man of few words failed to tell me this rather relevant bit of information until we had been married for several years. I was curious to see that two full Coke bottles were fizzing away in front of the empty seats at their table, but it didn't dawn on me that they were bait, intended to snare my best friend back into Geoff's life. Geoff had bought them, his way of not only impressing Linda, but ensuring that we would have to sit down and join them out of politeness. It worked and Geoff immediately started flirting once more with Linda, whilst I sat hesitatingly next to Mick who, due to his lack of words, seemed like the strong, silent type.

Mick nonchalantly took a gold packet of ten Benson & Hedges out of his jeans pocket and a shiny lighter out of the other, before offering one to me. I said no, because I'd never smoked, apart from the time when I was four when my older brother, Brian, persuaded me to take a puff from a cigarette he'd made with tobacco from tab ends he found on the street, and a crumpled Rizla paper that he'd 'borrowed' from our uncle. I watched Mick, with interest, as he slowly drew a ciggie out of the packet and placed it ever so slightly offside, between his lips. He flicked open the

Zippo with his left thumb before using it to spin the splint wheel in one continuous movement. After lighting up, he inhaled deeply, and held his breath for a millisecond before finally closing the lid causing it to click distinctively, at the precise moment he started blowing smoke into the already smoke filled room. I thought that action, made him look so cool and sophisticated, like one of the many film stars Linda and I had seen at the pictures when they did exactly the same. If he ever did read this, he'd be surprised by that comment as he's always said he thought I was aloof and uninterested during those first few minutes. My nose may have looked as though it was in the air, but it was a cover up for the butterflies in my stomach that I swear were wearing hob nailed boots.

Smoking gave Mick something to do with his hands whilst I nervously wondered what to do with mine, but at least the pauses in our stilted conversation were not that pregnant as, thanks to the juke box, they were filled in by the music that was constantly playing.

'When a Man Loves a Woman', by Percy Sledge, never ceases to transport me back to that night. Music really is magical; it can instantly remind us of a specific time in our lives the moment we hear certain songs. I never tired of hearing the Mindbenders' 'Groovy Kind of Love', 'My Girl' by Otis Redding, or Paul Jones singing 'Pretty Flamingo'. Mick told me that he was a bass player in a group called the Spell and once he started talking about them, he became more confident and animated, whilst I remained unconfident but fascinated. It was surprising how long we could make one drink last, as Mick didn't offer to buy another. I only had my bus fare home and enough money for one bottle, but even if I could, I wouldn't have dreamt of offering to pay for his, as unfair as it sounds now, boys were expected to pick up the tab.

Mick was a sixth former, well at least school described him as one; in truth he hardly went, so I simply thought he didn't have much money either. It's a good job my dad, Richard, a master plumber and publican, wasn't there as, in his eyes, real men paid their round, but we weren't in our pub, and it was Mick's way of keeping his promise to Geoff, by getting me out of the way as soon as he could. When Mick drained the last dregs of coke from his bottle, I couldn't do the same because my straw had had so much twirling and squeezing, that the ends were sticking together. Had I tried to suck up those last few drops, the noise would have made me resemble a three-year-old, not a good look for a teenager doing her best to appear sophisticated, despite forgetting to not annoyingly twiddle with her hair. My curfew time was fast approaching and feeling as panicky as Cinderella not to be late, I was dismayed that for several seconds, that seemed like minutes, Mick didn't stand up when I did. I mistook his lack of words as disinterest not realising that he wasn't as self-assured as he looked, but when he did, I was momentarily shocked by what was below his waist.

He was wearing pointed winkle pickers and tight jeans. Oh no! he was a rocker, and I was a mod, at least, that is, I tried to convince myself I was, and although I fell in love with Cliff Richard when I was six, I much preferred the Beatles, Small Faces, Who, and Kinks as opposed to rockers' favourites, Billy Fury, Chuck Berry, Gene Vincent, or Eddie Cochran. I thought deafening motorbike engines and leather jackets adorned with studs, spikes, and chains were intimidating, so ex-army Parka's with furry bits and quieter scooters were much more to my liking. Dolly-bird magnet, Vespas looked good and were economical doing 110 miles to the gallon, and their rival marque, Lambretta, gained even more attention when their SX 150 was advertised as having S.X appeal.

Bank Holiday clashes between mods and rockers had made it seem dangerous for opposing members to go out. The newspapers exaggerated the stories, feeding the myth that rockers and mods could never peacefully meet, and I believed that. However, that didn't deter me from fancying Mick any more than the conspicuous cigarette burn in his grey jumper did. Truth be known, if need be, I would have changed camps for him, in a blink of my false eyelashes.

In those few seconds, possibly the longest of my life, I thought that he wouldn't cross the line and be interested in a mod emulator in her green leather jacket and homemade black velvet choker. I was wearing something else too, of course, it's just that I can't remember exactly what.

I was wrong, Mick wasn't a rocker and wouldn't have cared less that I decided to copy mod icons, such as Cathy McGowan who fronted Friday night's 'Ready, Steady, Go' in her original Mary Quant clothes. The show's theme tune, 5-4-3-2-1 by Manfred Mann instantly makes me feel fourteen again,

Finally taking my eyes off Mick's two-inch heeled boots, instead of saying good-bye like I thought he was about to, Mick was pointing to the way out and then himself, and I realised that he was suggesting that he left with me.

The next bit was terrifying to a fledgling teenager trying to appear in control and nonchalant. He guided me towards the exit that was at the top of open tread stairs, and his gentlemanly 'ladies first' offer, meant this ultra-coy girl had to walk up the steps, with him following behind. I wished that I'd put my jeans on, but because I hadn't and was wearing a mini skirt I gained brownie points without realising.

As Mick wasn't a rocker, he didn't have a motorbike outside or anything else for that matter, except shanks pony. He didn't own anything, apart from his guitar, so no one could accuse me of being after his money. The bright evening outside was an extreme contrast to the darkness we'd just left, and I felt exposed knowing that the flattering light in the basement was no longer hiding any imperfections in my skin. It's torturous being a teenager when a spot feels like a mountain, thank goodness maturity does have at least two advantages, more confidence, less pimples. I needn't have worried because Mick offered to walk me to my bus stop, and we took our first steps of billions together. Maybe over romantic, I know, but the first paving stone that we stepped on together is still there to this day; I'd love to dig it up and give it pride of place in our garden.

I think Mick would approve, providing I promised not to put my cherished garden gnome on top. By way of explanation, the gnome, hand painted by my dad, shortly before he died, and a toby jug I now own were, according to him, tongue in cheek, his 'only' possessions. In all honesty, though, it wasn't far from the truth—he wasn't materialistic, and neither am I.

Mick grabbed my hand to guide me across the road, a convenient excuse to take it, as we walked to the other side of town. He asked if he could see me again and when I said yes he pulled out his well-thumbed diary to see when he could fit me in. He explained that as well as playing bass, he was the Spell's manager and needed it to keep a record of where they were playing, so even though squeezing me in wasn't exactly romantic, I was impressed and from that moment on we became Mick and Pat.

Dad said we sounded like two Irish navvies, not that he had anything against Ireland as his mum was born near Dublin and he was half Irish. I kept a diary, too, but kept mine a secret, so later that night I found a pencil and wrote: 'Met ? he's gorgeous I really want to get to know him better'. Amazingly, at the same time I was writing this, Mick was telling his mum, Madge, that he'd met the girl he was going to marry. Maybe because he's of Romany descent he's clairvoyant, but even if he isn't, his prediction came true. It wasn't until the next day when I was sure that his name really was Mick that I rubbed out the question mark and wrote it in. We agreed to see each other the next Friday and when he asked if I'd seen a film called *The Knack*, it threw me into a panic. I thought that if I owned up and said I had, he wouldn't offer an alternative, so I pretended I hadn't, and we arranged to meet outside W. H. Smiths.

Although I'd previously been going around with Tim, the boy who got in before Worzel did, sweet though he was, I didn't view him as a boyfriend but was flattered he showed an interest in me, and Mick was therefore my first proper date. I realised that although I liked Tim it could never have been anything more than a platonic relationship and I'm embarrassed to admit that it was mainly his Del Boy vehicle that enticed me to keep meeting him outside school.

The other girls seemed greener than our bottle uniforms whenever it appeared, you would have thought it was a Ferrari and although it was one wheel short of a proper car, we were all impressed that Tim owned it. Their envious reaction went some way towards making me feel a little more self-worth which was great because in truth I had none, but our time together was short-lived and ended when I faced up to the fact that I wasn't romantically attracted to him. We were going nowhere, apart from up and down the streets in a rattling Reliant Robin, so I asked him not to collect me anymore. Tim had the last laugh, however, when the next day as I was walking through the centre of Bradford to catch my second bus home, his pride and joy went screeching past me. Tim had another girl in the passenger seat, but he wasn't the fast mover that he appeared to be. I learnt that she was his real girlfriend and they had been going out for a couple of years. But now that Mick was asking me out, the earlier humiliation I'd felt when I saw Tim with another girl became instant, indifferent history and there were no hard feelings from my point of view. That short, sharp shock probably served me right for being so shallow minded, in seeing him simply because he had four wheels, sorry I mean three.

When Friday finally arrived, it took me most of the day to get ready and at long last, seconds after our arranged time I walked towards Mick as he waited patiently outside the shop. I attempted to look confident, something I was anything but, and just as I was a couple of feet away, several huge raindrops slid down the shop's overhead canopy and straight into my eyes. The running eyeliner made me look like a panda. Even worse, the water had loosened the glue on my false eyelashes that had detached themselves at the inner corners, causing me to blink madly in an anything but flirtatious way. I tried desperately to pretend nothing had happened, despite stinging eyes that were quickly turning pink. I must have looked horrendous but with hindsight Mick was probably more concerned with how he looked, so he didn't even notice. Nothing has changed much, as an experiment I wore a new coat recently without saying anything, to see if he'd even notice. I'll leave you to your own conclusion. Moments later, as we were struggling to find something to say, a pigeon flying over our heads decided to leave a good luck present on Mick's head. There was no way we could pretend it hadn't happened and were both so shocked yet amused and our feathered friend broke the ice far quicker than the sharpest arrow shot by cupid ever could, and as an added bonus my tears of laughter washed away the smudged eye makeup. I have never thought about it until just now, but who knows, had it not been for that bird, conversation may have remained awkward, and we may have had a different impression of each other. Mick might not have got his diary out for me ever again. I really should have thanked our feathered friend for possibly changing the course of our lives. If we'd been in a reverse position and my head had been the target, it would have been just too much. I would have probably given up, made a hasty retreat from a disastrous first date, lashes flapping no more as they slid down red cheeks, wet with tears of yet another humiliation. That would have been the end of the beginning. However, we made it to the film during which Mick, trying to be both impressive and helpful at the same time, gave me a running commentary of what was happening, not knowing that I knew just as much as he did.

The next night, he was playing at Stone Chair Club, Halifax, which seemed a long way away then, and asked if I would like to go along to watch. The distance didn't deter me at all, I didn't need asking twice, so I eagerly accepted. Little did I realise that part of the deal was that I had to travel there with his mum, Madge, who, of course, I hadn't met, and stepdad Albert. The group needed to set up before I'd even finished my Saturday job, so it was impossible for us to go there together.

I can hardly believe that I did go through with it, but I did, as I would have done anything to see Mick, including having to introduce myself to his mum and family. The plan was that I would go straight from work, have tea with his parents and go in their car to the club, where his brother David and another Pat, his wife, would be waiting. In the rush to get ready for work that morning, I'd forgotten my makeup and had to ask if I could borrow some from Madge; my desperation to impress my new boyfriend was even greater than the discomfort I felt in asking her. Her foundation for mature skin was too bright for my complexion, but I couldn't throw kindness back at her so continued to apply the vivid liquid. I needn't have worried, though, as Mick must have been getting used to my messy makeup—that is, of course, if he even noticed my orange, clown-like face.

Embarrassment with a capital 'E' was yet to come that evening. I walked into the club and there was Mick, singing away, I thought he looked so attractive, dressed in a blue shirt that suited him perfectly.

The Spell was a very apt name, as I was certainly spellbound, so much so that I almost didn't notice my tell-tale stomach-ache. David's Pat said she was going to the ladies and asked if I would like to go with her, I was so pleased because I knew I needed to get some Tampax from the vending machine.

Later in our relationship, Michael loved to tell me a joke about the little boy who after seeing an advert for Tampax, went into a chemist and asked for a packet and when the pharmacist asked him why he was buying them, the reply was 'because the lady on the telly said you can swim and ride a bike with them, and I can't do either'.

Because I didn't have any coins, I had no option other than to ask Pat and therefore bring her into my confidence, at least I thought I had. Of course, I didn't ask her to sign a confidential agreement, so she was perfectly entitled to later tell David anything she wished, and she did, and for some reason he decided to tell Mick. Thinking that my embarrassing experience was only between Pat and I and that was bad enough, it was only at the end of the night that Mick admitted he knew of my earlier predicament and asked if I was OK. I wished the ground would open and swallow me there and then. Because I was only fourteen I thought it was far, far worse than the eyelashes and Panda eyes, especially as I didn't think he would even know about such things; in my book it was a taboo subject and now my secret was known, not only to Pat but to Mick, his brother, and who knows, even Madge and Albert. I was absolutely mortified and felt like hiding and had I done so there's every chance I'd still be there.

I naturally hoped that our third date would be without incidence, after all third time is supposed to be lucky, but my wish was dashed when embarrassment decided to accompany me on that date too. We'd arranged to meet outside C&A, a clothes store that was very popular but even so, no one seemed to know what the letters stood for—probably not 'coats and 'ats' as many jokers claimed; however, it didn't matter one jot as it was a great place to find the latest teenage clothes.

Mick was waiting for me, and I could sense him watching me as I got nearer. Attempting to at least look sophisticated, I tried to walk like Sophia Loren, and I was doing OK until I realised something was making it hard to walk as my legs couldn't stride out. Glancing down I was shocked to see that my belt had slid down from my waist and was slowly slipping to the floor via my thighs. Hoping against hope that Mick hadn't noticed, I stopped, put my knees together, and let it drop to the pavement. Too humiliated to pick it up, I stepped over it and carried on as if nothing had happened.

Mick was polite and because he didn't say anything at first, I thought I'd got away with it, but well into our date he couldn't resist telling me he had, and we couldn't stop laughing as I'd relaxed enough by then to see the funny side. The fact that he'd initially spared my blushes made me like him even more. However, to this day, he still tells people it was my knickers that fell to the floor, but thankfully he's simply embellishing the tale for effect, and it was definitely only my belt.

PS: In case you are wondering, Linda and Geoff's romance remained in 1966, never to be reignited.

2

The Beatles

One night, after Mick and I had been to the Continental, we were late leaving, and had to run across town to try and get to my ten o'clock bus. Even though I'd be in big trouble if I was late, it was more important to me to try and look good and that's not easy when you're trying to run at four miles an hour when you can only do two.

We were almost there and gasping for breath, my face had turned redder than a baby's bottom with nappy rash. To make matters worse, one of my loosely tied black and white 'magpie' shoes decided to fly off my feet. The seconds retrieving it, meant I hadn't time to put it back on, so I hopped towards the bus just as it pulled away. All I could do was stare at the back of it, as the driver had no intention of slowing down to let me get on. It was game over, I thought I was going to get into massive trouble when I eventually got home, but I was wrong. Mick phoned Dad to apologise saying that I had just missed the bus and would be on the next one. Far from being cross, he couldn't get over how polite Mick was, so my new boyfriend went straight into his good books when, let's face it, it could have taken Dad quite some time before he felt positive about a boy going out with his young daughter—especially one who had no intention of getting a proper job, only of becoming a pop star.

I can't remember Mick ever going to school, how he got away with it I don't know, but in that respect he was a bad influence on me as I started to miss school myself so that I could be with him. We were happy in our own little bubble but playing truant didn't bode well as far as my exams were concerned. I was meant to be studying for my GCE O Levels, but my first priority was to be with Mick. I guess with hindsight, that wasn't a bad thing, as my future was destined to be with him, so that time was well invested after all. I became an expert at copying my mum's signature so I could forge excuse notes, the teachers must have thought I was a very sickly pupil. My parents really took to Mick, and sometimes during school holidays we would join them on days out. They didn't realise that we had stopped waiting for official holidays to enjoy many of our own exclusive, weekdays off.

Dad was never a confident driver, something I've inherited from him, and was doing a steady 43 miles per hour on the York Road to Scarborough when he was pulled over for speeding. We were in a 40-mph zone, it was the first and last time he was booked, in all the years he drove. You know, saying that I inherited my lack of driving confidence from Dad has just made me realise it's probably nothing to do with him at all, more likely Mick. Several years after our day trip to Scarborough when we were married, Mick gave me lessons before my fourth driving test, but his unique method was to whack me over the head with his newspaper, because he got so frustrated with me. Unconventional I know, and even though a husband teaching his wife is a terrible idea if they want to remain married, we survived—just. He literally hammered the lessons home as nobody else could or dared. I didn't find it funny at the time, no surprise there then, but I swear I wouldn't have a licence now if not for his persistence, I can't say patience unfortunately. Thanks to him, I'm a whizz at hill starts and can reverse around corners quite well, it's just the actual driving bit that's still a problem.

Once we reached Scarborough, my parents, in their usual busman's holiday way that they insisted was research, headed for the nearest pub, but this time Dad had a valid reason, that first pint would steady his nerves after his one and only run in with the law.

I'm making them sound like alcoholics, but they weren't, in fact apart from the odd Babycham and brandy if she was really pushing the boat out, Mum didn't drink at all. Dad limited himself to about three pints, unlike many Yorkshiremen, including David, who could get through eight or nine pints with no problem. Amazingly, most of them could still walk in a straight line, so you'd hardly know, apart from the odd slurred word at best or a complete inability to speak at worse. They thought nothing of getting in their cars afterwards so they could just about drive home t' wife.

Mum and Dad were happy to split up from Mick and me for a while so we could be alone. We climbed towards Scarborough Castle before sitting down on some grass to admire the view. Oblivious to what was about to come, I continued to chatter away to Mick only to be stopped mid-sentence when he handed me a note. I tentatively opened the folded paper worrying what he had written, was this the end? Had my incessant talking put him off? Was he wanting to finish with me? For once lost for words, I felt the blood rush from my face and my heartbeat was so loud that I thought my heart was about burst out of my chest as it rose up and down so quickly I could hardly breathe. I read his distinctive, large handwriting and it sent me into an even greater panic and this one was off the Richter scale. Far from wanting to end our relationship, he said he wanted to stay with me forever and although I felt the same, I was still only fifteen. My sensible head would have told me that I was far too young to contemplate anything of the sort, let alone a lifelong commitment, but I wasn't wearing it. Had my heart really burst out of my chest seconds earlier it wouldn't have made any difference as it didn't belong to me anymore, Mick stole it the moment I began to read his words.

How I wish I had kept that note but I threw it away, fearful that my parents might see it. We decided to go down to the beach where we saw something shiny in the sand. It was a plastic diamond ring probably discarded by someone who'd won it in an amusement arcade. Was it a sign that, sensible head or not, fate had decided that our future was to be spent together? Mick picked it up and although he jokingly pushed it on my engagement finger, we both seriously hoped it was. The highlight of the '60s for me, if you exclude meeting Mick and all that followed, was seeing the Beatles playing in Bradford at the Gaumont theatre 1964. It was one of the biggest picture houses in England when it was built in the '30s and had over 3,000 seats. It was John Lennon's twenty-fourth birthday and Beatlemania had arrived. Mick was there too, but because it was two years before we met, and we didn't know each other. The group travelled from London and although a traffic jam made them two hours late, they made it just in time for their two sets. I went to the first one, but Mick can't remember when he went so we don't know if we were in the building at the same time, maybe even feet from one another. From my seat, John, Paul, George, and Ringo looked about half an inch tall and it was impossible to hear them because of all the screaming. Even the minute image of them was intermittent, as everyone stood on their seats making it a real struggle to see over the shoulders of the person in front.

Mick made me laugh when he described going to the show with his friend, Eric. Mick turned towards him to gesticulate just how crazy he thought all the girls were, only to find his friend bouncing up and down on his seat, screaming, 'John, John,' as loud, if not louder, than they were.

'I'm Happy Just to Dance with You', 'If I Fell', and 'I Should Have Known Better' were all numbers that they played, but as we couldn't hear anything, they could have played 'The Wheels on the Bus,' and no one would have been any the wiser. I remember the girl next to me almost fainting, and I was distracted trying to help her. Much as I loved the Beatles, I didn't feel dizzy at all—I realised that the whole thing was mass hysteria and the girls who passed out, did so because that is what they expected to happen; it was a self-fulfilling prophecy. There was also an awful lot of kidding going on. The canniest fans realised that if they were 'rescued' and laid in the wings, they had a better chance of meeting their idols. They pretended to lose consciousness so that they could miraculously 'recover' if they came within inches of the fab four. It really was an amazing night and although the group were frustrated at not being able to hear themselves play, they must also have felt elated as the last time they'd appeared on that same stage, they were bottom of the bill supporting Helen Shapiro. They managed to escape from the thousands of teenagers around the theatre and headed for Halifax. Their road manager was a friend of Freddie and Rita Pearson who owned a country club there, called 'the Cavalier'. It was the ideal place for the Beatles to spend the night because the fans would have easily invaded any of the hotels in the centre of town. They did once stay at the Midland Hotel in Bradford, but it was before they were world famous and there wasn't a problem.

A police escort ensured that they were safely taken to the manor house. Its sheltered situation was perfect, and it was only a short journey. The owners and their family had been sworn to secrecy and, consequently, fans didn't know where they were staying, so they were left in peace. The two single beds that were slept in by John and Ringo are still there to this day, complete with their brass bedsteads. Subsequent guests have taken knobs off of them as souvenirs, so they have often been replaced, the originals long since gone. Luckily, the beds are too big to fit in a suitcase, otherwise they would probably have vanished many times over as well. Their restaurant bill was about £17, the equivalent of more than one week's average pay. The framed receipt for that meal of prawn cocktail and melon, smoked trout and turtle soup, steak and duckling is proudly displayed in reception and has been read by many Beatles fans, curious to learn about that special night. There's no mention of dessert, but as it was past midnight before they started eating, that's hardly surprising.

Even though it was John's birthday he went to bed first, leaving the other three in the bar, because he had toothache. That decaying tooth was no respecter of the fact that it resided in what would become one of the most famous mouths in pop history and was causing him agony. Fortunately, the hotel's resident ghost was more empathetic and respectfully controlled any urge to haunt him, otherwise it could have been more than just dental pain that kept the famous birthday boy awake on that wonderful night, well at least I thought it was wonderful, unlike poor Mr Lennon.

3

Butlins Beckons

Mick and I spent every waking moment we could together during the first few months after we met, and they were lovely but were cut brutally short after we'd been out one Friday night. I'd only been home a few minutes when Mick phoned me to say that he'd had a phone call from a group called the Beat Squad and they wanted him to join them immediately to play at Butlins, Filey, for the summer season. Mick didn't know them, but as they came from Keighley and the Spell had just played at Ryshworth Club a quarter of a mile away, it wasn't difficult to work out where they'd seen him play. To be asked to join them professionally, especially at Butlins, where so many famous entertainers and musicians had started out, was an offer he knew he couldn't refuse, so there was only one answer he could give. The phone call turned out to be one of the most important he ever received, as it was the first step towards him realising his dream of becoming a pop star.

Mick's ambition had been dampened up until that point because he was forever trying to persuade the rest of the Spell to turn professional, but at that time, the others were home birds and got cold feet whenever he mentioned it. For someone to phone him out of the blue, especially someone he didn't even know was amazing and too big an opportunity to turn down.

When they said immediately, it was no exaggeration as they asked him to set off the next morning. Fortunately, Bob, who was the Spell's road manager, was free and although he was sad that an era was about to end, he was happy to drive Mick to the holiday camp. There was no time to say goodbye to me in person, and I was beyond distraught. I cried all through the night and the next morning, my eyes resembled those of a boxer who had just gone ten rounds in a boxing match and lost. I looked so awful that there was no way that I could go to my Saturday job at Stringers bookstall, in Kirkgate Market, as I would have scared the customers. My eyes didn't have any whites left because they were completely red and the skin below them was even more puffy than my lids. I was right to be so upset because it would be another six years before we would finally be permanently together, as Mick didn't return to Yorkshire until we got married, so I learnt to be patient and waited.

When Mick broke the news that he was going to Butlins in Filey, I knew the holiday camp well because I went there for a holiday, only the year before, with Linda and her family. Seeing how upset I was and to cheer me up, my parents, who needed little excuse for a holiday, promised to take me there again with Linda and they kept their word.

The Beat Squad had their work cut out and deserved every penny they earned as they had to play for three solid hours during the afternoon and after a short break were back in the Sportsman's Bar for another boozy four hours every night. Mick's fingers must have got very tired!

Most campers left their worries at home and flung themselves into having a good time, they were a great and generous audience and lined up pint after pint after pint for the boy's, it's a wonder Mick, being the youngest, could stand up at the end of the night, let alone sing and play. There was a limit to just how much they could sensibly drink and even though there were plenty of volunteers to help 'get rid' of the extra pints, an awful lot was thrown down the sink. I think the calories in that beer must have kept Mick going though, as he can only remember having one meal a day. He called it breakfast but when he told me that it was always the same, two eggs and spaghetti on toast, which he ate in the campers dining hall, I thought it was strange to have pasta for breakfast until it dawned on me. He was right in that it was his breakfast but to everyone else in the camp it would have been lunchtime, hence the spaghetti. Even though I doubted at first that he only had the one meal, it was probably right and was the start of him losing weight. When I first met him, he was 11 stone but by the time we were married, only 9.

Holiday makers stayed in chalets that were about the same size as our garden hut and most only had a sink and the toilet block was usually some distance away. Mick remembers one such block was quite luxurious in that it had four big baths, but there was never any hot water, so his daily dip was cold.

People had to take their own toiletries but as Mick didn't have any, he always managed to find scraps of soap that campers left behind, using them to wash his hair too, surprising really as his hair always looked healthy and shiny. He had to get used to doing Sunday afternoon theatre matinees, something he'd never done before. It was good practice for the future, in fact the whole experience was, but he wasn't thrilled at having to put thick face makeup on that made even Madge's bright orange foundation look pale.

I didn't see much of him because Linda and I were too young to go into the bar without an adult. It wouldn't have been fair on Linda anyway, to spend all our time there as I'm sure it would have made her feel like the gooseberry I was the night I met Mick. Instead, we spent every night we could dancing in the ballroom to the Timebox, from Southport. They played great Tamla Motown numbers, 'Under the Boardwalk', 'This Old Heart of Mine', and 'Dancing in the Street', and were, I swear, every bit as good as the originals.

I didn't like rowdy pubs, anyway, especially as I lived in one, but I think that first came about because when I was little, we used to visit my Uncle Wilf and Auntie Gladys, in Barnsley, who spent their time looking after pigeons, eating, and socialising 'in't club.' The first two I liked, but the third I hated.

Side tracking here slightly, auntie's nephew, David Bradley, was plucked out of oblivion when film producers visited his school and chose him for the main role in the now classic *Kes* by Ken Roach. I felt so proud of him as he was extended family, after all. Ken Roach's method, of making sure David's performance was the best it could be, was cruel but worked. In a caning scene, David was told that the camera would pause just before the cane hit his hand. The look of pain on Billy Casper's (David's) face was genuine, as the shrewd director knew that no matter how good David was at acting, his portrayal of pain would never be as convincing as the real thing, so he lied—and the thwack was real.

Something I really like about Barnsley is that no matter how distant a relation you are, you are still family and referred to as 'our'. I loved being called 'our Pat' by everyone there, it always gave me a feeling of belonging. I've never thought about it before, but I guess that entitles me to call the '60s star, 'our David'.

While on the subject of actors, when I was at infants' school, I liked a boy in my class called Simon Rouse. Simon is now known to millions

as the 'old school' cop in the television series *The Bill*. It wasn't until
recently that I realised that he'd done so well, as I never watched the
programme. I must have had good taste even then; I'm pleased that he
has made such a success of his life.

While I'm name dropping, I may as well make it a hat-trick, but this
time can't make any claim to have known Charlie Watts, drummer with
the Rolling Stones. It was rumoured that he used to visit my Nana's next
door neighbour and when I first asked Nana if she had ever seen one
of the Stones next door, she thought I was talking about the contents
of their garden. I don't think she ever did see him and neither did I, so
it's probably not true but what a small world if it is. Oh, that has just
reminded me of another neighbour, when Brian asked her if she liked
Acker Bilk, a traditional jazz clarinettist in the '50s, she told him she
didn't know as she had never had any!

Mick didn't view Butlins through the same pink-tinted glasses that I
did, and cynically called it Butlitz. The standing joke among the staff
was that the blue coats and barbed wire were there not to prevent people
getting in, but to prevent them getting out.

Linda had a new boyfriend by the time we went there with Mum and
Dad, called Norman, and we had to do a double take when we saw him
as we were walking towards the dining hall. He, and his friend Clive,
never told us how they got in, maybe they'd tunnelled under the barbed
wire? If they had, it was miraculous, as security was as tight as Colditz
Castle, minus only its searchlights and guns. However, they'd probably
did what other day visitors did and paid, but even so they had taken the
trouble to travel 70 miles to get there and that in itself impressed Linda
and me.

We took them to the Hawaiian Bar we thought it was sophisticated
because it had plastic palm trees and played Hawaiian huha music—not
really, I've just looked it up—it was hula—I was close, not bad really,
seeing it was so long ago and after all, it's not something you hear every
day. It was dark in there, and if Norman and Clive really had been
fugitives, the fact that it hadn't succumbed to blue lights that made
anything white stand out, it would have been the perfect choice, as
the last thing two young men on the run would have needed was to be
fluorescent. I'm pleased to say that this time Linda's relationship didn't
remain in the '60s as she ended up marrying Norman.

The holiday camp was next to a long stretch of beach, Mick and I
never went there as he had so little spare time, but only four years earlier
I was on those sands with Dad making sandcastles with my bucket and

spade. I was ten and perhaps a bit old for such things but Dad's mantra when I was little was 'Seven years on the sands' but we both enjoyed it so much, that we went way past that, as neither of us wanted to stop digging together, in the end I'm not sure who was humouring who.

Mick must have had plenty of time to miss me, in between the rowdy performances, and I was over the moon when he told me again that he would like us to be together forever. His way of expressing his feelings was sincere, saying he wanted me to have his children, but he forgot to mention anything about getting married first! It was the closest he ever got to proposing as he never did by getting down on one knee or anything, but never mind, I couldn't have everything.

The thought of having children then, although it was way ahead in the future, sent my sensible head into a spin and even though I knew that I definitely wanted to be a mum one day. I muddled and spluttered, too inexperienced to give him a coherent answer.

Our holiday passed quickly, and Mick and I were forced to say goodbye, not knowing when we would see each other again, but at least we could do it in person this time. The journey home was awful, each mile was another mile further away from him. No doubt Mum and Dad must have wondered if they'd done the right thing taking me there, as I had to go through all the trauma again and was heartbroken for the second time in the space of a few weeks.

However, education wise it was a good thing, because I decided to do a year in the upper fifth form, knuckle down, and retake my exams. When Mick lived at home I was distracted, my mind being anywhere but on schoolwork. I spent hours sitting in on the Spell's rehearsals, and even though I did attempt to study, it was impossible to think clearly with the group belting out songs at a higher number of decibels than a Jumbo Jet, not that we had those at Leeds/Bradford Airport then, more likely just a few Dakotas. I suppose I could blame the fact that I only passed two GCE's on the Spell—nothing to do with me at all. With Mick many miles away, I had no excuse to feign illness, so I started to attend school regularly. I finally ended up with five GCE O Levels and several CSE's grade 1, the equivalent of O Levels, so that wasn't too bad I suppose, given my distracted circumstances and being the youngest in my class.

During those later terms, my attention was diverted again, because Mum became ill with acute stomach pains and it was only through my Nana's insistence that Mabel allowed the doctor to see her. She was whisked into hospital immediately as she had peritonitis, so Nana possibly saved her life, and it took my normally lively, sparkly, mum weeks to convalesce. I was given permission to go into school late, so that I could help at home and one day, being the only schoolgirl on the bus, I was asked by a man who got off at the same time as I did if I knew where the park was. I did and gave him directions and then he asked if I minded if he walked alongside me. Not knowing what to say and afraid of saying no, I said nothing, so he did anyway and far too closely.

As he continued his one-way conversation, I walked faster hoping he would get the message that I wasn't happy, but he speeded up too. He said hello to someone as they came out of a corner shop and the next thing I knew; he was exposing himself. I was so frightened that my blood flooded with adrenaline, and I sprinted to school. I dropped my pencil case in the panic but was too scared to turn back to pick it along with its scattered contents. I breathlessly told my teacher what had happened, and she called the police. It turned out that he lived opposite that corner shop. Nothing became of it, but at least I didn't have to go to court to give evidence. I wondered why, on earth, he'd done such a thing, little realising that a green gabardine coat and leather satchel were anything but unattractive to such sad characters as him. Needless to say, from that morning on, I never went into school late again, the dishes and bed making had to wait, but it was not easy to have to walk past his house every school day.

A few days into my new school term that September, Mick phoned me with yet another announcement to say that he was leaving Butlins to go to London with the Timebox. They were returning to a flat on West Kensington High Road that was rented by girls who allowed them to sleep on the floor. It was a large apartment and the Timebox saw no reason why Mick couldn't join them, even though they should perhaps have asked the girls' permission first. I was getting used to being parted by now and therefore this news wasn't as devastating as the first time he left me. I accepted that if Mick was going to achieve his ambition and make it in the music business, London was the place to do it.

The only way of communication was via letter or phone. We had a landline at home but there was no such luxury for Mick whilst sleeping like a vagrant on the flat floor. Whenever possible, he walked to the nearest phone box knowing that it couldn't be a very long conversation as he had to watch the pennies. You could hear pips after dialling a number to indicate that the phone was being answered and hearing them gave me butterflies whenever he pressed the A for answer button. Eventually, he began to reverse the charges, but we still had to keep the cost down otherwise I would have been in trouble with my parents, so the calls were frustratingly short.

I spent all my time looking forward to those brief calls that often came in the early hours of the morning and spent every night with one ear open, that doesn't sound quite right because the expression should be eye of course, but that wouldn't have helped me hear! I only slept properly once I'd either received his call or realised it wasn't coming at all. I was lucky my parents were night owls and didn't complain too much because it didn't enter Mick's head that he might be waking the entire house, as he often did, because he didn't know what day it was, let alone the time.

In those early, pre-fame, winter days, or more accurately nights, Mick had to jump up and down trying to keep warm in those icy phone boxes and felt lonely being so far away from his family. He spent many an hour walking the empty streets at night and there was no comfortable bed to go back to, the flat floor upon which he slept wasn't only hard, it shook constantly because the tube trains ran directly underneath the building.

Walking distracted him and whenever he went past a smart flat or town house he used to peer into the windows that looked cosy and inviting, but his desire to make it kept him going even when he felt like throwing in the towel and possibly even his guitar too.

A letter was inexpensive to send, and he had plenty of time to write and I began to live for those letters landing on our doormat. I often risked injury trying to get to them first because our Alsatian, Kim, got in the way as he too loved the letters but only because they were good to chew. I read and re-read Mick's large almost illegible handwriting, it's a good job that doing so had no physical detrimental effect on the ink, otherwise I would have worn it out. Mick's writing is still hard to read, and no one seems to be able to read it except me but that's only because I've had so much practice. When Mick first went to school, his teachers contributed to making his writing hard to read because he was naturally left-handed, and they forced him to use his right. Could that be because they went along with a centuries-old belief that the left-handed were children of the devil I wonder? Probably not, but in many ways that wouldn't have been too far-fetched as the school really was old school. I'd better not tell Mick about his possible connection with the devil, otherwise, knowing him he'll start chasing me around the house with an imaginary pitchfork as we've never really grown up.

It was round about that time when he was struggling to write and breaking scores of pen nibs that Mick had a play-fight with his friend, Eric, in the school cloakroom. Unknown to them, their head teacher was walking past. Pump bags flying in air and shouts of encouragement from their peers, caught Mr 'I'm So Important's' attention and they were literally whipped into his study accusing them of fighting for real. Eric was told to hold out his hand and with misplaced satisfaction, the cruel master canned his hand and despite the scream, trauma, and tears that the pain caused, that nasty head didn't hold back and the poor little mite was given a second helping. If anyone was related to the devil in that school, it was him. Turning to Mick the disciplinarian enquired, 'Which hand do you write with Jackson?' The now truthful reply, 'The right one sir' resulted in two excruciating doses of the cane of the opposite hand. Mick struggled for weeks to do the simplest things such as eating with a knife and fork, dressing or brushing his teeth until the blooded welts on his true dominant hand had healed. I've been a hypnotherapist for the past twenty years and, consequently, when Mick was recalling this incident to me recently, my professional experience meant I could immediately spot his eyes filling up ever so slightly. My now, seventy-plus-year-old husband was forcing back tears, because the memory of that burning pain is hard wired into his memory. The two little boys left that shameful scene, and by that, I mean the adult's shame, with bleeding hands. Madge was beside herself with rage and marched into the school tearing many strips off the bombastic head teacher, so many in fact that Mick was never put through such an ordeal ever again.

However, as the saying goes, every cloud has a silver lining, that incident taught Mick to never show weakness or admit defeat, two qualities that have helped cement his determination throughout life, particularly during his many ups and downs in the Love Affair.

4

A Cockney Curse and Liverpudlian Elvis Presley

A couple of days after he'd arrived in London and started living in the girls' flat, Mick began to look for a job among the *Melody Maker* and *New Musical Express* adverts. He saw that a club in Wardour Street, Soho, was holding an audition for a bass player, but no other details were mentioned. Feeling very nervous and unsure of himself because he knew that he had to find the club on his own, he set off on the day of the audition. He found the busyness of London exciting yet overwhelming, and although he had heard about Soho, he had no idea where it was. Thankfully, he discovered the *A-Z of London*, the fact that the metropolis warranted one, made him realise just how huge a place it really was. The centre of Bradford was tiny by comparison and the friendly locals were only too glad to point you in the right direction if need be, so the idea of consulting a map was foreign to him. Then as now, although he won't admit it, map reading wasn't his strong point which is why he used to delegate that task to me before SatNav came along. He managed to get to Soho but whether he was holding the map upside down, I don't know, he could not for the life of him find the street. In sheer desperation, as time was ticking away and he feared he might miss the audition, he decided that he'd better do what he hates doing and ask someone for help. Apart from the girls in the flat, and the conductor of the red double-decker bus that he'd just jumped off, it would be the first time he'd spoken to a Londoner. He approached a middle aged, dishevelled man and said, 'Excuse me, could you tell me the way to Wardour Street please.' He was in luck, the unshaven, stale-smelling Cockney could, but unfortunately, he spoke so fast and that, coupled with his accent, meant his reply was incomprehensible, so Mick replied, 'Sorry?' Mick was shocked, but had no problem understanding the loud, aggressive response, 'Are you deaf or just stupid?' and with no intention of repeating himself, the 'got no time for anybody' individual started cursing and to clearly emphasise a point, gave Mick the peace sign, but unfortunately it was the wrong way round.

Mick made it to the audition and once inside the building he forgot all about that unfortunate encounter. He unpacked his bass guitar, hoping that his nerves would steady and his fingers and brain would work in tandem, so that he could show what he was capable of. He was in for another much bigger shock, but this time, it was an exciting one as he was 'gobsmacked' when the outside door opened, and non-other than one of his childhood idols—the Liverpudlian Elvis Presley, known as Billy Fury, walked in. As the star, escorted by minders, approached Mick and the other hopeful auditionees, his overcoat was deliberately draped nonchalantly on his shoulders, and Mick thought he looked so cool, like someone out of the Mafia, and felt completely in awe.

He needn't have worried though, because despite his fame, Billy was still the friendly Liverpudlian he always was, and also wore a friendly grin beneath huge, quaffed hair that never moved, despite the huge draught that had sneaked through the entrance with him. Someone rushed to fetch a chair for Billy and the guitarists went through their paces whilst he listened and watched intently. After what seemed like forever for Mick, one by one, the other bass players were asked to wait in an adjoining room, until he was the only one left and was elated when Mr Fury said, 'Alright der, lar, you've got the job.'

One of the minders then asked Mick his name and age. Afterwards Mick kicked himself harder than he had ever done before, as he realised that there was no problem about his name, but he should have lied about his age as the devastating response was, 'Sorry kid, come back when you're eighteen.'

My ultra-deflated, then boyfriend, was devastated and returned to the flat and with no bed to get into, slumped on the floor feeling that he had just missed out on possibly the best and maybe even only musical chance that he would ever have. He now knows that it was probably a very good thing that he didn't get the job as he might have been in a backing group forever, and an even greater opportunity was waiting for him. The disappointment was still fresh in his mind when the next editions of the two papers came out, but his hopes were at least raised slightly when he spotted another advert for a bass player. Literally picking himself up off the floor after a fitful night's sleep, he dusted his *A-Z* down and set off once more in his search for fame. His heart must have dropped into his boots when he saw scores of hopefuls clutching guitars, waiting patiently in the queue that snaked around the building. Once inside Mick was dismayed when he saw how the other candidates were shown the door after only seconds of auditioning. The group's manager, Sid Bacon, whose son, Maurice, was the drummer, knew exactly what he was looking for and wasted no time in finding it.

Finally, Mick's turn came. The expression on the smartly dressed, rotund, business-like manager's face changed to interest and relief as he recognised that his search could be over. That optimistic look immediately helped to steady Mick's nerves and his trembling fingers stopped shaking quite as much. Before Mick even picked up his guitar or sang a note, his long hair, angelic face, and the way he spoke, meant that as far as Sid was concerned, this latest bass player certainly looked the part. His northern accent, at least to the Londoners, must have sounded reminiscent of a Liverpudlian one, again gaining instant points. Liverpool had given birth not only to the Beatles and Billy Fury, but many more top groups and it was considered cool to come from the north.

The years of practising playing his bass since he was eight paid off. Mick was asked if he knew 'My Girl', a song that, luckily, he had sang and played many times. The fact that he knew it well, coupled with his ability to sing and play at the same time, meant he sailed through the audition. Mick was accepted on the spot, and the remainder of the snaking queue was sent slithering home. The group he was auditioning for was called the Soul Survivors, the original line-up alongside Maurice already included Stephen Morgan Fisher, keyboards, and Steve Ellis, singer. Stephen was a good keyboard player after having spent many hours practising on his family's upright piano, and he had previously played with two school groups, the Beat Circuit and the Private Eyes. Stephen wasn't the only member of those two groups who went on to have a successful musical career as the singer Chris Ross, who was also in both groups, joined Glyndebourne Opera Company.

Stephen and Steve were friends before they joined the Soul Survivors as they both lived in Finchley, and they'd spent eons of time listening to soul music and went on to write several songs together. Luckily for them, Sid's handbag warehouse in Walthamstow was not far from their homes and it was there along with a place in Tottenham that the Soul

Survivors rehearsed. Steve had answered Sid's ad for a singer but only because one his mates suggested that he should go along to try his luck, and not wanting to turn down what he viewed as a dare, Steve accepted the challenge—and has probably been thanking him ever since.

'Keep on Running', a huge hit for the Spencer Davis Group, was the very first song that Steve learnt to sing with the group. I along with almost every other teenage girl in the country loved Steve's voice instantly, he was the perfect front man. They worked incredibly hard, an ethos that remained throughout the life of the group irrespective of any changes in the members. In the very early days before Mick joined them, they initially played anywhere they could often for free, sometimes even turning up to gigs uninvited.

They certainly earned their stripes and were anything but an instant manufactured group like the Monkees, the only similarities being that Sid, forever the perfectionist, wanted only the best musicians to accompany his fourteen-year-old son, so he placed ads in the most popular music papers to find them.

Sid's brother, Max, often popped in to see how they were getting on, he was a well-known actor, comedian, and drummer in the '30s 'Ambrose Band' (think Popeye music) that regularly appeared on the radio. Max was also in several films including a minor role in the 1968 *Chitty Chitty Bang Bang* based on the only children's book that James Bond creator Ian Fleming wrote (it was for his son) called *The Magical Car*.

The fact that music was in Sid's family's blood was one reason why he wanted Mo, as the boys called his son, to get involved in the business too, but he was equally motivated by the opportunity to make money on his substantial investment. Shortly after Mick joined the group, he practically snatched Sid's hand off when he offered him part-time work in his factory. It meant that, coupled with the meagre wage he received from playing, Mick would be able to afford to rent somewhere. Although it would, through necessity, be the cheapest he could find, a bedsit would at least have a bed for him to sleep in.

Lugging heavy boxes of handbags up and down three flights of stairs was not what Mick thought he would be doing when he first travelled down to the capital, but it did help him eat—at least most of the time. One day, however, when he only had a plectrum and a few coppers in his pocket, he felt so hungry, as he hadn't eaten properly for some days, that he really couldn't bare the emptiness in his stomach any longer, and hoped the assortment of coins he'd scraped together would be enough to buy something that would help him feel better. The short walk to the local shop sapped his energy, he was so weak, and when he got there he discovered that the only nourishing thing he could afford was one of many pickled eggs squashed into a grubby jar, so in desperation, he decided to take a gamble and steal some food. Simon & Garfunkel's 'Parsley, Sage, Rosemary and Thyme' was playing through a loudspeaker, mesmerising the young girl behind the counter. Her expression changed from one of boredom to dreaminess as she joined in with her squeaky voice.

Had she noticed Mick watching her like a hawk, as he planned how he was going to get past her till without her noticing, she would have been forgiven for thinking that he fancied her, and she might even have taken pity on him allowing him credit, but he couldn't take that risk, as by now, he felt on the verge of collapse. He helped himself to some freshly baked bread rolls, milk, and a large bar of Cadbury's chocolate, not the healthiest choice perhaps, but it would be filling and keep him alive at least. Feeling guilty, he walked around the shop for quite some time before furtively popping his loot into his jacket pockets.

He was lucky because Miss Squeaky Voice was distracted once more when 'The Last Train to Clarksville' by the Monkees began to play, and she stooped behind the counter to turn up the volume. Mick momentarily forgot he was in the middle of committing a crime and went back into musician mode, appreciating what a great record it was, even though he thought it was a rip off of the Beatles. Her bending down was the perfect opportunity to flee through the door, so Mick took it and he was back in the street in an instant and Miss Squeaky Voice never suspected a thing.

Once he was away from the shop, he checked to see that the coast was clear and there weren't any police around, and then scoffed the lot so quickly that, had he been caught, the evidence didn't remain hidden for long, as his stomach had shrunk so much that he brought it back quicker than it went down. As I'm very anti-crime, I like to think that when Mick did get his wages, he spent a lot of it in that shop, and they made enough profit out of him, to more than pay for his stolen food.

Mick forgave Sid, for the Dickensian working conditions he had to put up with, when Sid made an important announcement that made him think that all his Christmases were about to arrive at once. Sid had wisely decided that because the boys wanted to become a top group, they had to have top instruments. They were each given the choice of any instrument that they wanted, so Mick wasted no time in visiting St Giles Music Centre in London, after being told that price was no object. Mick now admits that shortly after he'd joined the Soul Survivors, his old school friend and former lead guitarist in the Spell, Steve Robinson, asked him what guitar he had, and Mick lied. Knowing that his pal would have expected nothing less, Mick boasted that he had a Gibson EB2 semi solid in sunburst.

I'm not as knowledgeable about guitars as it sounds as Mick has just told me exactly what make it was, I just hope I heard him properly. According to him, any young bass player's dream would have been to own a Gibson guitar and Mick's was no exception. Sitting on the top deck of a double-decker bus on his way to one of the most respected and famous record shops in the world, he pinched himself to make sure that it was really happening. He was way past the age when he could realistically be described as a kid, but he must really have felt like one, and better still, one that could have anything he wanted from a proverbial sweet shop.

There was no decision to be made, it just had to be the Gibson he told Steve he already had. Mick made his way towards the exit, carrying his new prized possession and because this time, he'd paid for his purchases, he was escorted out by a uniformed member of staff who reverently held the door open for him, touching his cap as Mick proudly walked through it.

Mick's head was spinning with excitement and also relief that he really did own that dream bass, because how could he have possibly looked Steve in the eye again if he didn't? Sitting on the bus that took him back to his bedsit, he would have been forgiven for thinking that Sid should have provided him with a security guard because he was carrying such an expensive guitar.

Sid wasn't the group's only manager for long, because after he'd invited representatives from Decca Records to hear the Soul Survivors, they loved what they heard and consequently, Sid formed a close bond with them. They were Decca's marketing manager, John Cokell, and in-house photographer, David Wedgbury, and they soon joined him as co-managers. David became internationally renowned for his photographic work that featured on many famous album covers of the time. His subjects included David Bowie, The Who, John Mayall, Lulu, Marianne Faithfull, and many others.

With artistic flare, David radically suggested that they altered their name to the Thin Red Line and in order to gain publicity, paint a thin red lines on each of their faces that extended onto their clothes, past their jackets and down their trousers. I remember Mick telling me about the plan and it seemed so far out that I couldn't believe that he was serious and thought that David was having a laugh, but he wasn't, he meant it. However, the boys thought the same as me and they refused to co-operate, fearing ridicule, but in the decades to follow, theatrical clothes and extreme gimmicks adopted by groups made the idea seem tame by comparison.

Who knows, it could have worked really well, and they might have been credited as the first group to use off the wall makeup, but only David had the imagination and foresight to see that. He was right about something else though, the name of the group had to be changed as there was an American group who were also called the Soul Survivors, so they renamed themselves the Love Affair after a television series. Sid must have been patting himself on the back for making such a good decision about investing in the best instruments his money could buy. His group may have sounded good before, but now they sounded fantastic, and Sid was confident that he really was onto a winner.

Decca liked the sound and image of Sid's protégés so much that a recording contract was drawn up straight away. It took slightly longer than normal to dot the i's and cross the t's because the boys were minors and their parents had to sign on their behalf, writing their signatures over a pre-decimal six penny stamp. Logistically it was not ideal because the signees lived many miles from one another, but that didn't deter anyone, because they were all confident that success was just around the corner.

Now that they were finally signed to one of the biggest recording labels in the world, all they had to do was find the right song to record. Not only were Sid's young stallions ready, they were chomping at their bits and raring to go.

Kenny Lynch was chosen to write that song for them, as he had co-written with Mort Shuman, 'Sha-La-La- La-Lee'. Kenny quickly came up with a song called 'Woman, Woman' but they were not overwhelmed. They sensed that they could do better, so although it was recorded it wasn't released, that is until much later in 2000 when it was put on a CD called *No Strings* produced by Angel Air, and even then it was probably just an attempt to keep it for posterity.

It was decided that 'She Smiled Sweetly' written by Mick Jagger and Keith Richards would suit them better. Chris Farlowe had a major hit with another of Mick and Keith's songs called 'Out of Time' so their management along with Decca thought that the group could be equally successful with a Jagger/Richards composition. It was to be overseen by the excellent Mike Vernon, who became a legendary record producer, so everyone thought it really couldn't fail.

Mick told me that it was while they were recording the 'B' side written by Steve and Morgan called 'Satisfaction Guaranteed' that he became overawed with emotion. Before explaining why, I must mention that Mick told me something yesterday that I had never realised. The songwriters whose compositions were put on the 'B' side of records were paid the same royalties as whoever wrote the hit on the 'A' side. 'Everlasting Love' must have made a small fortune, not only for Buzz Cason and Mac Gayden who wrote it, but also all those lucky enough to have written the 'B' sides of the song that has been recorded by numerous artistes.

How I wish Sid had thought to ask Mick to write the Love Affair's 'B' side, but it's probably because he didn't know how lucrative that would have been. If he had known and never one to miss an opportunity to make money, he would no doubt have written something himself even though he couldn't write songs, but hey what did that matter, ma boy?

Not only were the boys making a record (Mick's dream, since first nagging his mum for a guitar after seeing Elvis in 'King Creole'), it was being made in non-other than Abbey Road Studio 2, the same one that the Beatles were using, but not at the same time, I might add.

I've always been fascinated by all the wondrous equipment to be found in recording studio control rooms. All those nobs and faders just begged to be pushed and pulled, which of course then, really were, whereas now, they're manoeuvred with a computer mouse, but nevertheless they're still intriguing.

I'm not sure how many tracks were possible in those early days, just a handful I believe, as it wasn't that long after records had only been available in stereo. Nowadays, there are so many that even my old school triangle could have one all to itself, if it wanted to. My goodness how things have changed. Then, tapes the size of dinner plates and such sophisticated aids as tea towels were used to deaden sound when placed over snare drums, that otherwise might have sounded like metal dustbin lids blowing about in a gale. Mick remembers a sound engineer having a laugh, at their expense, by using an oscillator to produce such low frequencies that their internal organs began to rumble. Within seconds, all the boys were scrambling over each other, desperate to get to the nearest toilets.

I guess that's not surprising to anyone who has seen how a sopranos' voice can shatter a glass, but it was certainly a shock to them, and for once they didn't quite fully appreciate the joke, especially when they, themselves, were at the receiving end.

Although I was thrilled that the group were signed to Decca and had made a record—and I was very proud that they had—truth was, I wasn't really over enthralled with it. The tempo of 'She Smiled Sweetly' was slow, and I thought it was a bit of a dirge, it may have suited the Stones, but I felt that it was a depressing choice for five vibrant teenagers. Perhaps everyone else secretly agreed with me, but having got so far, maybe it was a bit like the story of the king's new clothes and nobody was willing to own up. That would certainly have accounted for the lack of money or effort spent on promoting it, and without valuable airtime on TV and radio stations such as Radio Caroline, it didn't stand a chance. Ironically, the summer after it was made, Radio 1 burst onto the scene, and it might have been easier to push the record onto up and coming DJ's, anxious to prove that they kept their fingers on the pulse of latest songs, but its release was a good six months too early, and by the time September arrived along with the new station, 'She Smiled Sweetly' was already dead and buried.

Steve admits that he never felt comfortable with the song because he wasn't a Rolling Stones' fan, as he much preferred Motown, Stax, and of course good old soul music that allowed his voice to fully express itself. Still, at least he and Morgan must have felt chuffed that one of the songs they had written, was chosen as the flip side, it's just a pity that as far as the 'A' side went, satisfaction wasn't guaranteed!

Fairly soon, thanks to the work in the factory, Mick had enough money to find a place nearer to where the group were based so he took the first bedsit he saw in Finsbury Park. It really was a dump but at least it was his own and he no longer had to catch several buses to rehearsals, carrying his heavy bass guitar and it stopped the roadies moaning about having to pick him up from distant Olympia whenever they went to gigs. There was only one bathroom shared between umpteen bedsit tenants and nobody, unsurprisingly, wanted to take responsibility for cleaning it. The bath water always cold (just as it was at Butlins) and he was never really sure if he was cleaner or dirtier when he got out because the bath itself was so disgustingly grubby. His former unpaid landladies, the girls, were pleased he'd moved out as there was now a lovely empty space in their hall where Mick's massive amplifier had spent most of its days tripping them up. Mick still remembers the winter day, when after walking three miles from his bedsit to Kings Cross Station, to catch the Bradford train, he was dismayed to find that the waiting room was closed. He was feeling shattered, the walk itself was no problem, but because he was afraid to leave his guitar behind, fearing it might disappear, he had to carry that and his suitcase. Their combined weight had used up every ounce of energy that his now emaciated body made. However, at least there were benches he could rest on. His relief turned to panic as he realised that his body was beginning to freeze as frost was forming on his fingers, so he pushed newspapers down his trouser legs and up his sleeves in an attempt to keep warm, but it didn't work.

Had Mick been carrying a violin instead of his guitar, it would have been more appropriate, but at least you know there was a happy ending. It was during those difficult, early days just after he rented his horrible bedsit that he wrote a song called 'Once Upon a Season'. It explains much better than I ever could, exactly how he felt, here it is:

> Creep in from the pouring rain
> Turn the key in battered door
> Climb the tired stairs in darkness
> To the top fourth floor
> Step inside smell the damp
> Throw my coat on the floor in a heap
> Light a cigarette curse the world
> What's there left to do but sleep
> I can see them round a glowing fireside
> Drinking coffee watch the movie warm inside
> I'm going back there in the summer wait and see
> And make them all so very proud of me
> Stroll the park on sunny day
> See the people passing by
> Breath in fragrant air and feel good
> Raise my head up to the sky
> But here I am and nothing's changed
> Although the sun feels warm upon my weary head
> I think that someday I might win through
> Then what's the use I feel I may as well be dead
> I can see them on a Sunday taking tea
> Sunday driving do the garden think of me
> I'm going back there in the winter wait and see
> And make them all so very proud of me

I needn't have worried, though, his mum was right when she said that her son was born so lucky that if he put his hand down the toilet he would find a box of chocolates, not that he would want to eat them if he did, of course, but she made her point. Unknown to Mick, whilst he was writing these heart-rending words, the biggest box imaginable was waiting for the Love Affair, but they had to wait until Christmas before it arrived.

5

The Marquee

Even though their first recording was never released for many years, and the second was a damp squib, the Love Affair's ambition was far too great to become deflated, so everyone simply got on with the job of doing gigs and searching for the final piece of their 'fame' jigsaw.

They played at all the top London clubs including Tiles, Flamingo, notorious for tough audiences and a favourite of Georgie Fame, and above all others, the Marquee that gave groups a fantastic opportunity to make a name for themselves because if they were successful, word about them, would spread in London and then throughout the rest of the country.

Mick became familiar with the Marquee in his first few weeks of settling in London, not because he went there, but because he got so used to seeing their adverts while looking through the musical papers for a job.

He had no idea that the club, once described in *Melody Maker* as 'the most important venue in the history of pop music', had been part of the London scene since the '50s when its owner Harold Pendleton first moved into premises in Oxford Street that had been home to the Marquee ballroom.

Harold didn't have to think of a name for his new, at first predominantly jazz, club as 'the Marquee' was perfect. There, the red and white canopy stripes were bright and eye catching, and added greatly to the atmosphere, they were admired by everyone and because they were so cheerful they instantly helped to put people into a party mood. It was there that the Rolling Stones made one of their earliest performances. Those stripes proved to be timeless because when the lease ran out and Harold moved to nearby Wardour Street, he was anxious to keep that successful 'logo' and went to great lengths to recreate the décor in the new place.

Although the outside was different, once the inside had been ripped out to create a space big enough to comfortably hold 600 or 700 people, and the familiar striped, circus theme (that suited the '60s perfectly) were in place, customers could hardly see the 'join' and felt instantly at home.

The first night it reopened, long queues formed, and hundreds had to be turned away, even though, as was often the case in future years, nearer to 1,000 were squeezed into the club that was meant to accommodate far less, but that was a time when it didn't seem to matter that much, only that everyone had a good time.

Complete with a small stage, no taller than a few feet, the club felt much bigger than it actually was, because of mirrors behind the few seats (because it was mainly standing room only) that were placed around its edges. The club didn't remain pristine for long as practically every famous group in the country launched their careers on that tiny stage (just as they had done in the previous premises), with the exception perhaps of the Beatles and the Kinks. There were probably others, of course, but not many and it would certainly be quicker to list who hadn't played there as opposed to who had.

Night after night, the likes of Georgie Fame, Fleetwood Mac, Joe Cocker, 10 Years After, and Free belted out their stuff making it impossible for the crowd to speak, but they weren't there to talk, they were a discerning, yet tough audience and the louder the music the better.

There was only one tiny dressing room and it had to be shared by everyone who was playing and if only its walls really could have talked, what amazing tales they would have had to tell. Silent they may have been, but they became the focal point of everyone in there, who read and usually contributed to the graffiti that could have been in *The Guinness Book of Records* as having the highest number of now, world famous autographs written amongst it.

Mick confirms that it was daunting when, before playing to a full house, they had to push their way through the throng to get to the stage or to get to the toilets as there was no such luxury as a toilet or basin backstage. At least there was a fire exit that opened out onto the back of the club, but more often than not it would be blocked with equipment in transit either to or from the stage as roadies did their best not to trample on one another.

As the years went by and sound systems got better, the volume of music increased relentlessly, and the club was constantly having to improve the sound proofing as best as it could. Just as the Cavern in Liverpool had daylight gigs, so did the Marquee, and even David Bowie honed his skills and flare for outrageous costumes, when he appeared there at lunchtime.

However, there was nothing quite like the nights, when hundreds of customers stood shoulder to shoulder unconcerned that music was so loud that it was probably capable of shattering an eardrum or two. Chewing gum was thrown onto the floor and drinks spilled (though not always of the alcoholic type, as the place wasn't licensed at first), and the unpleasant resulting stickiness didn't appear to matter at all, it just added to the club's cool reputation.

Steam bellowed from sweaty bodies and up onto the ceiling, before condensing into rivers that drenched those mirrored walls. It's a wonder that the audience could see who was playing through the dense cigarette smoke that added to the atmosphere in more ways than one.

The place was often so hot, that the dampness in the air reached saturation point and the moisture often caused problems for musical instruments. The most successful night in the club's history was when Jimmy Hendrix played there and the Beatles, Rolling Stones, and anybody who was anybody squeezed into the place to watch.

It was a never to be forgotten, once in a lifetime performance, even though Jimmy had to stop several times to tune his guitar that kept going slightly off key, and only then was he happy enough to continue playing it, often with his teeth.

Whenever Mick first came home to Bradford, we'd spend most nights in his mum's front room playing John Mayall and the Bluesbreakers *Beano* album with Eric Clapton, and when I finally got to live in London, I was excited to learn that they were regulars at the club, but not quite as regularly as Manfred Mann who played there over a hundred times.

Throughout all of this, the place was run by John Gee, an extremely likeable, dapper manager, responsible for booking all the artistes. Being much older than most of his customers he was a popular father figure who was married to his job and never happier than when he got onto the stage to introduce everyone. Though proud to have played a part in their destiny and pleased to see them do so well, whenever groups made it big, and that was often, he was sad because they would become so popular that the club couldn't accommodate their new, massive audiences. John knew that meant that they usually had to stop playing for him, and he felt bereft, as though part of his club's vast family (that included everyone from cleaners, bar staff, and bouncers) had left the fold.

Sid and John had one thing in common, they were more than familiar than most people, with the renowned '30s band leader Ambrose because Sid's brother had been the drummer in his orchestra and John had worked for them as a promotor and handling their tours.

Although the Love Affair had played at the Marquee, Sid was keen that, rather than just playing there sporadically, his boys got a residency, and he had no qualms about asking John if they could have one. Affable as ever, John said that he really rated the Love Affair but would like Mick to join him for a bite to eat, at the nearby Ship pub, whilst he thought it over. Mick found him to be good company especially as they both liked Frank Sinatra, a fact that impressed John because it was unusual for someone as young as Mick to like that type of music. John's admiration of the famous Crooner verged on the obsessive, ever since he'd been present at one of Sinatra's recording sessions, and whenever anyone else shared his passion, they'd instantly become his new, best buddy. Thankfully, that pleasant meal helped to clinch the deal and much to Sid and the group's delight, John informed them that a Thursday night's residency was theirs. The place then began to feel like a home from home for the boys, and between sound checks and opening time, they'd nip around the corner to the pub, to relax for half an hour. They always went back through the front entrance, as the bouncers knew them, and along the dark, dank tunnel leading to the main part of the club. Mick aptly named it 'the tunnel of a thousand smells' because it was—and to quote him, these are just a few he remembers—'tobacco smoke, beer, Coca Cola, minty chewing gum, male and female armpits (they're different), Tabu perfume, cannabis and all similar aromas left over from yesterday and the day before that and the day before that!'

The Love Affair's popularity grew in the club, they had the right image, and were a good 'together' group that produced an exciting sound. All that was missing was the right song.

The boys viewed their two previous recordings, 'Woman, Woman' and 'She Smiled Sweetly' as limbering up exercises, they were simply not the correct choices, and were optimistic that it would be third time lucky, and things would get better.

One day, when they were rehearsing before their Thursday night at the Marquee, Mick received a distressing phone call from David, to say that their stepdad Albert, who was an HGV driver, had been taken seriously ill with a brain haemorrhage whilst he was delivering goods to Liverpool docks. Without hesitation Mick knew that he had to get to him ASAP, all thoughts of making it in the music industry seemed insignificant, compared to that dreadful news. However, Sid saw the situation entirely differently.

Sid wasn't emotionally involved of course, and even though they'd had a setback with the recordings, he was confident that he was, at last (especially as they now had their residency), the captain of a ship whose destination of fame, was just over the horizon. As a conscientious businessman, he knew that his job was to make sure that the whole crew and vessel weren't destroyed before it got there.

Sid panicked when he thought that his bass player was about to drag it down by going AWOL. He told Mick that if he went, not to bother coming back. Sid must have found it difficult when he gave his callous instruction but having invested a large amount of money and time into the group, his business decision overrode any secret empathy that he had. He probably thought that the seriousness of Albert's condition had been exaggerated and therefore not that serious, but the group's future was.

Mick, on the other hand, could not believe what he was hearing, he knew he had to get to his stepdad but in doing so, Sid was saying he would sack him. It was still a no brainer for Mick, if he was being dismissed, then so be it, family came first. He loved Albert, who'd encouraged him in his ambition when others thought it was unachievable, they'd spent hours sitting together in their tiny front room, whilst Albert explained chords and the intricacies of music on their Philips organ, often using just his left hand to simplify things. Albert was a great stepdad, and having no children of his own, he treated David and Mick as if they were his. It was Albert who comforted Madge who had a hard time fighting her maternal instinct to bring Mick back home from Butlins because she worried so much about him. Just as the holiday season was ending and Mick told them that he was going to London, Albert stopped Madge from trying to make him change his mind.

Only weeks before collapsing, Albert came to Mick's rescue yet again when the recording contract with Decca was pushed under Madge's nose. She must have felt as though it was so final, all hopes of Mick ever returning home to her, dashed for good. Madge listened to Albert, knowing that hard though it was, she had to put her own feelings aside so Mick could get on with his life. Albert held one of her hands whilst she shakily wrote her signature on the dotted line, with the other.

Mick knew that Sid's instruction to never come back was the least of his worries at that moment, he just had to be at his stepdad's side, come what may. Mick jumped ship quicker than Sid could shout 'Stop!' leaving the captain no doubt worrying that he had given, not only a hasty order but an unwise one. The young bass player hadn't been gone long before Sid regretted his words and decided that no matter how long Mick had to be away, he would welcome him back, and make sure the new Gibson would be plugged in ready for his return.

Fortunately for Albert and Sid, it wasn't long before Mick could go back to London where, true to Sid's word, his Gibson was waiting for him, and Sid admitted he had been wrong to be so hasty. John and David Wedgebury started to really enjoy their roles as managers especially when they got involved in making suggestions for songs that they thought the group should record. John raved about 'A Whiter Shade of Pale' by Procol Harum because he liked the Hammond organ that featured so prominently and suggested it might suit the Love Affair. Although a Hammond keyboard did feature in 'She Smiled Sweetly', the record simply didn't have that certain something that could have made it into a hit. Procol Harum's record was fabulous, so why John could think that covering or even competing with it was a good idea, I'm not sure. Procol Harum's version was such a huge success that I can't imagine how anyone else could have done it any better. I think that if they'd gone ahead and recorded the song, it would have been their third disappointment, achieving nothing but a miserable hat trick.

Despite team Love Affair feeling confident in their own abilities, Decca must have lost patience, and lacking any foresight, they dismissed the group, wrongly believing that it was the correct financial decision for the label. It wasn't the first time that they'd made a gigantic mistake, of course, as they had famously turned down the Beatles in favour of Brian Poole and the Tremeloes, who happened to be auditioning on the same day as the fab four. Decca's reasoning was simple, the Beatles were from Liverpool, 220 miles north of London, so they thought they would save on travelling expenses by signing up Brian Poole.

Having experienced the thrill of recording, the group knew that they would allow nothing to get in their way now, not even being let out of their Decca contract, so they continued to rehearse hard. That work paid off because their renditions of songs such as 'Ride Your Pony', 'Rescue Me', and 'Knock on Wood', went down a storm everywhere they played and the number of fans they acquired grew tenfold each time they travelled up and down the country. That was all the encouragement they needed and even their thirst for recording was quenched for a short while when they made a few demos at a lesser known studio in South London.

By this time, Rex Brayley, a loveable, cheeky imp of a lad joined them as lead guitarist, I was going to say boy but that makes him sound quite young when in fact he was the oldest. Rex had previously been in a group with his brother called the Dae-b-Four, it was based in Hounslow and years after Rex left, the drummer Kenny Slade joined Joe Cocker's Grease band. Rex may have been the oldest, but he was also the smallest, yet his confidence more than made up for his size and he was great fun. Mick still thinks it's hilarious whenever he recalls the time after one of their gigs, and several joints and glasses of champagne, Rex announced that he was Freddie the frog and started to croak. The others thought his jumps were impressive but were not the least bit phased when Rex sprung onto the top of the chest height hotel bar with one leap. The reason Mick finds it so funny is that he, along with the others, actually, momentarily believed that their guitarist had really morphed into a live frog. They genuinely thought that tiny Rex had achieved the impossible by jumping nearly 5 feet into the air when he was only a few inches taller than that, himself.

After Rex joined, the line-up seemed stable, at least for a while; however, Stephen, who by this time was using his middle name Morgan to avoid any confusion with Steve, left shortly afterwards to finish studying for his A-levels. Although Morgan loved being in the group, he was persuaded to leave by his mum, Margaret, and several other of his relatives, who all had his best interest at heart. Mrs Fisher was a domestic science teacher and not surprisingly anxious that her son should follow in her academic footsteps. Her advice was sound of course as the odds against making it big were millions to one, especially as there were so many wannabe groups that never got anywhere.

The gap left by Morgan was temporarily filled, albeit for a very short time, by Peter Barden who went on to form Camel having earlier played alongside Rod Stewart, Mick Fleetwood, Van Morrison, and Peter Green who later joined John Mayall's Bluesbreakers. I never met Pete because he was with them for only a matter of weeks, before being replaced by Lynton Guest, who saw yet another one of Sid's adverts and rushed down from Leicester where he lived to join the other fifty-plus hopeful organists to audition.

Just like Mick, Lynton was enthralled with London and decided there was no way he would just turn around and go back home, even if he didn't get the job. Fortune was smiling on him, however, as he was successful. Mick was happy too as Lynton soon became his bedsit buddy, an improvement on previous flat mates—mice. The boys continued to travel up and down motorways and although it was usually boring and uneventful, it wasn't always the case. One journey comes to mind, I'm pleased I was still living in Yorkshire then, otherwise I might been with them. It was a miserably cold winter, but the fact that they were travelling to Liverpool from London gave them something to look forward too, as Liverpool was the 'in' place to be, because of the Cavern. The journey began in the usual way, their beat-up old Transit van, driven by their roadie, John Chapman, stopped at everyone's home to pick them up and after a quick roll call to make sure he'd remembered everyone, John headed for the M6. Now past the age, well only just in Mo's case, when their mums' insisted they had a jumper, coat, and woolly scarf in freezing temperatures, they never thought about wrapping up warm. Jeans, thin T-shirts, and jackets were what they insisted on wearing as they didn't want to look anything other than fashionable. Slumping in the van they all fell asleep due to tiredness caused by their 'must get on the road to as many gigs as possible' schedule. However, one by one, they woke up as they approached the north, and it was amazing what two or three ciggies did, and I don't mean each, they were sharing them because money was tight and cigarettes never cheap. Their nicotine fix had them sitting upright, renewing their abilities to speak coherently to one another, well, almost. Trundling up the motorway may have been as boring as ever, but cigarettes weren't the only things that were being ignited, their boyish senses of fun were too, because it started to snow. However, as they got further up the motorway, the flakes settled and inches became feet, and they began to get worried that they wouldn't make the gig. The communal puffing of the next cigarette became more urgent, and the John Players Special became a stub in record time and their moods almost as black as the packet.

They realised the disastrous consequences of a no show so early in their careers, so team style, they crossed the many fingers and toes between them. They knew that it couldn't really make any difference, but because they'd no control over the weather, it was the only thing they could do, apart from hope. Mick was the last to draw on the cigarette and needed to get rid of the red hot stub before it burnt his fingers. He opened the heavy, sliding door of the van to throw it out, thinking it would be quicker than winding down the window, little realising that action could easily have cost him his life.

Not only was it snowing, but a strong wind also decided to join in and was blowing between the door and side of the van, it was so fierce that it ripped the door from its runners, trapping Micks hand in its handle. The door detached itself from the van and its bottom edge began to scrape and bounce on the tarmac below, and Mick was still involuntarily holding on to it. Sparks were flying everywhere and the sudden excruciating pain in Mick's arm made him shout, 'What the f****'. Quick as a flash, Steve grabbed his right arm and using all his might, managed to prevent Mick from being dragged either out and under the van or onto the road where the drivers following would have had no chance to stop before running him over. It only took a few seconds for John to realise what was happening before slowing down, but meanwhile, Mick's shoulder was on the verge of dislocating because he was being stretched like an elastic band between the runaway door and Steve's vice like grip. Those few seconds seemed much longer to Mick as he saw his life flash before him, but he was incredibly lucky because his fingers suddenly slipped free of the handle and Steve heaved him back inside as the door flew away and disappeared out of sight. It had narrowly missed smashing into anything, before burying itself in a snowdrift near the hard shoulder.

(Wow! thank you Steve, you played a major part in our destiny, had it not been for your quick thinking, that could have been the end of Mick and I wouldn't be writing this book.)

After safely stopping the van, John ran back towards the battered door to assess the damage, hoping beyond hope that it was still useable, but it wasn't. All he could do was carry it back and throw it on top of the speaker cabinets in the back before heading towards the next services, where they could all grab a coffee. Comfort break over and feeling slightly warmer after a hot drink, they clambered into the van, bracing themselves for a very uncomfortable ride now that they had no passenger door, but their troubles were far from over, they were only just beginning in fact, because the van wouldn't start. No matter how hard John tried, it wasn't having any of it, almost as if it was sulking because it was minus a door, so John went to find a phone box to ask Sid what they should do.

Although Mick's arm, that later developed a horrendous corkscrew like bruise that wrapped around it like a snake, was sore, he and Steve decided to pass the time by having a snowball fight, it didn't last long because of the cold, so they soon joined the others in the van. By the time John came back with the good news that help was on its way, Steve and Mick realised that their mock battle had been a bad idea because not only did they have to contend with the freezing cold along with everybody else, but their clothes were soaked. That hope of being rescued was dashed snowflake by snowflake, as with not so much as a hot drink for comfort, time dragged towards evening. Services were not twenty-four-hour oases then and closed at night and when closing time came, they watched the staff scrunch their way out of the warm building, and into their cars. The tyre tracks that they left behind, eventually disappeared under one large eiderdown-like cover of snow. The eerie silence made them feel they were in Siberia, and even the beauty of the scene could do nothing to raise their spirits. They realised that it would probably be hours before they could be rescued as the adjacent road was impassable and deserted apart from the odd car being dug out by their owners who needn't have bothered as it was impossible for anyone to get anywhere. Desperate for warmth, the boys pulled the thin, plastic amplifier covers over themselves in a useless attempt to keep warm, but any comfort the makeshift blankets gave, didn't last, and all they could do was shiver and wait.

It was early morning before the snow started to thaw, they'd spent a good twelve hours outside (in truth, they weren't exactly outside but may as well have been), and at about ten o'clock they were relieved to see the other John, their manager, arrive in a small truck and he towed them to a garage. They did live to tell the tale, but not before Rex was almost hospitalized with hypothermia. Of course, they never reached the Mersey, Liver building, or Cavern Club, but as they hadn't caused the weather, all was forgiven and they survived to play another day, or more accurately, hundreds of more days. However, Mick may not have been able to play ever again, had fate not smiled on him once more, when they were appearing in Chatham, Kent, and he was in danger for the second time in a matter of weeks.

The group were used to the jealous behaviour of their fans' boyfriends, but they couldn't help getting angry themselves that night, when constant, sarcastic, and caustic remarks were shouted at them, and eventually Mick snapped and thrust two fingers at the hecklers whilst Steve started shaking his fist at the same time as mouthing 'F*** You!'

Later, when the Love Affair had finished the gig and the audience was slowly leaving, the boys started to help John pack up the gear before carrying it down the fire escape at the back of the building, where the van was parked. It wasn't until they'd nearly finished, and Mick was in front of Mo as they were about to make their last trip down the iron steps, when who should emerge from a badly lit passageway below, but the boyfriends, who'd been swearing at them throughout their last set. Mick's heart leapt into his mouth when he saw something glistening in the hands of the obvious leader—it was the blade of a knife. Although he was used to fighting with his fists in his early teenage years, a knife was something else, and he turned quickly around thinking he'd push Mo back inside and slam the door safely behind them—but a gust of wind beat him to it. The only trouble was, he was alone outside and Mo, though thankfully safe, was inside the building on the other side of the steel fire door. Mick fumbled for the door handle before realising that there wasn't one, so he immediately turned around knowing that the last thing he should show his aggressors was his back—or fear. He was hoping and praying that Mo had gone to summon help, but meanwhile he figured out that his best plan was to stay at the top of the stairs and if possible, play for time.

As the leader began climbing the steps, Mick looked around him in the hope that he could find some kind of weapon to keep himself distant from the threatening blade. Luckily, a metal mike stand, waiting to be loaded, was to hand, and he picked it up, knowing that if he struck someone with such a heavy piece of equipment, it would cause them serious injuries, but this was no time for hesitation, he had to defend himself. Armed with the stand, Mick looked intimidating as he stood his ground, and the knife bearer stopped climbing towards him and Mick could tell that his opponent's confidence had taken a dive and he was wondering what on earth to do next. He didn't want to go further up and felt he couldn't retreat backwards either and lose face, as his fellow gang members were huddled at the bottom egging him on. Obviously searching his mind for inspiration, he shouted at Mick, 'Come on you B******, come on.' At this point, Mick recognised the irony of the situation and partly out of fear and partly out of black humour said to the knifeman, 'You've got to be crazy if you think I'm coming down to you,' following through with a nervous, but nonetheless effective, mocking laugh.

Mick thought back to his school history lessons about the Battle of Hastings and in a flash appreciated, for the first time, the wise words, 'If you have the high ground, stay there'. What would have happened next in this confrontation, we shall never know as, at that moment, John and three burly helpers followed by a couple of even burlier bouncers appeared at the top of a nearby alleyway; the knife wielder and his gang decided the odds were no longer in their favour, quickly disappeared, and left Mick to play another day.

6

Dedicated
Follower of Fashion

In those early days when the Love Affair were still unknown, the gap left behind in my life in Yorkshire was huge, but I was still at school and too young to follow Mick and had to get on with things as best I could. The '60s may have been in full swing, that is if you lived in London, but in Bradford the momentum wasn't quite as quick, and lounging around in coffee bars drinking coke, of the fizzy kind, and frothy expressos was for most people my age as exciting as it got.

There were hardly any shops that sold clothes exclusively for teenagers, but Chelsea Girl did, and we girls flocked into it, anxious to wear the latest 'in' dress so that we could look groovy. Of course, when you are only fifteen, you're easily influenced by so many things, especially pop songs. In those days it was the title that registered with me, not so much the actual words, and I really liked the Kinks 'Dedicated Follower of Fashion'. Even though its eleven-week run in the charts had finished by this time, every juke box, radio, and shop continued to play it over and over again. Ray Davis's voice certainly got stuck inside my head for months, the title subliminally, I'm sure, made me think that I just had to be a follower too. To wear something that had gone out was thought of as unforgiveable and had we young followers of fashion been told one day that birthday suits were in they'd have been instantly sold out! Clothes of the same price were hung together, most being around £3 or £4. I had to work three whole Saturdays before I could afford just one of the cheapest dresses. If you think about it, they were anything but cheap to me, so I had to be inventive to stop appearing like a one-dress woman, I'm exaggerating of course, I didn't only have one dress, I had three. Thankfully, mum liked to look fashionable, so rummaging through her clothes to see if I could borrow anything was usually successful.

With so few shops to choose from, it wasn't unusual to go out and see other people wearing the same thing as you. Far from being upset, we had fun comparing how we'd put things together, and by personalising outfits, we could convince ourselves that we were part of the in-crowd—whoever they were. I was so happy when my Nana gave me her old fur coat that had hung behind her cellar door since the Second World War. It was a perfect fit and no one in Bradford had one like it, it was absolutely fab, despite the bald bits that made it resemble a well-loved teddy bear. Back then wearing real fur was what everyone did if they could afford to. Madge had saved for years for the deposit on a mink coat, and it is beautiful. I said 'is' because she left it to me in her will, saying she hoped that I would enjoy wearing it as much as she had. I can't tell you how touched I was the day she told me she wanted me to have it. Even though I can't wear it anymore, I can't just throw it away when it was her most cherished piece of clothing. She must have felt like a millionairess wearing it and she certainly looked like one. I tried to justify owning both coats by thinking that as the animals had been killed many years before I was even born, there was nothing I could have done to bring them back. At least the mink's beautiful fur is still being appreciated as I occasionally take it out of the tissue paper it's wrapped in, stroking it reminds me so much of my lovely mum-in-law. Oh, I'm feeling sad now, I adore rabbits, cats, dogs, and all animals so the thought of them dying and fond memory of Madge is bringing a lump to my throat, so quickly moving on.

There were plenty of role models to copy, particularly Sandy Shaw, Cilla, and Lulu. Eyeliner was used to draw long lower lashes that made us all look constantly startled. No self-respecting girl would go out without long false lashes, at least the lower ones gave some sense of balance. Dusty Springfield may have had a fantastic voice but her distinctive habit of painting the whole of her eyelids black didn't become particularly popular with many younger teenagers. She was always immaculately turned out, and took hours to get ready, especially as her hair was fastidiously bouffant in style but by her own admittance she was not a fashion icon. Mick and I loved her voice, she was so talented and capable of mimicking so many other singers as her range was tremendous. It's sad to hear that although she really was a lovely person, she lacked basic confidence, quite possibly due to her harsh father. It has even been said that sometimes she felt very uneasy in front of the cameras whilst in the Top of the Pops studio and needed encouragement to leave her dressing room. Of course, much of what is said about performers is untrue, I find it hard to believe that, as was once rumoured, she often sang just one line at a time whilst recording, as it makes her sound incapable but of course, if she did, it could simply be down to her desire to be perfect.

It was Twiggy, who first thought of painting on lower lashes after seeing them on a rag doll and they were a big part of her image along with her slim, androgynous figure. Teenagers tried to emulate her, but because she was so slim, it wasn't easy and surprisingly Empire line dresses were popular too, even though they appeared to add a couple of stones to your weight. The seam under the bust made the wearer look pregnant, which of course very few single teenagers were, as it was considered scandalous and the schoolteachers at my school drilled it into us that we had to be sixteen before we could marry. In the six years that I went to an all-girls school, to my knowledge, only one pupil out of a constant 700 became pregnant. It was surprising that there weren't more teenage pregnancies than that, as the pill wasn't legally available for unmarried girls until '67; even then, it was only prescribed sparingly. Then again, maybe it wasn't that surprising as sex for the majority of 'good' girls wasn't considered an option until marriage. That was quite contrary to the swinging label given to London, but I should imagine that what I've just said applied to most other places in the provinces.

The arrival of the pill did, however, mean that a growing number of girls could take songs such as 'All You Need is Love' literally, because if they were on the pill, they didn't have to worry about being left holding the baby. When the news got out about that one pupil at my school (her condition was described rather crudely by some as 'having a bun in the oven'), whispers about her spread like wildfire. The Kinks must have got stuck in the other girls heads too, because rumour had it that one of them was responsible, but of course, more likely than not, it was just idle tittle tattle, nothing more. However, the temptation to pretend that those loose Empire line dresses were maternity ones sometimes proved too much to resist, and some girls, naturally curious to know how they'd look one day, found cushions useful props in finding out. It's just as well that was simply an innocent girly giggle, I suspect most boys would have been shocked had they seen them doing it, mistaking the girls' fun for wishful thinking, and then worrying they may get trapped and forced into a shotgun wedding. Oh, that has just reminded me of 'Shotgun Wedding', a hit in '65 by Roy C and later recorded by Rod Stewart, both are great in my opinion. A film was made called, *In the Family Way*, directed by

Roy Boulting, starring Hayley Mills and Hywel Bennett and was popular with its predominantly young audience. However, the title was chosen because it was attention-grabbing to attract filmgoer's attention only, as the story was actually about the opposite problem, it focused on a marriage between sixteen-year-olds that wasn't consummated.

One striking, '60s fashion was to wear black and white. I had black and white shoes, bag and dress, complete with black and white plastic raincoat and hat. I must have resembled a penguin. Miniskirts made it impossible to walk anywhere without constantly hearing whistles or car horns, especially when worn with white, knee high leather boots that Nancy Sinatra was constantly reminding us were meant for walking. It was fun, and no one ever got upset by it, such was the light, vibrant mood of the day.

If I walked down a busy road wearing my white mini-dress with a tasselled hem, and wasn't tooted at, I'd begin to worry, thinking my resemblance to Hiawatha was perhaps over the top and was only reassured by the next horn blower or cheeky comment shouted out of a wound-down car window.

Making the most of that black and white fad, discos often had blue strip lights that I earlier said were missing in Butlin's Hawaiian bar, that made white material fluorescent. That was fine from a distance because if you were watching someone under those lights the effect was quite something, but up close, dust and bits of fluff on dark clothes, also became luminous and everyone looked as though they had the worst dandruff ever. I hated those lights apart from when I was wearing my favourite multi-coloured dress, because it lit up like a psychedelic rainbow. Anyone who looked serious while dancing under those indigo lights was most likely trying to hide false teeth that remained dark as they didn't illuminate, unlike natural ones that sparkled far more than Pepsodent toothpaste could make them. Obvious false teeth weren't good at attracting the opposite sex, but then again, neither was an unsmiling face. I remember Mick telling me that he thought I looked like the girl in a popular Maclean's toothpaste ad that we saw whenever we went to the pictures, I thought it was the most flattering thing anyone had ever said to me. I was elated and flashed him the most confident smile, I just wish he hadn't gone on to explain that it was her face that made him think of me, not her beautiful teeth.

Monday night was a favourite with teenagers, as the Mecca started to hold discos especially for them. Boys stood around the dance floor, eyeing up the girls, but most were too shy to ask anyone to dance, but they did their best to look sophisticated, but as they were often eating ice cream cornets, bought on the upstairs balcony, it wasn't easy.

In their defence it really was hard for boys to ask anyone to dance as the girls formed tight circles around their handbags, it must have seemed very intimidating to inexperienced Romeos. Those circles stopped the girls feeling vulnerable, kept their handbags safe, and had the added advantage of stopping any unwanted attention. That security meant they could ignore the boys' stares and be left alone to enjoy songs such as 'The Clapping Song' by Shirley Ellis.

The Beatles and the Rolling Stones were played constantly, and a divide of a different type was formed as it seemed mandatory to like one but not the other. Linda was a Stones fan and so it made the sleepovers we had more fun, as her bedroom was covered in magazine pictures of the Stones and mine, John, Paul, George, and Ringo.

That was before I met Mick, when I would never have thought in a million years that before long I would have a boyfriend whose photo would be pinned up on the bedroom walls of thousands of other girls. We spent hours trying to convert one another, good practice I guess for debate, 'debate' being one of the more obscure subjects at school along with Latin. I was so pleased at the time not to learn Latin, though to be honest I wasn't even sure what it was. Latin would be useful now, when trying to work out the meaning of words and I regret that I didn't learn it.

Occasionally, Linda and I would go to the pictures to watch a Doris Day film, we thought her beautiful clothes were amazing because they were so brightly coloured and co-ordinated, a world apart from the aproned, granny-shoed, flowery-frocked look of many women we saw in our mill town. Oh, I mustn't forget to mention their wrap-around pinafores, jumbo-sized plastic shopping bags and big purses that were needed to carry their silver and heavy coppers. They also had a few paper pound notes, but they managed to hang on to them for quite a long time because even a 10 shilling note went a long way towards the food shopping. These full-time housewives were probably only in their forties but nowadays, most seventy-year-olds look far younger than they did. If they were trying to look a bit smarter than usual rather than leaving their hair rollers at home, they'd cover them with a silk scarf but headscarf or not, they always remembered to wear bright red lipstick, thick face powder and thin drawn on eyebrows. I used to borrow Mum's eyebrow pencil to turn a mole on my right cheek into a beauty spot thinking it was glamourous.

Although I told my peers at school that my boyfriend was living in London I knew that most of them thought I was making him up. Unlike

Tim of the three wheels, Mick never met me outside school because he was rarely home and even when he was, it was a long walk from his house, so I learnt to ignore sarcastic comments made by many a doubting Thomas, but it didn't bother me too much because I knew he was real.

7

Jailed for Climbing Eros

Now, it would be easy in a book with this title to imagine that a milestone event like getting engaged would warrant a chapter all to itself, but our engagement was such a nondescript affair, and so low key that if we took that saying literally, the key wasn't even on the floor, but way below ground, at basement level. I'm not even sure exactly when we did get engaged as we didn't have a cake, announcement, or receive any cards. That was fine by us, I don't think it even occurred to us to have a party, so we simply went into Bradford, looked in Young's jeweller's window and chose my ring. Anybody else's reaction wasn't important to us and perhaps they didn't take us seriously thinking it wouldn't last.

You can imagine how thrilled I was with my sparkly diamond solitaire, but it didn't convince school friends that I really was engaged, after all, none of them could tell the difference between my diamond and the paste ones you could buy in Woolworths.

However, their scepticism did get to me when I had an almost equally important announcement to make. I was so proud, when Mick told me that the Love Affair had made 'Everlasting Love' and I couldn't wait to tell the girls, but they acted as though it was an everyday occurrence and pretended to be unimpressed. I guess I wasn't mature enough to realise that they were simply jealous, and they weren't mature enough to share in my happiness.

Sometimes life on the road for the boys was, to say the least, rather messy. It would perhaps be wise for anyone who suffers from emetophobia, or is very squeamish, to miss out the next few paragraphs. I wasn't going to include this snippet here, but Mick thinks I should as he thinks it's funny, I only hope that others do too but it very much depends on your sense of humour and the strength of your stomach.

'Everlasting Love' had been recorded, but it hadn't been released when the group were booked to play at a venue in Clacton-on-Sea. It had been a great night, the audience seemed to sense that the group they were watching were on the cusp of success. Their intuition added greatly to the atmosphere that left the owner a very happy man. The tills in the bar had been ringing constantly and he knew that the profits from the drinks, together with those from the sold-out ticket sales, would be a record (if you pardon the pun). The place was buzzing.

When the boys had finished playing, they were surprised and pleased to see that the owner had laid on a 'well done and congratulations on making a record' feast of sandwiches and trifle decorated with hundreds and thousands.

Although there was loads to get through, it took no time at all for most of it to disappear, and Mo, who after all was still only fifteen, and being a boy, acted like the typical child that he actually was, and could not resist finishing off all of the rest of the over-sweet, large trifle, washing it down with copious amounts of his first ever champagne. Roy, their then roadie, was also feeling tired and was not looking forward to the challenge of getting his rather drunk yet elated charges into their monstrous Ford Zephyr. He needn't have worried as for once they were as good as the spread they'd just consumed, and the gentle hum of the limo engine lulled them off to sleep in no time. Unfortunately, peace didn't last long, as he could hear a groan coming from the back seat and glancing in his rear mirror he saw Mo sitting upright and even though the internal light was dim, he thought he could make out a distinct green tinge around the young drummer's gills, who, as luck had it, was sitting next to the window. Mick was next to him and although not many cars had electric windows in those days, theirs did, so Mick, quick thinking, pressed the button and thrust the almost unconscious head, of the trifle guzzler out of the window. Too out of it to think about the best direction he should face, Mo felt slightly better once most of his share of the celebratory buffet was ejected onto the road, but not quite all of it, as plenty of the trifle, with its hundreds and thousands topping, had blown straight back onto his huge, fashionable, Afro perm—he was facing the wrong way.

Cigarette smoke and sweaty bodies was one thing that the boys were used to sharing but vomit was something else, so the by-now wide awake and unamused huddle pleaded with Roy to stop. Roy was equally repulsed, but he also took his responsibilities very seriously and was not going to risk crashing the car, no matter how unpleasant or pungent the air inside it was. It was another few miles before a motorway services came into view and the novice drunk had sunk into a fairly deep stupor by the time the car pulled up in front of a Little Chef. All except one jumped out, and were about to go in when, I'm not sure if it was out of pity or devilment, they decided they'd better go back and collect their drummer. He was incapable of walking on his own and had to be supported one on either side as Roy and Mick led him inside.

'What 'r we doing? he can't sit with us, he'll put us off our food' objected Roy, so without a second thought, they propped Mo up at an empty table nearest the door. They then joined the others who were in unsympathetic fits of giggles at the dishevelled, comatose, figure that had been unceremoniously dumped alone, all the while pretending that they didn't know who he could possibly be.

Unbelievably, they were ravenous again, and so they gave their requests of burgers and chips to the motherly waitress who readily took their orders, before heading towards the lonely customer yet to be served. Perhaps she needed glasses, but it was only when she was within a couple of feet of Master Bacon that she let out a screech, dropped her pen and pad and ran screaming into the kitchen, shouting for her boss.

Maternal or not, she then hurried back out again towards the boys, and looking almost as white as Mo, demanded that they either left immediately or (looking as though she was about to be ill herself), insisted 'If you want burgers, you'd better sort out 'im out, over there wi' 'undreds and thousands in 'is 'air....'

Even though it took the whole of the next day and the one after that for Mo to completely recover, his summing up of the situation? 'Well, it beats going to school!'

I never think of Mick as having a criminal record or of myself as being a gangster's moll, but I guess you could say that the former is true. However, I am pleased to say that far from being a jailbird in the usual sense, Mick only found himself behind bars as a result of a deliberate attempt by their managers to gain as much publicity as possible for their new release. The record came out just after Christmas '67, and first entered the charts at No. 36, possibly helped by the fact that previously, Sid, it was rumoured, gave a gift of £200 (equivalent to about £4,000 today), to Radio Caroline, in return for them playing the record several times a day. Even though everyone was wowed over by it, Sid wanted to make absolutely sure that it would climb further up the charts. Sid didn't part with money easily unless there was a pay back, so he must have known that this record was worth backing to the hilt, even though he had to dig deep into his own pocket. Robert Knight's version had already reached the American Top 20, having been released several months earlier and was hot on their heels in the UK at No. 40. There was a real urgency to find an alternative way, apart from the obvious one of continuing to grease various palms, to help the Love Affair win the race to the top.

The stunt they came up with got them arrested and worked better than they'd dared hope, because the story made headline news in the national papers and was reported on the evening television news. The original idea was thought up by a professional publicist, affectionately known as Biffo the Bear, after a character out of Beano. The plan was for the boys to have their photos taken on and around the statue of Eros, in Piccadilly. I don't know if Biffo had done his research to make sure the statue could bear any weight or not, but if he had, he would have discovered that although the base is bronze, the statue itself is hollow aluminium, otherwise the archer would never have been able to stand on one leg without toppling over.

Perhaps Biffo decided not to take any risks that might result in injury to either his clients or Eros so he didn't instruct any of the boys to climb on Eros's back because he himself might well have been dragged before a jury, one that was attempting to ascertain not only who was to blame, but who had squashed who as a result of an ill-advised piggyback ride. It happened on a cold, dull, early January afternoon when, full of optimism, the Love Affair couldn't wait to do their bit, thinking it would be fun. After asking if they were ready, Sid gave the boys the nod to start climbing the famous statue and they readily obliged. The cold air bit into their skin and icy fountain water drenched their coats, but even that didn't dampen their enthusiasm, as they were enjoying every second, so much so that they forgot all about their soggy uncomfortable clothes.

Mo tried his best to climb high, but knowing him as I do, I don't think mountaineering would have been his choice of sport at school, any more than it would have been mine, and he struggled to make it beyond the first tier. Ironically, unlike me, he now goes to the gym every day, though I suspect his favourite bit could be sitting in the sauna. The others managed to get higher up, near to the statue's foot, and Sid told them to start clapping and sing 'Amen' to make as much noise as they could to gain the attention of people going by.

One person stopped to watch, then another and another and within minutes, the small crowd became a big one. Drivers thought something interesting was going on and slowed down to see what all the fuss was about. Twenty minutes later, the enormity of the disruption was beyond belief, the West End traffic ground to a complete standstill. Meanwhile, a member of their entourage phoned the newspapers pretending to be a shocked little old lady exclaiming that, 'It's a disgrace, pippies are desecrating a national monument.' Police and reporters were at the scene within minutes. When asked to get down, the boys glanced at Sid, who was shaking his head, wanting to draw out the event as long possible. Fire engines, with sirens wailing and lights flashing screeched up alongside them, adding greatly to the drama. They were told that if they didn't come down, hose pipes would be used to blast them off. Looking at Sid for guidance, they were relieved that he gave them permission to get down, another even greater and possibly painful soaking would have turned the staged drama into a real one, especially if they or anyone else got injured. As soon as their feet touched the pavement they were arrested and now enjoying what was turning into a farce, the boys squirmed their bodies as if in pain when their arms were forced behind their backs. Mick accidentally on purpose, knocked the helmet of the policeman who was restraining him, it perched at an ungainly, comical angle, causing the wearer to stagger in an undignified manner as he struggled to get Mick into a waiting Black Maria. You would have thought that they were acting in a film instead of the situation being for real, but it was simply a game to them, one that for once would not get them in trouble with their managers.

They continued to be amused actors in their own play and egging each other on, they messed about for all they were worth. Rex shouting at the top of his voice, 'Help, brutality! police brutality!' did nothing to endear himself to the police officers who must have been frustrated that they couldn't show their true feelings in a more demonstrative way, as they were surrounded by hundreds of gawping witnesses.

They were allowed home after being released on bail, which was paid for by Sid and John, and everyone was delighted that they had to appear at the famous Bow Street Court because they knew that it would attract further publicity. The next day Sid's wish came true, his boys' faces were in every national newspaper. Had he had to pay for such exposure, it would have cost him many thousands of pounds. The saying that all publicity is good publicity was working. Mick remembers the first day in dock with great amusement and gratitude. They were charged with causing an obstruction and disturbing the peace. Unbelievably, they pleaded not guilty, hoping that they could drag things out. Their defence in court was that it was the public causing the obstruction, not them, the drivers chose to go slowly past and the public to stand and stare, they didn't make them. A young police officer, while being cross-examined by the group's barrister, was put under such pressure that he fainted in front of the packed court that included reporters from the major tabloids. Even the police couldn't help but let their faces slip into a smile for once, as Mo took his oath. When the clerk of court placed a Kippah on Mo's head, it appeared to hover above his huge Afro hair style, making it resemble a pea on a drummer (sorry, couldn't resist). The rest of the accused burst out laughing and couldn't contain their amusement, even when the judge sternly warned them to be quiet, otherwise they would be in contempt of court, and he would send them straight to the cells. The only thing they could do was try and make themselves invisible, by sliding below the dock out of sight, which they promptly did. Covering their mouths with their hands to stifle their giggles made things worse, their stomachs hurt with laughter, and Rex, who should have visited the toilet earlier than that particular moment, was lucky the judge wasn't aware of the convulsing guitarist's soggy, satin trousers. Bellowing at the boys to sit up straight, some people might have thought it justified if he had flung them in jail and thrown away the key.

Mo later described the scene from his point of view. All he could see was four pairs of feet doing a mid-air dance in an otherwise unoccupied dock. The court could hear snorts and sniggers as Mick, Lynton, Steve, and Rex tried not to choke. They had turned the whole scene into absolute chaos and the best Mo could do was take his handkerchief out of his pocket pretending to blow his nose in a futile attempt to hide his own laughter. They had to attend court two more times after that before the verdict was reached. At least over the years since then, Mick and the others have paid enough in taxes to cover those court costs many times over, so knowing that makes my conscious a little easier.

I was stunned at just how well Biffo's idea had worked when I saw their photo in the *Daily Mirror*. I'm not sure if my Dad was proud or dismayed when his customers insisted on crowding around his morning paper so they could take a look at the headline. It was obvious that the judge was frustrated when he fined them the most that he could, a paltry £11. Only days before, the fines had been increased considerably but because the incident had happened before that, he couldn't fine them more. Mick couldn't help being cheeky and as he was paying his fine he quipped 'There, that'll buy you a few more truncheons and whistles', no doubt leaving the clerk furious at his arrogance. It was during the final hearing that the group learnt that 'Everlasting Love' was rocketing up the charts, leaving Robert Knight in its wake. That free, national publicity had helped them beyond measure.

Nearing the end of school and having passed my meagre five O Levels and a handful of GCSEs, I was keen to find a way of moving to London to be near Mick. I'd turned seventeen and was engaged so my parents knew that I was determined to get there and resigned themselves to the fact that they couldn't or, more accurately, shouldn't stand in our way. Even when the group were in the charts and Mick had money at last, he used to bring home the odd teaspoon or milk jug from hotels to add to our growing numbers of tea towels and saucepans that I'd collected for our bottom drawer. Although I didn't approve of him pocketing things, as once in jail is enough for anyone, I did think that it was a romantic thing to do because it proved to me that he was serious about us sharing our future together.

The unfussiness of our engagement reminds me, very much, of Mo's wedding to Pam a few years later. They were married in a registry office with no guests present and asked a passer-by if they would mind being their witness and photographer. That photograph is as perfect as any professional one, they look so lovely—let me rephrase that, Pam looks beautiful and Mo so happy. It was less stressful but equally as romantic as any traditional wedding and must have also made that passer-by's day, and they probably talked about it for years afterwards.

Now, here's an interesting little snippet, yesterday, Morgan posted a Love Affair video on Facebook that he'd just come across that was made in '68. I was thrilled as there are so few about and I had never seen this blast from fifty years ago. They are even walking across a zebra crossing, a whole year before the Beatles were immortalised doing exactly the same on their Abbey Road album. You could say the Love Affair got there first, even though it's a different crossing. Mo had his Samoyed dog with him in the video, whose party piece was to greet everyone by softly nose-butting them in the groin. Sid thought it was so amusing that he decided to call him Chummy. I asked Mick if he remembers making the video and he does, especially trying not to fall off their bikes as they rode them down the steps behind the Albert Hall. He also said that he recalls seeing some attractive mews houses nearby that he dreamt we might own one day.

The video is on YouTube headed Love Affair—'A Day Without Love video 1968' (it has a bright orange band across it).

8

Belfast

The sparkle of my engagement ring was representative of our optimistic view of our future life together, but looking back now, we have had to face many ups and downs, a true roller coaster in fact, yet on reflection (no pun intended), every moment has been precious in its own way.

In the '60s, most children didn't waste any time between leaving school and starting work, and they found a job as soon as they could, that is if they weren't going onto further education. In true form, despite my aim to move to London, I was working within a few days of leaving school. Some of my friends were going onto college and university, but it wasn't the foregone conclusion for most pupils as it is now. I was an expert on the top twenty at this time, and because I had to bridge the gap before finally moving south, I replied to an ad for a sales assistant at the largest record shop in Bradford, called Vallances; it seemed ideal for me. I got the interview, and wore my Mary Quant, bright orange, corduroy coat that I'd bought in the sales. It was too long for me at first, so I chopped several inches off the bottom before stitching it by hand, leaving a lumpy hem. I was upset when I realised that I looked like a huge orange, so I added a wide belt with a shiny golden buckle that squashed my middle in sufficiently enough, to convince me, if no one else, that I was then as curvaceous as Marylyn Monroe. With hindsight, I attracted lots of attention whilst wearing it, but not necessarily for the right reasons. Vallances was in the heart of the town, and on a clear day anyone standing on the surrounding moors would have been able to see me quite easily, because my coat was so bright.

I remember being shown into Vallances' tiny staff room to be interviewed by the general manager. He asked me if I'd like to take my coat off, but I refused because I was nervous and would have struggled undoing all the shiny buttons and gigantic belt. A heater was blowing, and the temperature combined with the smell of a discarded, half-eaten pickled onion sandwich made me feel queasy, but I tried not to show it and concentrated on his questions. Thankfully, there was no more mention of removing any clothes and I was relieved because I'd only just met this man (must add, that even if I'd known him a long time I still wouldn't have taken any clothes off just because he asked me—I don't want people to get the wrong idea!). I felt he was in rather too close proximity to me, as there wasn't even a desk between us, just a smelly plate and the door behind us was firmly shut.

Any fears I had were unfounded as I realised that he was very nice and extremely 'proper' even if his choice of interview room left a lot to be desired. The questions were a doddle to me and when I correctly answered, 'What are the top three records in the charts?' he was obviously impressed, little knowing that I had a vested interest in knowing what was, so he offered me the job there and then. It seemed such an easy question and I wondered why there weren't many after that, but I now realise how knowledgeable he must have thought I was. If anyone asked me that same question now, I wouldn't have a clue.

I was over the moon and flounced down the steps to the ground floor, the orange coat must have made me look like a Belisha beacon, but I was unaware of the astounded stares belonging to the rest of the staff. How did I know they were looking at me if I was oblivious?—well it's simple, one of my new colleagues told me they were.

My immediate manager was Mavis, now my closest friend. Although she seemed much older than me at the time, she wasn't really, but her sophistication and knowledge of the job made her seem as though she was. She was kind and calm, and no explanation of my role was too much trouble. I was in awe of her immaculate make-up and hair but most impressive of all, her lipstick never came off or even faded, unlike my own which disappears almost as soon as I put it on, it's one of life's little mysteries. The record department was on the first floor with a large sloping window that overlooked Market Street, I could adapt a favourite joke of Mick's about car salesmen and say that we didn't look out of the window in the morning because that would have left us nothing to do in the afternoon—but I won't.

There were three of us and it was immediately apparent that it really was a crowd. I felt unwelcome by the third girl and couldn't for the life of me know what I had done to upset her. No matter how friendly I tried to be, her iciness never went away and the iceberg that grew between us made it impossible for me to reach out to her and make her a friend. I would have loved to have simply melted it away, but she made it impossible, so I had to resign myself to simply accept the status quo. However, she wasn't unpleasant, so for the sake of our jobs, we managed to work reasonably well together, even though I suspect she felt like putting flags out the day I left. It really was a teenage girl's dream, listening and discussing the charts as part of your job and there was never any shortage of attractive boys who hung around the counter. We had to be nice to the customers, so flirting and talking to them was encouraged.

Anyone could ask for a record to be played to them as they sat comfortably in a small private listening booth. Every Saturday we were crowded, not necessarily with genuine customers who wanted to buy something, but teenagers whiling away the hours in the warmth of their own enclosed space. On Saturdays the shop was so full that our customers had to split themselves between us and two other music shops nearby, it's a wonder those stone pavements didn't have a well-worn path down their middles because so many teenagers, budding musicians, and members of local groups walked on them. One notable group, whose members Mavis remembers popped in regularly, was called the Elizabethans, later known as Smokie. They went on to sell over 30 million records playing to millions of fans throughout the world. Not many groups can boast that they played in the Kremlin, but Smokie did. 'What Can I Do' was a huge hit for them in Russia, and after Vladimir Putin saw them play at president of Kazakhstan's birthday party, he became a fan of theirs and invited them to play at a New Year Celebration. There they played to 1,500 people, including Russia's top military and church leaders. Those dignitaries weren't exactly dancing in the aisles like Smokie's usual fans, but the group felt honoured, especially as it was their second visit in five years. I think it's fascinating that the first time they were there, they were served wine from Joseph Stalin's personal cellar, but the last time, it was plain old Australian Shiraz. Actually, Shiraz sounds fine, unlike the menu, which included octopus carpaccio. Mick and I occasionally eat calamari, which I guess is similar, but the thought of octopus is a tentacle too far as far as I'm concerned. I think, subconsciously, I'm afraid that if I ate it, my mouth would fill with ink or, even worse, my tonsils might get strangled by the octopus desperate to get out.

Even though Mick never went to Russia, certain early events in Smokie's career were almost identical to those he experienced. Smokie and Mick all had dealings with Mark Jordon who was Mick's agent when he was in the Spell, they all played at Butlins, but unlike Mick's full season, they only stayed a week. Smokie and the Love Affair were both signed up to Decca, but they never got anywhere with the label as their contracts amounted to nothing and only days before Mick was first on *Top of the Pops*, Smokie made their debut television appearance on a regional programme called *Calendar* for Yorkshire TV.

When I first saw Smokie on TV, I really liked them, but even though they were all from Bradford, it would be many years before Mick and I became friends with their bass player Terry Uttley, who was the granddaddy of the group, and a nicer man you couldn't have wished to meet. As a Bradfordian, I felt very proud of Terry and Smokie's achievements, especially as they big-heartedly played at no less than twenty-eight Annual Smokie Gala Dinner Dances, raising hundreds of thousands of pounds for our local hospital's Annette Fox Leukaemia Research Fund. In fact, it was through that connection and not music that we met Terry.

Mick and our son, Ben, used to be works drivers for Radical Sportscars, and Mick was approached by Professor Liakat Parapia, a consultant at Bradford Royal Infirmary, to see if he could donate a prize for their dinner dance auction. Mick said that he and Ben would take two people around several laps of a Grand Prix race circuit. Terry was the highest bidder, wanting it as a treat for his grandson. When they turned up at Donington Park Circuit, those several laps turned into many because our two appreciative guests loved it so much and were excellent passengers. Not everyone could be so cool, as many people had trouble to even walk after getting out of the passenger seat, while others had to run to the toilet, wishing perhaps they hadn't indulged in the traditional racers breakfast of coffee and a bacon sandwich.

Mick and I were shocked and devastated when (coincidentally driving through Ilkley, less than a quarter of a mile from Terry and his wife Shirley's home of forty years) we received a call from one of his daughters, Holly, to tell us that their father (loved by everyone who met him because he was exceptionally likeable) had died—only four weeks after their mum. I was so touched that she should even think of ringing us at such a tragic time, but she explained that she and her sister, Lisa, wanted his friends to hear the heart-breaking news before it was announced publicly. His girls certainly share Terry's approach to life and 'kindness' (that just so happens to also be a former name for Smokie) is so apparent in his daughters, no wonder he was so very proud of his family.

It's hard to be precise but at a guess I'd say that for every ten records listened to at Vallances, only one would be bought. No rules or regulations were made, nobody was thrown out, and the relaxed atmosphere was perfect for me, especially when customers were buying the Love Affair's records. I felt we were doing our bit to help the group, even though they were 200 miles away.

Miss Iceberg wasn't the only person that gave me the cold shoulder though, the other one belonged to a middle-aged woman in washing machines (by that I mean washing machine department she didn't actually climb into the drums), who liked to rule the roost and was not impressed when female staff her age were slowly being replaced by younger ones.

One of the long-serving delivery drivers there passed our pub on his way into work and offered to give me a lift each day. He became my human alarm clock and often saved my bacon on the days that I overslept; he would sound his horn and then patiently wait in the van as I hurriedly got dressed. I can forgive that former me for sleeping in as it was often a struggle to have a decent night's sleep living above a busy bar. The clatter of glasses, sound of laughter and chatter, and general noise along with the stench of smoke from hundreds of cigarettes came through the floorboards of my bedroom every night.

I often had to wait until midnight before it got quiet. Mum and Dad liked to relax watching a film in the room next to mine and I couldn't escape noise completely, until about two or three in the morning, because the walls were thin.

Living in a pub was not what I had selfishly hoped it would be; it destroys any normal family life because I hardly saw my parents as we kept different hours.

Those walls, though flimsy, proved they were thick enough to contain a lethal fire, in the kitchen next to my room, that started shortly after Mum had made Dad's supper. Luckily, I was living away in London at the time. I've never thought about it before now, but had I been in my own bed when it happened, the only exit was through the burning kitchen and that would have been terrifying and possibly fatal for me. Mum had left the chip pan on, a major cause of fires in those days. She'd intended leaving it for a few minutes but misjudged the timing. It overheated and caught fire, the flames spread in seconds and the kitchen and contents were turned into charcoal as the dense smoke poured out the open sash front window, which, in turn, helped fan the flames into a frenzy.

I was devastated because my white pet budgie, who I really loved, died, overcome by smoke. Mum's Pekinese was much luckier, the firemen were able to revive him with oxygen. There mustn't have been much happening that week, as news of the fire made the local paper's front page, alongside a photo of Chang and his rescuer, a handsome fireman. (I think Mum was a bit jealous!)

Thanks to that other gallant man, my van driver, I was never late although he did risk me making him so, but I know he enjoyed listening to the antics of the Love Affair, so he must have thought it was well worth it. It's sad to think that Vallances isn't there anymore, although the building it was in still stands, it is on the site of the Swan Arcade that was well-trodden by J. B. Priestley. In the '60s there was a huge mural painting of the Beatles on the showroom wall. It was several feet high and possibly still there beneath decades of wall covering, I would love to know, but probably never will.

Maybe one day, it'll be discovered like pyramid tomb art, but I doubt if that building will last 5,000 years even though its architect claimed that it was one of the sturdiest in Bradford. The large windows can't have been that strong though, as they were once smashed as fans arrived in their hundreds, waiting for the arrival of the Bachelors who were there to promote their record. That scene was familiar to Mick because a very similar thing happened to the Love Affair that was equally dramatic on one of their many trips to Ireland. They were on yet another tour, in Belfast, and the promoter owned several record shops, one of which was called A1 Records. A canny businessman, he saw a golden opportunity to not only advertise the tour, but his shops too. He arranged the deal in such a way that it included a public appearance in his Gresham Street branch on a Saturday afternoon. Not giving it a second thought, knowing they would be in the city anyway, the boys didn't mind and thought that a quick record signing and a few autographs would hardly eat into their day and weren't unduly concerned. They welcomed being away from their hotel, it was good to be doing something a little bit different, so they happily piled into their chauffeur-driven car to take them there. Messing about as usual, they didn't take much notice of the fact that their driver wasn't exactly sure where it was. They did, however, hear the reply of a middle-aged local who, when asked for directions, told their driver, in an attractive, lilting accent, that he needed to 'turn right *before* the last set of traffic lights'. It took them the remainder of that journey to compose themselves enough to face their fans as their stomachs ached with laughter. Even though their driver's sense of direction wasn't impressive, his previously unknown psychic one must have been, as he managed to get them there, following the aforementioned instructions to the letter. Little did they realise that they would be risking getting seriously injured or even killed during the mayhem that followed. The promoter had earlier arranged for all his delivery vans to drive around Belfast with banners and tannoys announcing their arrival. The crowds gathered and eventually the police had to erect crash barriers. They escorted the Love Affair's car through the throng until, risking life and limb themselves, they ushered the boys through the main door of the shop but not before the roof of the vacated car buckled in as several girls stood on it to get a better view. The screaming fans were completely hysterical by this time, and they made famished, scavenging vultures swooping on their prey seem tame by comparison. Realising that the crowd really was beyond control, the group had to get away from the situation and fast. The police pushed them up an emergency exit flight of stairs, this particular type of emergency though, could never have been envisaged by the person who placed them there. The old, wooden steps designed originally to hold just one person at a time started to give way and Rex was last and almost at the top when he had to be pulled by his arms, to safety just as they collapsed completely, sending dust clouds, plaster, and debris everywhere.

The boys could hear the deafening sound of the old stairs crashing down and at the same time screams and shouts and the breaking of glass. The large shop windows were shattering too, unable to sustain the weight of the many bodies pushed against them. Mick isn't sure if any fans were injured, but hopefully they weren't as he would surely have been informed and remembered if they had. The scene that followed was a bit like a police chase in a movie but instead of being chased by police, the police were ahead of them showing them where to go as they all escaped over the rooftops to safety.

As frequent visitors to Belfast ever since they first released 'Everlasting Love', the Love Affair were staying at a hotel in the centre of Belfast (possibly shortly after 'Bringing on Back the Good Times' was a hit in the summer of '69). Mick was shaken out of his bed by the tremor of an explosion. Nobody was evacuated as it was becoming common place, so he simply climbed back into bed and went straight back to sleep again. How cool, considering that the bomb was so big that it destroyed much of the adjoining building.

Back to Vallances. When I wasn't busy selling records, I was quietly scheming how to achieve my ambition of getting to London. Mum had said that as we were engaged, I could go, but on the condition that I found a job where living accommodation was included. It was her way of ensuring that Mick and I didn't live together. He was away touring the UK and Europe much of the time, and even if we had, it would have been a very lonely existence, so it was a wise instruction in more ways than one. However, Mick and I often think that if we'd bought a flat together, it would have been a great investment, particularly if it been in the centre of London as it would be worth millions of pounds now. Oh well, it's easy to be wise after the event.

I was still working at Vallances when Mick had a few days off and was back home after he'd had three hectic months of touring, due to the success of 'Rainbow Valley'. We went with some friends to a night club in Leeds. It was unusual for us to venture far, and I can't even remember why we'd decided to go out on that night, but we did. We thought that we'd slipped in unnoticed, but we were being watched by hidden eyes, whose owner wanted to make trouble for us. They'd phoned the police, wrongly reporting that we were in possession of drugs and almost as soon as we left to head home, we could hear police sirens and were surprised that we were being followed. The driver overtook us and flagged us down, we pulled over behind the flashing lights but were puzzled why we were being stopped, but it became obvious when we were bombarded with dozens of questions. The accusation was a complete fabrication, and the seriousness of the officers turned into friendliness as they realised we really were innocent, and their interrogation became one all about Mick's records and experiences in the group. We could tell that, although it was a busy Saturday night, when they should have been in pursuit of real criminals, they were fascinated by the novelty of speaking to Mick. They may have been police officers, but they were also young men and in awe of Mick, wishing perhaps that they were in his position, and they seemed in no hurry to get on with their jobs. One of them squeezed onto the backseat, whilst the other leaned nonchalantly through the open passenger window and within minutes we were having a good time, and we felt as though we were in the presence of new friends. They momentarily forgot they were wearing police uniforms and their official demeanour softened, revealing two very likeable fans of the Love Affair with great senses of humour. Even though the officers thought they had a genuine reason to stop us, thinking an arrest was imminent, far from being disappointed that one wasn't, they were chuffed that after asking Mick for an autograph, he wrote in his name on the last pages of their notebooks. The person who called them would have been very annoyed had they realised that, because of their malicious phone call, we thoroughly enjoyed that meeting, far more than the time we'd spent in the club. That night wouldn't have stood out and I wouldn't be writing about it now, so whoever they were, I'd like to say thank you.

On a different but similar occasion, while in Sweden where they were getting used to being stopped and searched for drugs, the Love Affair had an idea to brighten up the intrusion next time it happened. Knowing that Alsatians get excited by the smell of aniseed balls, they hid the sweets in every small orifice of their Jaguar. They couldn't wait for the police with their sniffer dogs to stop them so they could see what would happen. When they were eventually stopped the dogs went crazy, and the officers were frustrated that they couldn't find anything other than aniseed balls. It was worth all the dog hair and drool left behind, as on this occasion those Swedish boys in blue, so different to our Leeds policemen, were too sulky and pompous to ask for autographs. The only signatures they wanted was on statements admitting guilt, so they left with their own tails tucked firmly between their legs, whilst those belonging to their four-legged friends wouldn't stop wagging after enjoying their treats.

They say that a prophet is never welcome in his own country; the person that wrongly accused Mick when we were in the nightclub in Leeds that time was not pleased to see him and certainly no kinder than Leon Hickman, a Bradford reporter who wrote a piece in our local paper shortly after Mick was on *Top of the Pops*. He said that the long overcoat Mick was wearing, as he stepped onto the platform in Bradford Exchange station, made him look like a veteran from a doss house. Mick's mum was incensed because the comparison insulted her. It took us all our time to stop her from going into the *Telegraph & Argus* office to tell him off, even though in truth his additional paragraph about Mick getting off the first class carriage of a Pullman train delighted her, as it was confirmation that her youngest was, at last, doing well.

9

I Move to London

Knowing how I would get to London was no easy task as, of course, I couldn't research the internet because it didn't exist, and I didn't really have a clue how to start going about it. Thanks to having enough GCEs to allow me to apply to teacher training colleges, I thought that might be a good idea. Dad thought otherwise, don't ask me why, but he had a down on teachers and dissuaded me. My love of children has caused me to often regret that decision, as a short spell doing work experience in a nursery during my last school term confirmed that it would have suited me well—provided the children were over five. Looking after tiny ones meant spending most of the day wiping noses and bottoms and fastening buckles or laces on the cutest of shoes. Gorgeous though the babies were, being a nursery nurse wasn't for me.

One of the pub's customers worked for our local Inland Revenue and suggested that, because I had the right qualifications, I could apply to be a tax officer, immediately jumping up a grade and getting a decent salary, especially in the capital. I didn't realise that working for the Inland Revenue wasn't a popular thing to do, but it paid well, and I didn't really care as long as I could get to be near Mick. What the job entailed was irrelevant to me and when he explained that I would be able to stay in a hostel, that's all I really needed to hear. He brought an application form to me, appreciating the free pints Dad gave him in return for his help. Relaxed by the alcohol, the rather serious and usually sober taxman actually tried to quip a joke, telling Richard that he enjoyed the Bradford

Hotel's 'returns' far more than the ones he had to deal with at work. For the life of me, I can't remember going for an interview, maybe my head was too stuck in the clouds for me to remember such a mundane thing, but however I managed it, I did get the job, it was in Holborn.

Perhaps I was the only person in history to get so excited about going to a tax office, but I couldn't wait, and luckily Mick was in the country when I was due to start and managed to arrange to come home so that he could go back down with Mum and me. Mum obviously wanted to make sure I was OK and that I really was staying in the hostel and hadn't sneakily made other arrangements. The three of us left Dad at home so that he could look after the pub, but strangely enough, I wasn't too upset at saying goodbye. Although he meant the world to me, the thrill of finally setting off towards my new life overrode any sadness that I would usually feel.

Living in my own bubble, one that was more exceptional than most teenagers, due to our unusual circumstances, I knew surprisingly little about London. Although I had passed through briefly when I went abroad with Susan my first best friend and her family, we never got out of the car. I'd never set foot on the streets that, according to the Dick Whittington story I'd read as a child, were paved with gold and as Mick was also there seeking his fortune, and it was turning out well, I almost believed they were. The full extent of my knowledge of London, was that it was where my Uncle Jim, Mick, and the queen lived, though not altogether of course. Oh, and most importantly to us, it was where *Top of the Pops* was made.

South Kensington, to me, was simply the address where the Inland Revenue hostel was, I didn't realise that it was one of the most expensive parts of London. It was perhaps as well, because if I had I known, I might have thought that I was about to go up in the world, when in fact the hostel was one of the dingiest and depressing places imaginable.

The journey to London was fine and without incident, but we had misjudged our arrival by twenty minutes, which was not bad considering it took five hours to get there.

I tentatively rang the bell of the unloved front door. In its prime, the house would have been lovely when it had an immaculate white exterior with pillars, an ornate wrought-iron fence festooned with flowers and glistening door furniture. Now, the paint was peeling badly, the garden covered in weeds, the fence long since gone, and only iron stubs remained. The huge house had five floors and originally must have belonged to a very wealthy family with servants. If you ever watched *Upstairs Downstairs*, you'll know exactly what it would have looked like in its heyday, but that was decades earlier and the hostel was a stark contrast to its neighbours, many of which were still in pristine condition. Mum stood on one side of me and Mick on the other holding my suitcase, as we waited for several minutes in front of the unanswered door. On the verge of turning away thinking that we had the wrong house, I was both pleased, and not pleased, to see that the door was partially opened by an intimidating, middle-aged woman who peered around it. Her face was scarred down one side, her cold eyes that were almost as small as a weasel's, and the scowl that she wore did nothing at all to make me feel welcome. 'Yes?' she enquired curtly. I explained who I was, and then she snapped, 'You're late, he can't come in' whilst pointing at Mick with an accusing finger. I could sense that Mum was wishing that I would change my mind and turn around, but I was determined that having come this far, in no way would I allow the warden, as she was known, to put me off. Mick had no choice but to leave us to it, so we stepped inside the empty hallway, the smell of boiled cabbage was overwhelming. Our footsteps echoed as we approached the still grand staircase, its hard metal handrail may have steadied us as we went up, but it did nothing to soothe our nerves.

A second door was pushed aggressively by the warden, and I was dismayed by what I saw, behind it there was a dormitory with six ex-army beds and dilapidated furniture that any proud Yorkshire family would have thrown out. A girl a bit older than myself was reading a book but our unexpected arrival must have startled her, and she jumped off her bed in a panic. I was puzzled by the strange crinkly noise that her mattress made as she did.

I learnt that it was made out of straw and when I got into my own bed later that night, it was so uncomfortable, and I realised that my mattress was too. Anyone looking at the scene would have been forgiven for thinking that she was behaving more like an inmate in a prison cell than a young, trendy, teenager in swinging Chelsea. I put my suitcase next to a bed and not wanting to spend any longer there, we quickly left and went to check Mum into a nearby hotel. It only had two stars, but it seemed luxurious compared to the hostel. I think the person who chose the furniture for the hostel had taken the latter part of the title civil servant too literally, I was sure that even the scullery maids that once live there would have had better rooms. Mum pleaded with me to at least spend the night in her room with her, but I'd made my bed, this was my new life, so although the mattress was awful I decided I'd better literally lie on it. The coldness of the night continued, and I don't necessarily mean temperature wise. Feeling lonelier than I had ever done in my entire life, I got into bed wondering what the future would bring. I wished that I hadn't been so quick to turn down Mum's offer to stay in her room; however, I was soon distracted by a commotion coming from the bed opposite me.

The rustling of the mattress was already familiar, but giggles? when I finally braved myself to peer over my scratchy sheets to see clearer, I realised that, unbelievably, given the strictness of matron, the girl opposite had sneaked her boyfriend in, totally unaware that she was, in my eyes at least, risking being hanged, drawn, and quartered at dawn.

Wishing I wasn't there, I stuffed my last two tissues into my ears and slid as far down my awful bed as I could. In that instant my stiff upper lip disappeared, I cried, no sobbed is more accurate—I sobbed as silently as I could and not wanting to use my improvised ear plugs because they were doing a reasonable job, I blew my nose on the sheets.

I didn't really use the sheet to blow my nose on, I just put that in for effect, but even if I had, I think I could have been excused for feeling so defiant. I don't know how I managed it, but I soon fell asleep and when I woke up the next morning the bed opposite was empty, her boyfriend must have sneaked back out of the filthy window that was propped open with a brick, and the sound of rush hour traffic was clear to hear. I decided that she must have gone down for breakfast smugly keeping her sexy secret to herself.

Years later Mum confessed that she had spent most of that night feeling so upset that she also shed quite a few tears, but typically, she put a brave face on things, and I never guessed as we met up to say goodbye. She had all her makeup on, and it effectively disguised the distress she was feeling, as she prepared herself to go back to Yorkshire, but I did know that she really didn't want to leave me behind in that awful place.

The look on her face, as we said goodbye, made me realise that she wanted to say, 'It's not too late to change your mind you know.' But she didn't, and I've been grateful to her ever since, for allowing me to stay. I didn't tell her about the nocturnal visitor, as I'm sure she would have acted differently and insisted that I ended my adventure there and then, even though it had barely begun.

The lump in my throat made it hard to speak as we waved to one another as she disappeared around the corner of the road leaving me wondering how on earth I would pass the time before starting my new job in a few days. I decided to phone my Uncle Jim, Dad's brother who lived in Richmond, to let him know I'd arrived, as promised. Uncle Jim never forgot his Yorkshire roots, he was born in Scarborough and when my grandparents moved to Bradford into a very overcrowded terraced house, a fairly well off spinster aunty, called Gertie who lived in London, adopted him. I remember him visiting us when I was tiny, and like Dad, he loved children and he used to take me on walks as I held onto the big comforting hand of my favourite uncle. I was so impressed with his 'funny' accent it reminded me of the way people I'd seen on the television spoke. Dad won a few hundred pounds on the pools just before I was born, and had enough money to later buy a television, that no one else we knew could afford. He bought it especially for Queen Elizabeth's coronation in June 1953 when the sitting room above our plumbers shop was crowded with neighbours, friends, and relatives. Dad told me that the television impressed them as much if not more so than the occasion itself. It was surprising that the floor didn't cave in with their all their weight.

Although I was oblivious to all that excitement because I was too young, I do clearly remember, eighteen months later, sitting on Dad's shoulders when I was three years old. The Queen and Prince Phillip were visiting Bradford and they went straight past the shop door. Before they came into sight I didn't have a clue what was happening and was simply enjoying the atmosphere as hundreds of people lined the street each one waiving a paper Union Jack flag. When the royal couple's maroon Rolls-Royce reached us, it was inches away from my right foot, enclosed in a best shoe, bought for the occasion. My other foot also had a best shoe on it, but stayed firmly pressed against Dad's chest, lucky really, otherwise I could have been pushed off his shoulders by the jostling crowd and dragged behind the royal procession—the bottom of my party dress caught in the bumper of the royal limousine. That's amazing, I've been within inches of Her Majesty the Queen; how many people can say that? And she almost took me on part of her first nationwide tour of England as its queen, if not by the hand, then by the hem of my frock.

I'm digressing—back to her hometown and the hostel, I'd almost forgotten about that. On hearing how miserable the hostel was, my lovely uncle insisted that he drove to collect me so that I could stay with him and my Auntie Edith until I started my new job.

As a child I'd loved watching Hayley Mills in *Whistle Down the Wind* and was fascinated to hear she went to the Old Vicarage, a nearby school, the same one that my cousin Barbara went to. Sooty and Sweep were the only celebrities who lived near me, so I was impressed learning about the Mills family and went for several walks near their home, hoping to see Hayley or her dad, John, but I never did. I was sad when it was time to leave my uncle's house, but needs must, I had work to do. He gave me a lift back and I left him in his car, waved goodbye and made my way towards the grim front door of the hostel carrying my suitcase. Had he taken it up the steps for me I think the warden might have appeared again but this time, just like a character out of a vampire film, I imagined she'd be holding a wooden cross in front of her for protection, shouting, 'You can't come inside—you're a man'.

10

Her Majesty's Mini-Skirted Tax Officer

Alone again in the hostel with nothing else to do, I decided it might be a good idea to familiarise myself with all the rules that were pinned on a noticeboard and as I was wading through all the do's, don'ts, and 'forbiddens', a smartly dressed girl came and stood next to me and asked if I was new. I liked her and she seemed so knowledgeable because she knew a lot about the hostel. She told me she was twenty-two and I was impressed with her easy confidence and instantly felt safer than I had two seconds earlier. She explained that she'd been there for a week, and I was surprised to learn that she didn't work for the Inland Revenue as apparently, the hostel was also for young ladies regardless of where they worked, it just so happened that the tax office made use of the premises. Her name was Sheila, and we arranged to meet up in the canteen. Comfortingly, the hostel, suddenly, didn't seem as bad. I had a new acquaintance, one who smiled and seemed pleased to see me, but not nearly as pleased as I was to meet her. I was grateful and relieved to have made a friend quickly and easily, but I guess I must have looked extremely vulnerable, somewhat of a country bumpkin compared to her southern sophistication. I was dismayed to find that boiled cabbage was still being served along with school dinner type food. However, I was hungry, and Sheila and I spent a pleasant time getting to know each other. I was interested to hear that she was a 'temp', and she noticed the puzzled look on my face as I'd never heard of such a thing. She explained to me what it was, and I thought it sounded great but felt that I needed to close the gap of five years between us before I would be competent enough to be one myself.

Sheila took me under her wing, explaining how to catch a tube (up until then the only tube I'd used was one with toothpaste in it), to prepare me for my introduction to a city that was so alien. I wasn't expecting such a big culture shock on that first day. It was dark, wet and different to anything I had ever experienced, and I found the rush hour scary. However, I somehow managed to make my way from South Kensington to Holborn, without mishap. I was literally, to use a northern expression, 'gob-smacked' at the frantic, huge, white-tiled, draughty underground network, where people ceased to be individuals but part of a vast pre-occupied army, where it was every man for himself.

The long escalators that took commuters down into the bowels of the earth were as foreign to me as they must have been to many of the overseas visitors that mingled among the city workers. It was impossible not to read the adverts that followed one after the other as they appeared to move up or down the walls as I stood still on the stairs. Each ad portrayed wealth or a lifestyle that I hadn't realised even existed, they were like little windows into a wondrous new world. Once on the platform, that I hoped was the right one to get to Holborn, the clatter of the trains and whoosh of air that followed as they disappeared into the darkness of the tunnel, had me completely spellbound. The shiny rail tracks had a magnet-like quality that had a way of drawing you towards them, a feeling not dissimilar to that, some people sometimes have when looking down from a great height. I didn't realise then that those rails had, in fact, claimed the lives of many unfortunate souls who jumped on them deliberately. Hopefully if they'd taken alcohol, drugs, or medication, they wouldn't have known very much about it, their senses deadened to pain. On a more positive note, I had seen war films and knew that the underground had protected thousands of people during air raids. I could almost hear their voices, as they accepted their new norm as they chatted and helped each other, a common enemy helping to bring them close to one another, like one huge family, the British bulldog spirit instilled in each member. How ironic that only twenty years earlier, in the war, people in the underground would have been so accommodating and friendly and there I was, in peace time a young girl, alone, obviously confused and rather afraid, yet no one offered help or even smiled at me.

Those commuters seemed soulless; they were like tiny parts of a huge machine that was operated by an unseen controller. Had the controller been the Fat one in *Thomas the Tank Engine*, then at least I would have been surrounded by familiarity and the tube trains would have had smiley faces, but happy expressions were nowhere to be seen. I kept my eyes glued to the horizontal maps inside the tube trains as I was always scared that if I looked away for a second, I would miss my station. I counted off each stop and realised that some places were familiar but only because I had often played Monopoly. The first tiny victory was mine, however, when I did manage to get off at the correct station and I joined the crowds on the ascending escalator and even though my pulse must have been racing, I calmed down a little as I glimpsed at the adverts again, momentarily forgetting why I was there. Seconds later I timidly, yet determinedly, arrived at my new place of employment, with only minutes to spare.

Once inside the tax office I was fine, as the outside world may as well have been a thousand miles away, because there, in contrast, everyone seemed to move at a snail's pace. I felt as though I could have been a token on a Monopoly's board, visiting jail away from the chaos of London, but the next move involved much more than using a get out free card or paying £50.

I was about to be introduced to the world of not only inheritance tax, but corporate, wealth, super and whatever other type the Inland Revenue had dreamt up to replace the money squandered by the government. The public did come into the front office to sort out any tax problems they had, but as I was a newbie, I was kept hidden in the back. I was put next to a middle-aged woman, and it was supposed to be her job to show me the ropes. She left me dangling on those ropes every afternoon after lunch, as bang on cue at one fifteen sharp, she returned to her desk and promptly fell asleep. It didn't seem to matter as no one was perturbed by my sleeping mentor, not even when she had a cold that made her snore louder than ever. I was amused and realised just how futile the hierarchy was because there I was, a complete novice, one step up the ladder already, being served tea in a China mug as opposed to a pot one, simply because I was 'officer' grade. I knew nothing at all about the job but because I'd passed a few exams, I was considered superior to other people who knew the job inside out because they had worked there for a long time. The next grade up from me was served tea or coffee in a cup and saucer and the one above that a better quality one, and so on. I can't imagine what the overall boss must have drank their elevenses out of, but I imagined it would be something gold, encrusted with diamonds and perhaps the person giving it to them had to curtsey! How anything got done amazed me. The filing clerk, Sam, was ancient, with grey everything and spent the whole day chatting and moving in slow motion. He filed big brown envelopes marked 'deceased' at a rate of about six an hour. I used to think that it wouldn't be long before his body seized up altogether, rigor mortis would set in by which time his assistant would be filing away an envelope with Sam's name on it, alongside all the others.

One memorable day, my colleagues learnt the real reason I was there— that I wanted to be near my fiancé who just so happened to be in the charts at the time, and the dull tax office became unrecognisable, as one person and then another started singing 'Rainbow Valley'. Eventually the whole place was alive with the sound of music, well I'll rephrase that, with the sound of singing or more precisely still, attempts at singing and it was possibly the happiest moment in that office's history. It wouldn't have been unreasonable for people visiting the front desk and hearing 'Rainbow Valley' to imagine that there really was a pot of gold hidden somewhere, as at that time, tax for high earners was obscenely high. Those taxpayers must have been full of resentment hearing the words 'Sun always shines down in my rainbow valley' as they imagined tax collectors in the back clawing at their hard-earned money, rather like magpies swooping down on millions of pounds worth of glistening coins. When the Love Affair were at their peak, they were paid vast amounts of money but retained very little due to crippling tax rates. As a result, their managers decided to let the group have numerous roadies, book into the best hotels, and have expensive parties because they were all tax offsetable and if they hadn't, the tax man would have benefited even more. The cynical song 'Taxman' by the Beatles, that contained the words, 'There's one for you, nineteen for me', summed up the feelings of not only the pop industry, but every honest, hardworking taxpayer in the country.

It was interesting to watch the face of any person asking me, during those brief few weeks, what I did, because when I told them I was a 'tax officer' they instantly looked nervous of me, even when they were completely innocent of tax evasion. I hated scaring people, they were often so ill at ease to be in my presence, even when this particular tax officer had only just turned seventeen and wore a mini skirt.

11

Düsseldorf-Battle of the Beans

I never usually took much notice of song lyrics on records because I couldn't make them out, that's probably because, half the time, they weren't particularly clear, at least to my ears they weren't. Any attempt I made at singing competently was a non-starter, as the best I could do was a bit of dum dee duming or la la-ing in place of all the words that I didn't know. In fact, Manfred Mann's hit 'Do Wah Diddy Diddy' could have been written with me in mind, as those meaningless words suited me quite well, along with the Small Face's 'Sha La La Lee', the only problem with the latter was to know just how many la la's there actually are. I loved those two songs despite my lyrics conundrum, but I don't think I could say the same thing for Rex, whenever he heard Burt Bacharach's dreamy 'Trains and Boats and Plains' as he was terrified of flying. He was fine in trains and boats but whenever he knew he had to get on a plane it was torturous for him, the mere thought of an airport could have him reaching for a stiff drink. He preferred to sit in the middle of three airline seats, reassured to have someone at either side of him, and looking out of the window, for him was out of the question. On one particular flight to Düsseldorf, he was sandwiched between Mick and Mo when the plane started to experience extreme turbulence. Everything from coffee cups to passengers' teeth shook so violently that every person's stomach must have produced the same feelings as those experienced on a hairy ride at a pleasure park, but without the thrill. Mick and Mo had to pin Rex down as they knew that given half an opportunity, he would have tried to unfasten his seatbelt and run for it, but where to was anyone's guess. The moment they let go of him, he was up and off towards the exit, and they decided to let the air hostess deal with him, knowing that her pretty face would be much more effective at calming him down. Fortunately, it was a short flight and Rex's torment was over the minute they touched down, but Mick was surprised to see that the armpits of Rex's thick winter overcoat, that he'd worn throughout his ordeal, was drenched with sweat, such was his terror. Waiting patiently to disembark, Mick saw that Suzi Quatro and her entourage were on the plane and he silently hoped that she hadn't witnessed the commotion, as it was not conducive the cool image they tried to convey. He couldn't help being concerned that if not Suzy, then her minders were probably having a giggle at poor Rex's aviophobia. Little did Suzi or the Love Affair know that what lay ahead during the eccentric festival they were about to play in, would make even Rex's fears seem small by comparison to the fear generated by the huge, irate audience they were about face. German promotors, in their usual efficient way, had worked out how to effectively keep the Düsseldorf concert flowing, so that the audience didn't have to wait between performances. It was quite simple really, or so they thought. As it was taking place in a football stadium, they arranged to have two stages— one at each end. German performers would have one stage and British the other. As soon as one group had finished, 'all' the standing audience of thousands of people had to do was 'simply' rotate 180 degrees, and hey presto within seconds the next turn was ready and waiting. Sorry I'm lapsing back into my Dad's Yorkshire phrases, but how many ways are there to describe performers, groups, artistes? Not that many, so 'turn' does at least give a bit of variety, and nothing could be more fitting under the circumstances.

What the promotors hadn't taken into consideration was that, at that time, British bands ruled the world and other nationalities attempted to emulate them as best they could, but there was always a slight feeling of jealousy and resentfulness over the fact that good though they were, they didn't quite have that certain elusive something. It was inevitable that given the confrontational position of the opposing stages, that the promotors had created an 'us and them' situation, pretty much like those that took place during every football match. Whenever the German stage was occupied, there were huge cheers and applause no matter what the standard of the playing. However, as soon as it was time to do the inconvenient, and disruptive turnaround, the audience were ready to show their disapproval by jeering and booing. I wouldn't have been surprised if they had been provoked more by the silly revolving system than by any antagonism felt towards the British side. Word had got back to the boys in the dressing room that it wasn't going to be an easy gig, so when it was time for them to show, they braced themselves as their roadies guided them into the tunnel leading onto the pitch. Feeling like gladiators about to face wild beasts in the Colosseum, they wished each other luck and closed ranks, so that their modern-day quintet was better equipped to face the battle ahead. The tunnel had security people and crash barriers down each side to stop fans from assaulting the performers. Mick was, therefore, taken aback when, half-way down, one girl managed to break free and lunged towards him. Perhaps the news of the intimidating throng on the pitch made his imagination overactive because for a split second he thought she was going to tear his hair out, that is until she started to kiss his well-worn, grubby desert boots that had absorbed almost as much sweat, from being on stage, as Rex's heavy coat. Even though they all enjoyed the adulation they received, Mick thought her action was over the top and he squirmed at the thought of his unwashed boots being kissed by someone and he was swamped in embarrassment, not because of the state of his boots, but because it was so demeaning for her. However, his embarrassment was momentarily forgotten as they approached the holding area next to the stage where groups waited to go on. The Crazy World of Arthur Brown was about to come off, but not before reaching the climax of Arthur's theatrical performance. His high-pitched banshee screams and burning helmet with flames, so fierce they would have not looked out of place in Hell, had worked the hostile audience into an even bigger frenzy. Drama was in the singer's bones, so lapping up the atmosphere he started goose-stepping whilst gesturing a Nazi salute—the audience erupted and their displeasure was reaching boiling point, and who could blame them? Mick watched with dismay and thought 'Thanks a lot Arthur, you're meant to warm the audience up, not set them on fire too!' However, the show went on, and miraculously after the demonised singer was surrounded by security and escorted away, the audience swivelled round, switched off their anger and started to cheer as the next German group began to play, but that stint didn't last long.

Marmalade, an experienced group, was next up on the British stage. They had hundreds of gigs behind them, even before they recorded another song, that was of my ilk, their smash hit, 'Ob La Di Ob La Da'. Such was the effect of Arthur Brown's 'warming up' that from the beginning of their set, coins and pots of yogurt were thrown at them. Marmalade were anything but shrinking violets, having cut their teeth, playing to tough Glaswegian audiences, so they played on courageously, until their singer, Dene Ford, got a king-sized Jaffa orange full in the face. Enough was enough for Dene, so he stormed off followed by the others. It was 1-0 to Germany.

The audience swung around, this time a little prematurely, but again their mass demeanour changed in an instant, and they waited patiently for the group on their own 'side' to finish setting up. The Love Affair knew that they were on next, so they took deep breaths and climbed onto the stage, to face the music, in more ways than one. As soon as the audience were facing them, the swearing, jeers, and boos started up again, so the group replied with their own extremely loud version of the appropriately titled number, 'Stop in the Name of Love'. The crowd became more enraged at the boys' unmoved defiance and escalated to throwing anything they could lay their hands on, including fruit and vegetables. I queried this with Mick as it sounded rather odd, the fruit I could understand, but vegetables? However, he confirmed it was true, they really did. The straw that broke the camel's back for the Love Affair was when an unopened can of Heinz baked beans hit Mick right in the bass. It exploded, showering its contents everywhere, but not before leaving a crescent-shaped dent in Mick's newly acquired pristine, white, short scale, Fender Mustang. Fortunately, it went between the volume and tone controls and the bridge, otherwise had it hit them direct, then his guitar would have been unplayable, putting an end of their side of the battle. Even worse was the thought that had the tin landed on Mick's head, it could have killed him. Mick and Steve, with instant telepathy that fellow musicians develop, looked at each other and simultaneously mouthed 'F*** 'em' and brought the number they were playing to a sudden halt. Mick marched over to the amps and turned them up to mark eleven so they could mount a counter assault. (Mick had to explain to me that there isn't really an eleven, his little joke!) He started playing the bass riff of 'Everlasting Love', that was possibly the most iconic piece of music to be played that day. Several bars into the song, to everyone's amazement, including their own, the audience changed attitude, most likely out of respect for the boys not succumbing to the beans. Britain 1. Düsseldorf 1.

The Love Affair completed their stint to huge applause and the promotors decided not to follow up with a German group after all, and Cream were on next. If the audience thought that the Love Affair were loud, that would only have prepared them in a small way to what they were about to receive. Some drummers play with enthusiasm, some with intent but Ginger Baker played with hate, and his death-defying looks challenged anyone to hurl a coin, orange, or large can of beans.

Regrettably, a few days later, Mick decided to exchange his damaged instrument for a new one, but had he known that future trends would go crazy for any rock memorabilia, he would definitely have kept it; after all, nowadays, people pay way over the odds for even a pseudo-distressed guitar.

12

Home Alone at Christmas

Sheila became such an influential part of my London adventure that it's impossible to know how it would have turned out had it not been for her, and I am sad that we haven't been in touch since, and often wonder what became of her. I guess without her, it's quite possible I'd have plodded on in the Inland Revenue and who knows might have even risen to the grand ranks of those who warranted a China cup and saucer. I very much doubt that, though, as I wouldn't have been at ease, had I continued to be part of a scheme that, disguised as legal, was stealing money from hardworking people at a scandalous rate.

Sheila rescued me from the clutches of the South Kensington warden when she told me that she rented a bedsit in Earl's Court and her flat mate had just left and asked me if I would be interested in sharing it with her. Would I? Of course, I would. Who in their right mind wouldn't have jumped through lots of hoops to escape that regimented, cabbage-infused, dreadful place? The bedsit in Earl's Court wasn't far from the hostel, so we went over to see it that Saturday. As we approached, I could tell that it was a vast improvement on the hostel. The street had the same wealthy feel to it as those in South Kensington, but every house was pristine, painted white and I was pleased to see that her bedsit blended in because it was newly painted. It was in the basement with its own front door and had a cosy, almost secret feel to it. I immediately imagined Edwardian cooks scurrying up and down the steps, hurrying through that door into what would have been a large kitchen, fresh from their food shopping trips to nearby Harrods. Once inside the cosiness was even more so, as it was small, just one room that contained twin beds but hallelujah! they had proper spring mattresses and were covered in homely, pink cotton bedspreads. There was also a small table and two worn but comfortable easy chairs next to a double wardrobe. The kitchen was almost a cupboard but not quite even though it was not much bigger than one. It reminded me of my childhood when we had a freestanding kitchenette and a sink hidden behind a cupboard. It had a small sink, electric hob, and several essential utensils and pieces of mismatched crockery. Next to that was a slightly bigger cupboard, I mean room, with a bath, toilet, and basin where every possible surface was covered with Sheila's vast assortment of toiletries. Sheila had filled the whole place with welcoming bits and bobs, and it felt homely. I especially liked the candles squeezed into Chianti bottles in straw baskets that were adorned with layers of different-coloured wax. I had no hesitation in saying that I would like to share it with her, as I loved the place; from then on, it became 'ours'.

For the first time since leaving Yorkshire, I felt that it really was going to be possible to feel at home in London after all. Moving out of the hostel was a doddle, I only had my small suitcase to carry and Mum's £20 note, securely hidden in my bra, was more than enough to cover my deposit and a week's rent.

Sheila had lots of amazing clothes, including several angora dresses, the likes of which I'd never seen before. Those coupled with her impeccable taste in make-up, accessories, and blond, cropped hair made her look like Julie Driscoll.

I settled in well and although Mick was busy touring a lot, I never felt lonely thanks to her friendship and kindness in taking me under her wing. I think she enjoyed showing off her knowledge and I was certainly grateful to her. Her family lived somewhere near the south coast, so it wasn't too far, and she went to see them quite often. It was nearly Christmas, and she was as excited as ever to be making plans to go back home. It didn't over concern me that I didn't have enough money to travel back to see my own family, because even if I had, it was the busiest time of the year for them in the pub and I would have had to spend most of it alone, upstairs. In any case, I was looking forward to spending Christmas Day with Mick, because we would have the bedsit all to ourselves. He was playing at the Dreamland ballroom in Margate on Christmas Eve, and I couldn't wait for him to join me. Our Christmas dinner of Heinz tomato soup, brown bread, and honey might have been rather unconventional, but that didn't bother us. Even if I could have afforded a turkey it wouldn't have been much good without an oven.

Our only regret was that he had to dash back to the Winter Gardens at Weston-super-Mare for Boxing Day evening, leaving me alone in the afternoon once more. I really hadn't thought much further than his visit and had made no plans for the rest of the day. It was only after we'd said goodbye that it dawned on me that I had hours to spare and no idea of how to spend them.

I settled down to read a magazine when the lights suddenly went out— the meter needed feeding. The natural light from the window wasn't good, especially as we were below ground, and it was winter, but I felt my way to the scrap of a hall, where it was situated. I had plenty of shillings to put in it and felt reassured that even if I did run out of those in the next couple of days, I could always change the 10 shilling note I'd kept for emergencies. I pushed a coin into the meter and turned the dial so it would drop into the box, but the dial only went so far and stopped. It wouldn't budge any further, the coin was jammed. I gave it a hearty bang, nothing—so in desperation I took my boot off and hit the coin with the heel, but it made no difference. Ten minutes later, after trying everything I could to dislodge the shilling, I realised that it wasn't going to move. As it was Boxing Day, I couldn't phone anyone for help and began to feel slightly sorry for myself. The temperature in the all-electric flat soon dropped and the darkness and silence confirmed that I was in trouble, I couldn't even make a hot drink to console myself, as just like the hob, the kettle was electric. There was only one thing I could do, so I put my coat on locked up and headed towards the Pancake House, a few hundred yards up the road. There I could at least treat myself to a pancake and a mug of comforting hot chocolate. Sheila had introduced me to the place, and I thought it was fab, never having tasted the likes of maple syrup before. I must have developed a degree of amnesia even then as, on a different occasion, she took me to another restaurant that she liked, and we had spaghetti bolognaise and I was convinced that it was the first time I'd eaten it. I had completely forgotten that I had it when I went through Italy on my one and only previous trip abroad. I think it was more the way in which we ate it that accounted for my temporary loss of memory. She showed me how to twirl the pasta on a soup spoon, but not before the waiter had sprinkled freshly grated parmesan cheese on top and asked if we'd like some black pepper. I'd never had black pepper before and I wasn't sure, but Sheila assured me that we did, so when he scuttled away and returned with the biggest pepper mill ever (it must have been in huge demand), he ignored my outstretched hand to take it from him, and started to grind the pepper onto my pasta, in a most theatrical way. I felt embarrassed, not realising that was what waiters were supposed to do. I wasn't used to being served like that, it reminded me of Mum doing everything for me when I was little—he was doing all things that she did except spoon feed me! When we first sat down, he put napkins on our laps and what with the pepper performance and then his refusal to let me pour my own wine, I thought he was being paternal because he thought that I was incapable of covering my own knees, using a pepper grinder because it was too heavy or pouring wine from a bottle without spilling it. I have to admit that I don't really like waiters behaving in such subservient ways. Even though I would have loved to have lived upstairs in times gone by (I would have had to treat servants like one of the family though), I also would have been quite at home downstairs, so you can see my dilemma and perhaps sense my uncomfortable feelings, when people treat others as though they are superior to them or *vice versa*, it just doesn't sit well with me.

As soon as I got outside our bedsit, the bitter air rushed up my sleeves and around my knees (I'm a poet and …. Oh, do shut up Patricia, this bit's supposed to be tear jerking.) How I wished at that moment that I wasn't wearing a miniskirt because even though I had tights on, my legs felt very cold in the near freezing temperature. It must have been the thought of having my favourite pancake or even ignorance of how depressing the position I was in could potentially be, but I wasn't worried at that point. After all I had the recent memory of the previous hours spent with Mick to sustain me, and delicious food to look forward to. It was only when I reached the café, and it was shut, that the truth of my predicament hit me. I was cold, hungry with nowhere to go except a bedsit with no power. I toyed with the idea of phoning Mum and Dad from a phone box, but there was nothing they could do, and I didn't want to worry them, so decided to leave them with the illusion, that I was fine, thriving and possibly partying the day and night away. One or two restaurants were open, but were beyond my budget and fully booked anyway, so I had no alternative other than to return to the bedsit, that for the first time since staying there, seemed anything but welcoming. As soon as I stepped inside, without thinking, I automatically flicked on the light switch, but of course the Christmas fairy hadn't magically fixed it in my absence. It was too dark by that time to even read, so I stumbled into bed, fully clothed, popped my orange corduroy coat on top of the bed for extra warmth and with only a glass of cold water to drink and a couple of stale rich tea biscuits to eat, I shuffled down under the covers. For once I wished that I was in the pub's bar, at least the constant noise would have been company, the coal fire warming and with a Babycham in hand, I could have literally drown my sorrows. Those 200 long miles away from home felt like 2,000. I'd come full circle from the hostel, because in a matter of only weeks, there I was again, feeling bereft in a single bed, crying into my pillow, but not using the sheets as a handkerchief as this time, I had to wash them myself. At least there wasn't a commotion coming from the other bed, as of course Sheila's was empty and silent. I eventually fell asleep knowing that tomorrow was another day, and my 'home alone' Christmas would pass, and it did.

When Sheila returned she was surprised to hear my tale of woe as the meter had never caused a problem before. She knew that I wasn't looking forward to returning to the tax office, so she did her best to cheer me up, by suggesting that perhaps I should leave and become a temp like her. 'After all,' she said, 'the pay is almost on a par with what you're getting now, and you'd get out and about and meet lots of new people.' I decided to give it serious thought, but it didn't take me long, I decided that the tax office had served its purpose of enabling me to live in London, and it was time for a change. After checking with Sheila's employment agency that my typing speeds were good enough for them, I registered as a temp and as soon as my notice was up, I found myself working in an estate agents. It was small and friendly but as the houses they sold were in and around the Royal Borough of Kensington & Chelsea, it was light years away from the uninspiring agents in Bradford. You could buy a house in Yorkshire for a few thousand pounds as opposed to tens of thousands of pounds in London. As I sat typing descriptions and purchase prices, I couldn't get my head around such massive amounts of money. They were so confusing, my eyes glazed over at the price tag of property in Cheyne Walk and neighbouring roads such as St Loo Avenue (can't quite make my mind up if that's posh or not as I'm not so sure I'd like to have that as my address!), as there were so many noughts after the pound signs. It was only later that I realised that I should have taken more notice of those details and requested to accompany one the agents on valuations, to see how 'the other half' lived. As it was, I just worked foggily, away on autopilot, my mind somewhere else, as I waited for pay day. I did enjoy answering the phone though, because I never knew which interesting person would be phoning next, but how I wished that the company had a different name. No matter how hard I tried to sound sophisticated because we were agents for such exclusive homes, I found it impossible,

Mick taking a break between sessions at Butlins, Filey looking pretty much the same as he did on our 'blind' date.

I was certainly spellbound when I first saw Mick playing with his group aptly named the Spell. Mick arranged for me to go to his house, introduce myself to his mum and stepdad, have tea with them before travelling in their car to watch him. A tall order for a fourteen year old, but I was so besotted with him that I braced myself and went along with his plan. I couldn't go earlier when they had to set up, as it was a Saturday and I was working in Kirkgate Market, Bradford. *Left to right:* Mick, Martin, Tony and 'Big' Mick.

A rare couple of photos of us together, the first one (*left*) is near Scarborough, the place where we found a plastic 'engagement' ring on the beach that proved to be so prophetic for us. … And the other (*right*) is somewhere very cold at the British seaside—(not sure what's under Mick's right arm, answers on a postcard perhaps?).

Above left: Mick with Mum & Dad on one of our many days out we shared. They both really took to him, even though he didn't intend getting a 'proper' job. It's fortunate that they didn't realise that we had numerous other unofficial days 'off' of our own, from school, otherwise I'm sure he wouldn't have been nearly so popular.

Above right: Mick's debut professional gig in the Sportsman Bar, Butlins, Filey. The first of scores of pints bought by an appreciative audience is next to him. Unknown to the generous customers, most had to be poured down the sink at the end of the night as his group couldn't drink them all.

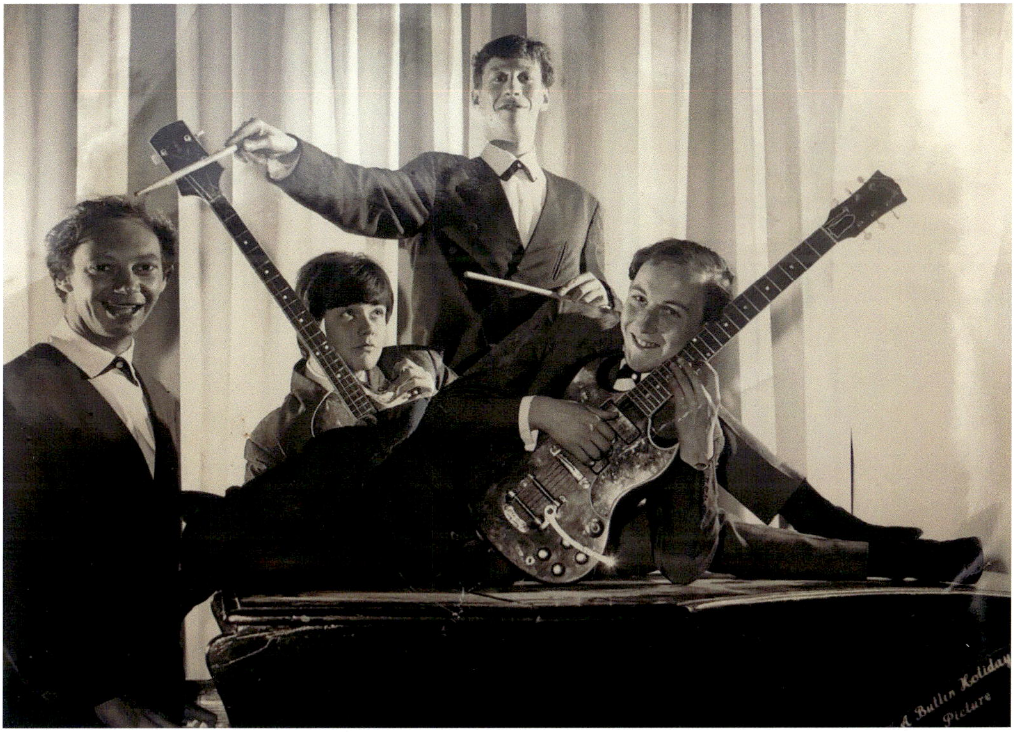

Mick with his first professional group, the Beat Squad at Butlins, Filey. I know I'm biased but no wonder they wanted my baby faced boyfriend to join them and with literally no notice. I was beyond distraught because it was another five years before we would be permanently together again.

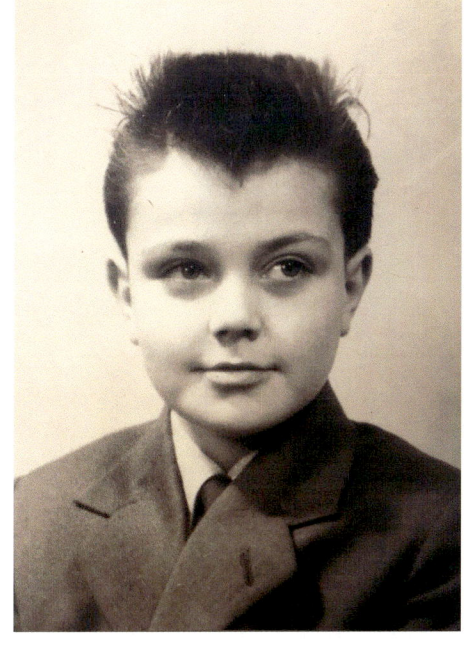

Above: Mum, Dad and me, well prepared for my 'seven years on the sands'—seven years before Mick and I first met.

Right: The first time Mick cut his own hair aged nine, and for the most part, he's still doing it.

Pre-mobile phones and laptops. How I treasured Mick's letters, and still do.

Above left: I'd have never guessed, in a million years, that shortly after covering my bedroom walls with magazine pictures of The Beatles, I would have a boyfriend whose centre fold photo would also be staring down at thousands of other girls.

Above right: The downside of being pop stars. A snippet from my scrap book confirming that the boys were under constant threats from jealous boyfriends.

The day the Love Affair climbed the fountain of Eros, Piccadilly in London. You can tell it's before they started their ascent as they are nice and dry. It was worth them getting soaked, as the stunt gained them thousands of pounds worth of free publicity. They were fined a paltry £11 each, only days earlier the fines had been increased considerably but because the incident had happened before then, the frustrated judge couldn't charge them any more.

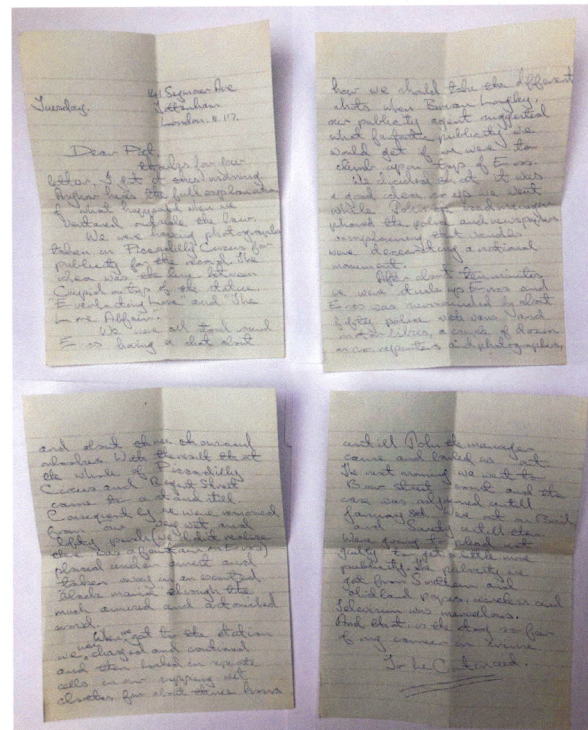

Mick's newsletter describing how the group brought the centre of London to a standstill after climbing Eros, and their subsequent arrest and appearance at one of England's most famous magistrates courts, Bow Street.

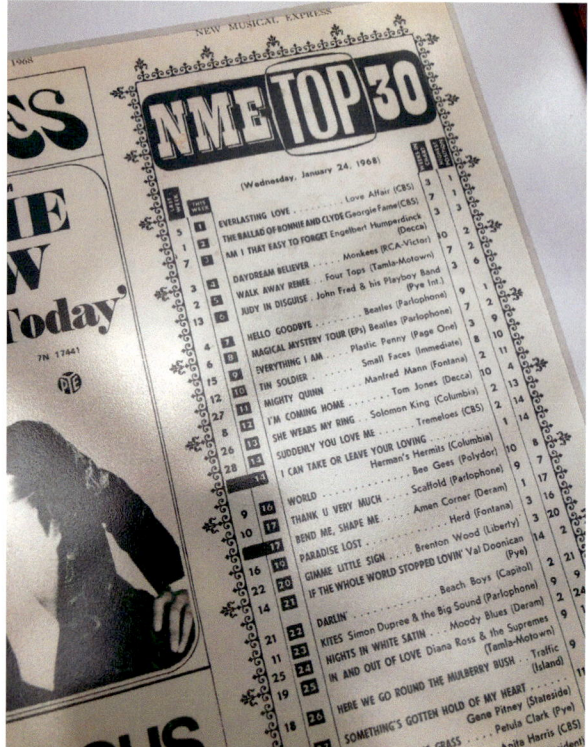

I was so, proud of the Love Affair when they became the youngest group to reach No.1. Mick's mum was right when she said he was so lucky that if he put his hand down the toilet he'd come up with a box of chocolates!

Mum & Dad's pub might have been their 'happy place' but it was also where a serious fire and heroic rescue took place. There's Kim our Alsatian, possibly looking out for the postman so he could get to Mick's letters before I did, as he loved to chew them.

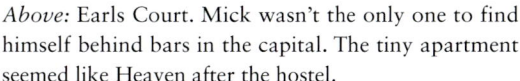

My amateurish attempt at producing a half decent scrap book wasn't very good I'm afraid. It's falling to bits now and yellow with age. Fortunately, the individual lengths of cellotape that I dedicatedly stuck over the magazine photos have gone part way in preserving them and the job did give me something to do at least, when Mick and I were apart.

Above: Earls Court. Mick wasn't the only one to find himself behind bars in the capital. The tiny apartment seemed like Heaven after the hostel.

Right: Inside the bedsit at Earls Court but I'm not home alone, nor is it Christmas! I've just noticed the electric blanket switch, it was no use at all when my coin for the electric meter got stuck and all I could do was get into bed and shiver (at least my bargain Mary Quant, bright orange coat with a lumpy hem, came to my rescue as a make shift extra cover).

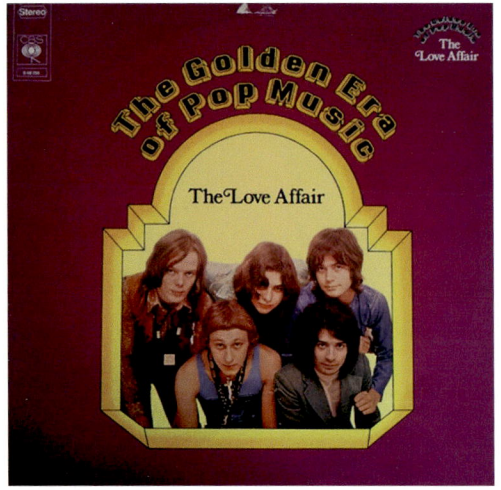

Front and middle cover of a German double, 24 track album called 'The Golden Era Of Pop Music'. Even though videos of the group made in Europe were often puzzling, for example having girls dancing behind the boys with machine guns, they were imaginative and have stayed the course, unlike all the footage from 'Top Of The Pops' and other British shows which has been wiped from the tapes, I guess in the name of economy.

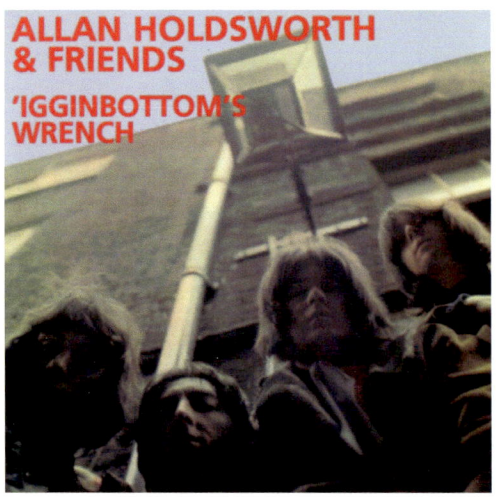

'Igginbottom were instantly offered a residency at Ronnie Scott's, playing alongside John Williams. Ronnie became our surrogate 'uncle' and his club felt like home. It's so sad that Steve Robinson (who was our friend when we were all at different schools), Allan Holdsworth (from Keighley, now also part of Bradford) and dear old Ronnie are no longer with us.

Outside Elcot Park Hotel, scene of the extraordinary, never to be forgotten few days that we spent there as the group rehearsed for their tour of the UK, sponsored by Yardley cosmetics. The boys look as though they were told not to look at the camera, either that or maybe, just maybe, they are keeping an eye out for the hotel's resident ghost!

Mick says this is one of his favourite photos of me, that's really flattering as he usually compares me to a hamster ☺

Above left: I really like this photo, mainly because for once the boys are genuinely smiley, and look so much friendlier than when photographers asked them to look cool. Note the ever present cigarettes are being smoked as per usual but Mick and Rex at least look as though they are trying to hide them behind their backs.

Above right: Mick's mum Madge and me outside his house in Bradford Moor. It's where he was brought up and I sneaked to when playing truant from school. Thankfully, her terrifying ordeal, when she chauffeured us through overwhelming numbers of screaming fans, was long since over.

The Shipley Times & Express photographer asked me to pose for him so he could practise his skills. I do look serious but I guess that's what I thought 'models' were meant to do!

Left: A studio media publicity shot: Rex Brayley (guitar), Maurice Bacon (drums), Mick Jackson (bass), Lynton Guest (Keyboards), and Steve Ellis, vocalist. Mick in his favourite turquoise leather jacket that mysteriously went missing.

Above: Rex is centre stage here; he may have been the smallest in the group but he more than made up for that with confidence, he was good mates with Keith Moon whose notorious behaviour rubbed off onto Rex who revelled in being what Mick's mum would have described as 'impish'.

left: Poor Steve, who was a mod, detested having to wear frilly or satin shirts like the ones Rex and Mo are wearing here as they were so not him.

Arriving at Schiphol Airport, Amsterdam, 22 March 1968. Lynton is obviously enjoying being in the middle as he's the only one looking vaguely happy. Mick was glad to have him as an early bedsit mate, a big improvement on Lynton's predecessors – 'mice'! *Courtesy Nationaal Archief—Dutch National Archives*

It never ceases to amaze me how the Love Affair's music is constantly re-released in some shape or form throughout the world. This CD was produced in 1992, twenty years after the original group split up. 'Everlasting Love' has been viewed nearly twenty million times on YouTube and its latest claim to fame, is that it is on both the promotional sound track and film track of Sir Kenneth Branagh's wonderful, award winning film, 'Belfast'. I was thrilled because not only were my great grandparents Irish, but Dame Judy Dench, my favourite actress, is one of its stars. Thanks to the film, the song is gaining fans in America, so even though their proposed tour of the states, sponsored by Geest bananas, was cancelled at the last minute, 50 years ago, it is now their version as opposed to Robert Knight's that is being listened to by new friends across the pond.

A serious 'business meeting'. *Left to right:* Morgan, Mick, Mo, Rex (not sure were Steve was, behind the camera perhaps?).

Mick and me in cousin, Bevan's sports car. Thankfully I didn't know about the dodgy brakes at the time. I must have been excellent at being an invisible fiancée as photos of Mick and I together at that time are practically non-existent. This day was captured on Mick's mum's 50s cine camera, the film was later put onto video tape and stills taken from that.

At any rate some time
this next year. No, you don't
have to pinch yourself, I
mean it. I think its almost
time that you and I got
married, that is, if thats
allright with you. Anyhow
we can discuss things in
more detail when I get home.
Well thats about all for
now my love, give my regards
to the family and Kim and
Ming. I'll see you soon.
I love you,
     All my love,
     Michael.

Above left: Message from Sweden - 'It's almost time you and I got married.'

Above right: Signing our lives away? Not really – we've lasted 50 years and still counting.

Mick and me on our very first sofa. Being next to Mick relaxing at home is still the place I like to be the most.

So much has happened of course in over 50 years but nothing compares to the thrill of being blessed with our daughter, Suzannah, son Ben, and three beautiful grandchildren.

Above left: And just for posterity … here's an updated photo of Mick and me, resting after collecting bags of conkers with our family.

Above right: A recent (January 2022) visit—for old times sake—to Ronnie Scott's with Mo Bacon (drummer in the Love Affair). Not only is Mo a great drummer—amongst his other many qualifications he's Suzannah's Godfather and the best, jovial bear hugger on the planet!

because my 'r's sound more like 'w's.

It was never more obvious than when I had to repeat the company name several times a day 'Good morning' or alternatively 'Good afternoon, Bwitton, Bwook and Bwown'. My considerate employers never commented, but Mick still pulls my leg about it.

Like many commuters, I was, by this time, travelling on the tube, like a pro (hmm, perhaps I had better rephrase that) and I was proud that I was no longer flummoxed by London transport. However, whenever my boss and his wife offered me a lift home in their car, a journey that took us past St James's Park, it was a treat to be above ground and see where I was going, so I always, readily accepted.

I got used to seeing Buckingham Palace guards with their stunning red uniforms and black bearskins and I felt I was almost on nodding terms with Her Majesty. Of course, I couldn't be sure if she was in, as the flag that's flown above the palace when she is, wasn't always visible from the back of a car, but I liked to think that she was. I found that thought comforting, after all I'd 'known' her since I was a little girl! I've just looked to see if that estate agency still exists, there is one called Brown & Brooke in South London, but no mention of Britton. I wonder what happened to him, or indeed if there is any connection at all.

13

Passively Smoking Pot was Terrifying

I think it's time to talk about the Love Affair again. What I write isn't necessarily in the right order or set in stone, these are simply memoirs as far as either Mick or I recall. If all the members of the Love Affair were here now, we could compare notes; though, in all probability, we may still not come up with exactly the same recollections because, of course, everyone sees and remembers things from different perspectives, and it was a long time ago after all. Everything here is written in good faith, and things did happen that are best left unsaid, and as my hairdresser also commented recently, it would be much 'juicier' if I told all, but that is not my style because the last thing I would chose to do is deliberately upset anyone.

When I was with the group, I simply observed, often totally bemused, or confused, and at times I was dismayed by their behaviour as I thought their 'looning' often went too far. I was brought up in a way that could be described as relaxed, yet firm, so when the boys thought it was hilarious to throw sandwiches around, inappropriately poke fun at someone, or behave arrogantly I didn't like it. However, from their perspective, they really did think they were just having a laugh so perhaps I should let them off and say it was simply 'high jinxes' fuelled by high spirits. The words 'You were so pristine, and I felt kind a mean' from 'Six Form Lovesick Blues' fitted this time too, I might have appeared aloof, but most of the time, my silence was only because I felt unsure of myself and rather shy— 'You were so pristine, and kind a green' would have been more accurate.

You may think I'm making it up when I say that I didn't realise that one of, if not the main reason the boys were often sillier than the silliest schoolboys, was because they often smoked hash. It seems unbelievable I know, but I really was unaware at first, and Mick never made me any the wiser. I know that makes me appear incredibly naive but it's true. I didn't even know that it's possible to passively smoke cannabis until the day we went to a party at CBS Records. It was reminiscent of a scene in a Peter Sellers film, where posing as a dentist, he inadvertently inhales laughing gas and becomes overcome by laughter. I must have inhaled the equivalent of a joint, but unfortunately it wasn't laughter that overtook me, but paranoia. I think that paranoia affected Steve a little bit later, too. After the party he invited us back to his place along with Rex and his girlfriend Judy. The journey there was memorable, not because Rex gave us a lift in his Aston Martin but because not only did its wheels bump into the edge of several pavements, Rex drove straight across a roundabout, and I don't mean one that was painted on the road, but a real one. Unlike me, Mick never forgets a car, and when I read this bit to him, he informed me that Rex's car was a pale blue metallic DB4.

After we'd settled in his apartment, Steve's started showing Mick a book he liked but misinterpreted what Mick was meaning when he responded, 'Yes, it's a great book, one you could pass down to your children'—he also thought the book was really good, but Steve thought he was being sarcastic, saying it was childish. It would have been unnatural if they didn't have the occasional skirmish and there was very little middle ground, as they tended to be either falling out with one another or the best of mates. Mick liked Steve, and was happiest when they were getting on fine, which was thankfully was most of the time. I also liked Steve but being in awe of the adulation he got from fans, I was too shy to even strike up a conversation with him, that awful insecurity of mine getting the better of me.

At the time I was affected by passive smoke, Mick was lodging with Morgan's family and I was sleeping on the floor in their house as Morgan had hospitably offered us the dining room as a makeshift bedroom. My head was next to a glass display cabinet containing a white marble sculpture of a man's head that made me paranoid as I became convinced that it was going to jump out and attack me. I spent a terrifying night keeping my eye on it and felt as though I couldn't move, even though I wanted to, and the trepidation stayed with me until dawn. It's not an experience I would care to repeat and as a result, I have been suspicious of, and have kept away from, drugs ever since. I might have been scared of that ornament, but I loved going with Mick to Mrs Fisher's house because it was family home, I was so attracted to what most people take for granted—a homely house as opposed to living in a pub, above the shop or more accurately at that time, a rather nomadic existence. It was the first time I'd ever seen a dishwasher and was both intrigued and impressed by it. In truth, the dishes didn't come out particularly clean as it often was in serious need of salt and rinse aid, but I didn't realise that I just thought the odd bit of dried on food was normal due to the pots not being washed by hand. Mrs Fisher's pots were actually China and willow patterned and I've liked it ever since, especially as it illustrates the Chinese tale of a young couple in love, eloping and transforming into doves. Perhaps subconsciously, I associated the fable with Mick and my own story, although not identical of course as we were never doves, we did leave our nests so to speak, and would possibly have eloped to London, had my parents not been so understanding in letting me go anyway. That sounds too sweet and gooey, so quickly moving on. Mrs Fisher liked to take time out from her busy life and simply sit down and talk to her family. I found it an eye opener that they could sit around a table and actually have a sensible discussion about interesting topics other than tap washers and the price of sausages. Every family is different, of course, but I was impressed, even though I didn't feel particularly qualified to join in, as I had, like a lot of seventeen-year-olds, rather tunnel vision because if things didn't directly apply to me, I wasn't that knowledgeable about them. I'm happy to say that I have improved and love to talk about lots of different topics, no surprise for you there then. Is that really an improvement? I think Mick might agree to differ on that one.

Morgan was going out with Rex's ex-girlfriend, Pauline, and she and I got on really well, she was kind and like Sheila was very knowledgeable about the London way of life, no surprise really as she had been born there. She and I became good friends and the four of us often used to go out together. Consequently, I have always had a soft spot for Morgan, he's a gentle soul, dedicating his life to music and, more recently, photography. Thinking back a moment to seeing the Beatles, would I have ever dreamed then that one of our future friends, Morgan, would one day be a member of Mott the Hoople, recording with Yoko Ono, or playing the organ for Queen? I don't think so.

Another person I really liked was John Chapman, the group's main roadie, he was a hardworking, protective asset and was a rock upon which the boys could always depend. His parents were also kind enough to take Mick and Lynton in as their lodgers after Mick moved on from

Morgan's. They were homely and lived in Tottenham, and I liked John's mum and although her name was Dolly, she certainly wasn't a bird, though she did appear to pleasantly rule the roost, and Bill her Irish husband seemed quieter, no doubt grateful to have such a competent wife. Bill was a tailor and Dolly, I think I'm right in saying, was an east ender, but if not she certainly sounded like a likeable Cockney to me. She worked on the buses and was so down to earth that they made Mick and I feel instantly at home. Mick and Lynton were lucky to stay there.

As members of the youngest group to have a No. 1 hit record, the boys found themselves in exceptionally different circumstances to those of typical teenage boys. I'm certain that such success would have gone to the head of almost anyone so young. They really were having a ball and who can blame them, they were enjoying every moment possible. I was going to say, and no one got hurt, that isn't strictly true, but whenever anyone did, it was not deliberate. None of their behaviour was meant to be vindictive, though, but some people do like to throw cold water on success, but as the saying goes, even bad publicity is good publicity. Bad press worked wonders for the group again, when after the Eros incidence, they shocked the nation by making an astonishing, shocking confession, but this time the ripples spread much further.

14

Mick Exposes the Pop Industry's Biggest Cover-up

Climbing Eros certainly turned out to be a stroke of brilliance, bringing them much-needed publicity. When all the fuss died down, and the story was yesterday's news, John and Sid began to wonder if they could find a way to follow that genius plan and get even more publicity. Well, the answer came much quicker than they even dared to dream, providing they were willing to take the risk. Of course, climbing Eros and being arrested was a gamble, the prank could easily have backfired, but their fans were young and the sense of rebellion that tends to lurk below the surface of many a young mind meant that, far from being a mistake, it worked in their favour. When I first met Mick, the things that really attracted me to him, apart from his obvious good looks, was his honesty and willingness to help anyone in trouble. I loved it whenever he stopped to help someone if he thought they needed it. He would help old ladies or blind people to cross the road, sometimes when they didn't even want to—and I'm not joking, it happened. If someone fell, he would help pick them up despite his own back being troublesome afterwards.

When Mick was asked if he would be the spokesman and whistle blower on what turned out to be a hugely controversial topic, his honesty meant he didn't hesitate and was helped by the fact that he thought there was nothing to hide, even when almost everyone else in the music business thought that there was. Everything is never as it appears, particularly in newspaper reports or television news. For example, the footage shown of scores of teenagers screaming in the airport when the Beatles first set foot in America looks impressive, but apparently a lot of those girls had been paid to do that. Even Cliff had his suspicions that something wasn't right when he sang 'Congratulations' at the Eurovision Song Contest in 1968. Two countries he was extremely popular in gave him a nil score, causing him to drop to second place when he was favourite to win. Decades later he was informed by a very reliable source that it had been fixed.

Jonathan King was at the pinnacle of his career and had his own TV show, *Good Evening, I'm Jonathan King*. It went out live every Saturday on prime television opposite *The Monkees* on the other side, and when the boys were guests, most of the nation was watching one of the two programmes. Sid, John, and Jonathan King thought it would be a great opportunity to attract media attention, not only for the group but for the show itself, by admitting that the only member of the group who performed on 'Everlasting Love' was Steve. It wasn't obvious that it had been prearranged, and Sid and John were right once more, their disclosure turned out to be publicity gold. With hindsight, it's easy for me to say it was gold because it all worked out for the best, but it could have had the reverse effect. Not that JK would have suffered, as it wasn't his neck on the line and he knew it would benefit him whatever the outcome, as people would be talking about his show, but it was hugely risky for the Love Affair. Sid and John underestimated just how much talking would be done as it became a huge issue and debate that lasted for months and brought more publicity than they dared hope. The fact that they went on to have great success was testament to the fact that it was yet another inspirational decision.

Mick wasn't worried about telling the truth, after all it was common practice at the time for lots of groups not to play on their own records, and everyone in the industry knew, but the general public didn't. As professional musicians, every member of the Love Affair was capable of being on the recording too, after all they'd played live to thousands of people by that time, not forgetting the top London clubs. Not playing on the record all boiled down to one thing, money—and time is money. The record companies and group managers had one objective only and that was to make a profit and whenever they decided to use session men, it was because it was an ideal situation for everyone. Studio time was expensive and seasoned session men were used to the studios, it was their place of work and could therefore do the job in half the time, so they churned out hits one after the other, it was how they earned their bread and butter.

The day 'Everlasting Love' was recorded, Mick, Mo, Rex, and Lynton did as they were told, it didn't bother them in the least that they were not joining Steve in the studio and were more than happy to have a day off. It must have felt strange for Steve, not to have his buddies with him, but I imagine he was also happy knowing that his soulful, distinctive voice, couldn't be duplicated by session men. His voice has hardly changed and when I first listened to his much more recent album, *Boom! Bang! Twang!*, I was instantly taken back to all the excitement of the Love Affair's gigs; I could listen to him all day.

Steve's parents along with Mick's didn't really appreciate what was going on and both sets thought that perhaps their sons should get 'proper' jobs. Steve's mum, bless her, hankered after him getting a job as a manager in the Co-op and would have been made up if he had, after all, he'd been promised the position after working hard as a delivery boy for them. Had she known that the first job Mick took after leaving the group was in Morrison's supermarket, stacking shelves, she would have been very impressed I'm sure. I certainly was, knowing what guts it must have taken to go from one extreme to another, but we were newlywed and he'd left the group, so the time had come for him to actually get one of those proper jobs but that's another story.

Steve has had an impressive long musical career since leaving the Love Affair, but it was broken for a period of time when he got married and had a family. In order to support them, he admirably he took a job at Shoreham Docks that offered more security as well as a decent wage. That job had the advantage of helping him get back into first-class physical shape—that is, until tragedy struck when Steve described it as having an altercation with some 2-ton forklift blades. The pain and distress must have been indescribable for him, and it took him eight long years to learn how to walk again, but he finally won through to pursue his music once more. Steve's not only been gifted with a voice that thrills millions of fans, but he also never fails to give his best, singing from his heart, explaining that 'Even if you're knackered, you've got to want it, to pull it out of your boots and do it properly'. The day that Steve found himself alone in the studio with a forty-piece orchestra so that he could record 'Everlasting Love' must have been incredibly nerve-racking for him, so much so that someone handed him a brandy so he could feel calmer, even though, being only seventeen he didn't usually drink it. He was asked to pretend to sing in a lonely booth, while the technicians did what they had to do to adjust the sound. The rules were that he had to sing live with the orchestra and Steve was so spot on that he only had to sing it twice before it was in the bag—his boots had given up a perfect rendition of that fabulous song, one that Tony Blackburn said, was his all-time favourite from the '60s. Now that's what I call an accolade! That wasn't always the case though because when Tony first heard it, he said he preferred Robert Knight's version and it wouldn't be a hit, but it obviously grew on him. It just proves that critics are often wrong and do sometimes change their minds. Another example was, that when their cover of 'Everlasting Love' was played on *Juke Box Jury*, Lonnie Donegan said he didn't think it would be a hit either.

The Jonathan King interview made uncomfortable viewing in parts because Steve and Lynton who were only of school age, along with Rex, who was all of nineteen, stood in the background, looking for all they were worth, as if they were being interrogated by a headmaster. They were young and not experienced enough to hide their anguish and uncertainty of whether or not what Mick was saying would be the death knell for them. Rex crossed his arms protectively and the other two looked incredibly guilty, even though they had done nothing wrong. I don't know where Mo was, perhaps as he was only fifteen and the 'baby' he couldn't face it. Mick remained calm and controlled and deftly traded banter in his soft northern accent like an intellectual impresario. He explained why it was only Steve that appeared on 'Everlasting Love.' 'We're musicians and I hope, competent musicians but it takes a great deal of time before you become accustomed to conditions in the studio, for instance you don't all play together, you play instruments individually, it's terribly different.' Nodding in agreement, JK then asked, 'You don't feel as though you're cheating the public in anyway?' to which Mick who might have surprised some people because he was confident replied, 'No because the public must have bought the record for the sound, they liked it and made it number 1. They didn't buy it because the Love Affair made the record. The record came before the Love Affair really.' JK was pleased with the way the young bass player was handling his questions and then asked Mick, 'Do you think you could have played on the record?' and without hesitation he replied 'I don't think we would have done it as quickly, but had we had the time we would have done it just as well. We didn't cheat the public, because Steve sang on the record and this is the sound of the Love Affair, Steve's voice.' At that point Lynton took the opportunity to explain that they had played on another TV show in Manchester along-side an orchestra.

I'm not sure if their host was quite prepared for Mick's next quip. 'I suppose I could turn around to you Jonathan, because you've made records, and say that you sang on your record, but it didn't also go down on the label that Jonathan King sings on this record supplemented by

Fred Bloggs and various other session men.' Interestingly Jonathan King's body language gave away the fact that he wasn't quite expecting Mick to say that, because he instantly fiddled with the top of his shirt as the boys giggled. He must have literally felt hot under his collar at that statement. Unperturbed, however, he kindly rounded up the interview saying:

> I'd like to say that as someone who's been inside the business for some time, that I've known that groups often do not play on their records. I know that there are at least three records in the top twenty at this very moment, that I know the groups did not play on the record, although it says on the label that they did. I don't think there's anything wrong with it, I go for sound, I think the only thing that's wrong is when they conceal it. I think the Love Affair should be congratulated for being honest, they're very capable musicians, I heard them playing last night and they were very good.

The producers of the programme had earlier filmed the reaction of people in a nearby record shop when they were asked how they would feel knowing that a group hadn't played on a record. The only negative reactions came from the people who were older, and the younger ones didn't mind at all. The group then knew that despite their tricky live television admittance, that it couldn't have gone any better, most of their fans were under seventeen and the survey boded well, and they were right. However, producers of *Top of the Pops* weren't best pleased with that interview and threatened to blacklist them from appearing on the show. Mo has even been quoted as saying that one of the executives demanded that they bought his wife a dishwasher if they wanted him to change his mind, but they refused to comply. I don't know if that's true or not. That's just reminded me of the time when Sid apparently offered five whole pounds to the sound engineer at the Wembley Empire Pool Poll Winners Concert to 'Make my boys sound better than anybody else,' and he was serious, but I doubt if it worked; they sounded no different to everybody else to me.

I remember sitting several rows back from the front of the huge Wembley stage, but although I was proud that the Love Affair were appearing as best newcomers, I was actually more excited to see Cliff Richard. I had loved Cliff since the age of six and had never seen him live before, it made my year.

Of course, when 'Everlasting Love' became a success and entered the charts, the boys were thrilled to finally be on *Top of the Pops* where they did their first stint of many appearances. Had the producer had his way, though, then shortly after that first show, they would never have appeared again, but this time, it had nothing to do with the Jonathan King interview but Mo. Perhaps because he was so young, the fact that he was on his favourite show, may have gone to his head and he was feeling super important. The floor manager seemed to take forever to sort out whatever he had to sort so Mo became bored and decided to have a cigarette. The only problem was, he didn't have a match or anything so addressing the person nearest to him he clicked his fingers and then pointed to the Dunhill in his mouth and demanded 'Hey, you—light'. Unbeknown to Mo, that person happened to be covering for Johnnie Stewart who was the usual producer, so the stand-in must have been well experienced and respected. It took the camera crew all their time to prevent him from punching the young upstart as he was so angry that he could hardly get his words out. As a result, no one within earshot was in any doubt that had it not been for the group's further hits, Mo and the Love Affair might never have set foot in that studio ever again. He must have been spitting feathers when his colleague, Johnnie Stewart, had to have them on every week until it reached No. 1. Only when the record began to crawl back down again could they be dropped, as the show's policy was to feature groups and singers whose numbers were rising but never when they were going down.

Hopefully, all was forgiven, when only twelve weeks later the Love Affair were on the show again, as their second huge hit, 'Rainbow Valley', entered the charts. 'A Day Without Love' was the group's third major hit of 1968, a year that culminated with them appearing on the prestigious Christmas Day show, when *TOTP* featured all the No. 1's from the previous twelve months. Not many people can say that they have been in the homes of 14 million people at Christmas! I did go to the studio with the boys when they were on *TOTP*, but I don't have much recall about it now; that surprises me because you'd think that I'd never forget going to such an iconic show; however, I do remember being asked if I would mind mingling with the studio audience while the group were on and as a result was herded here and there by floor managers, who did a great impression of old-fashioned policemen on traffic duty.

Again, I'm not 100 per cent sure, only pretty, that one of the people doing the rounding up was Peter Stringfellow because he started dancing with me. Dancers were pushed in front of various cameras for optimal shots that gave the impression that the studio was much fuller than it actually was. I guess some of the Love Affair's nonchalance, through growing familiarity with being on television, must have rubbed off onto me too. I got used to their celebrity mind-sets and such occasions were, sadly, almost taken for granted and viewed as the norm, which of course to them they increasingly became. Perhaps if the outside of the studio had been higher in profile, more like a theatre and the *Top of the Pops* name and those of whoever happened to be appearing that night, were 'up in lights' then it would have helped me remember better, but it was indistinct, swallowed up in the BBC building at Lime Grove, in Shepherd's Bush. In those days we didn't have mobile phones, I wish we had, as I could have taken hundreds of photos and it would have made recalling details much easier. Surprisingly, much of the equipment in the *TOTP* studio was old and therefore not in tip-top condition and once when a different live programme was being made there, it suddenly had no picture due to an aged camera developing a fault and going up in smoke, short circuiting all the others in the process. My acceptance of being in such famous building meant I wasn't as much in awe as I would be now, after all I think respect and reverence only really comes with maturity and knowledge. However, I think that even then, had I realised that the studio had once been the home of my childhood heroes, Andy Pandy and Billy Bunter, I would have been very impressed.

The Love Affair appeared on the show roundabout the same time as Pan's People were making their debut. The dancers were loved by everyone, as young girls wished to emulate them and of course males of all ages were entranced by them. The girls worked incredibly hard whenever they were needed to fill in the gaps left when a celebrity couldn't be there. Often there would be a last-minute change in the number they'd rehearsed, and they had literally a day or less to change their routine and costumes because they had to start from scratch. They never failed to deliver and were the first dancers who were a group in their own right, always the same line-up with the same choreographer; in fact, they became more famous than many of the groups they danced to, and deservedly so.

The show was often chaotic because of tight deadlines and forever changing charts and that is what made it so enthralling, as it often went successfully on air, only by the skin of its teeth. I don't think there were any major disasters but those who worked behind the scenes must have had many interesting stories to tell. It's funny really to think how there was such controversy over groups not playing on their records, when it was perfectly acceptable for them to mime to records on *TOTP*. It was so blatant and there wasn't any attempt to hide the fact that the performers weren't playing and singing live. The catch phrase 'spin the disc' was used as a cue in the mid-60s, when it aired from Manchester, for Samantha Juste, to place the pick-up arm of a record player onto the records. The camera would then cut to the artists who would pretend they were playing their instruments and then lip sync to the words. In fact, I think part of the appeal of the show, at this point, was to see just how well or badly the stars did and audiences were joyfully amused or critical when the poorest performers, some of whom must have been mortified at the thought of going out 'live' in front of millions of viewers, were way out on their timing. Those viewers didn't realise, of course, that each group or singer was allocated a mere thirty earlier minutes in the studio and to familiarise themselves with the set, find their spot, and patiently wait as the lighting engineers got on with the job of making them look as good as they could. Once that was done, their record was played through a small and fairly quiet speaker so they could practice miming and some of the crew would be placed strategically around the set, to represent the audience. It was then a case of 'next' and they then joined the artistes' conveyer belt, to wait for their live appearance that night. How nerve-racking must that have been for some of them, especially the newbies?

There were no such nerves though at one run-through when Steve Marriot mesmerised the whole studio with his amazing performance, when everyone was stunned how he could achieve it with only about five watts of volume, a pretend audience and no lighting effects. Steve was no stranger to acting though, because as a child performer he played the Artful Dodger in *Oliver* in the West End. He stood on a cylindrical podium, no larger than a small coffee table and about two feet high, with the other members of the Small Faces close by. The record they were miming to was 'Tin Soldier'. Remember, no audience, no lighting, no loud amplification, no actual playing of instruments or actual singing, just miming and the playback speaker was no louder than the average television set. As the track started, a switch in Steve's soul must have been thrown and his silent singing and air guitar were in perfect sync with the music. As his feet shuffled and stomped, his body gyrated and with his eyes closed and grimacing face, it was easy to see that in his mind, at least, he really was in front of a massive live audience. The energy that he generated was electrifying (and this was only a rehearsal) and when the track finished, everyone gave him a standing ovation—there is so much more to being a pop, rock performer than just singing and playing a guitar.

The policy on miming was changed in the '70s when the Musicians' Union decided that everyone had to sing for real to backing tracks that were made especially for *TOTP*. I think that the seed of that decision possibly sprang from Mick's admittance, but it took several months for it to sprout.

The boys became pros at television appearances, including *Doddy's Music Box*, *Lift Off*, *Crackerjack*, *Colour Me Pop*, *Whistle Stop*, together with many European TV shows. It's so frustrating that despite all this, and the group having Top 10 hits in many countries, there are only a handful of recordings left of those appearances. However, when you think that, likewise, only five complete recordings of *Top of the Pops* in the '60s have survived, then it's not surprising that there is so little left of the group's work, and I guess we are lucky to have any footage at all. If it hadn't have been for Maurice Gibb of the Bee Gees recording the show on an early reel-to-reel home video recorder and later giving it to the BBC, then the footage of the boys performing 'One Road' in 1969 wouldn't have survived either.

Because the group travelled extensively throughout the whole of Europe and Scandinavia, three rare surviving videos were filmed there and very strange they are too. It's only because I spotted the same face belonging to a girl in a bowler hat, dickie bow, and glasses on both the 'official' 'Everlasting Love' video and 'Gone Are the Songs of Yesterday' that I oh so cleverly have worked out that they must have been made on the same day. Mick remembers being absolutely frozen and been told to think warm while making them and is embarrassed by them now. Having girls dancing to 'Rainbow Valley' with rifles and pretending to shoot them into the air was, to say the least, incongruous. Only recently I came across another video that I hadn't seen before; it was possibly made in Austria. It was fascinating and lovely to watch for the first time, a film that was made so long ago. Looking at it now, when thousands of pounds are spent on current-day videos, the limited budget then makes it look rather quaint, but the director did at least try and make it interesting, and as it's shot outside among trees, it's quite refreshing compared with those made in studios. I'm just pleased that they have survived. There is a small snippet taken at of one of the poll winners concerts, when the boys wore evening dress. The image is very grainy and there's no sound, but I like it anyway as a memento. I think it was put on YouTube by the person who had the presence of mind to film it, and I'm glad that they did because I'm frustrated that, throughout their five years together, so little has survived.

15

Ronnie Scott's &
'Igginbottom

In 1969, when the Love Affair were at their peak, Mick and I met up with Steve Robinson. That meeting led to one of the most respected British guitarists of our time, Allan Holdsworth, finding his first real steps towards becoming well known to guitar aficionados. Allan was one of the greatest guitar players ever, he told people he didn't start playing until he was seventeen, but he was actually fourteen and sounded as though he was born with a guitar in his hand. Three months prior to our meeting up in Bradford, Steve had started playing with Allan and two other friends, Mick Skelly who played bass, and Dave Freeman the drums. Steve was anxious to get Mick's verdict on their music and hoped that if he liked what he heard that perhaps, he could help them.

Like them? We were blown away, they were unbelievable. We'd never heard anything like them before and it was an easy decision for Mick so he couldn't wait to get back to London to play their music to Mo and Morgan.

Although the Love Affair were signed to CBS, the three Ms—Mick, Mo, and Morgan—felt that Decca's new progressive subsidiary label, Deram, would be more suitable for their discovery, and they were right. Mick christened them 'Igginbottom's Wrench. It only took Hugh Mendl, who was a record producer and A&R executive with Decca, five minutes to decide to sign up these shy, self-effacing musicians. As Hugh has been described as having a name that deserves to be spoken of in the same breath as George Martin's, it really was a magical opportunity for

'Igginbottom. When Decca famously turned down the Beatles in 1962, Hugh was the only person there who wanted to sign them up, but his recommendation was overruled by Dick Rowe, and the fact that he rated 'Igginbottom highly too, bowled everyone over with excitement. The resulting album, *'Igginbottom's Wrench*, was amazing especially when Alan, Steve, Gi, and Mick Skelly aka 'Igginbottom along with Mick, Mo, and Morgan recorded the whole album in only one session, from 9 p.m. until 9 a.m.—with hamburgers and plenty of coke to keep them awake. Mick was justly proud to have jointly produced it with Morgan and Mo, as well as writing and performing on the second track, 'Out of Confusion'. Hugh, meanwhile, was credited with being responsible for some of Decca's other, most important, signings including the Rolling Stones, David Bowie, Genesis, and John Mayall's Bluesbreakers. He was therefore a man who definitely 'knew his stuff' as Mick once comically understated.

'Knowing his stuff' meant that Hugh was sure his good friend, Ronnie Scott, would be willing to give the young members of 'Igginbottom a hand by allowing them to play in his club. Never one to allow grass to grow under his feet, Mick arranged to meet Ronnie the next day. Feeling as though they were in the presence of a kindly uncle, the three Ms were warmly welcomed into Ronnie's office, as several minders stood to attention outside. Once more an important decision was made within minutes. After Ronnie heard 'Igginbottom's tape, he rated them so highly that he invited them to play in his club. They became part of the headline act downstairs, alongside John Williams and Barney Kessel. No. 47 Frith Street, Soho, is still home to the club and was a hive of activity in Swinging London, but in their innocence, 'Igginbottom didn't realise what an amazing achievement it was for them to impress Ronnie in the way that they had, and to be honest, neither did I. We all just took it in our stride, as though that sort of opportunity happened every day.

Totally bewildered in many ways by the goings on, Steve, Allan, Dave, and Mick did, however, take to Ronnie Scott's and were instantly at home on the famous stage, and I for one couldn't have been prouder of them. The reaction of the audience was one of total disbelief that youngsters from 'up north' had such talent.

This is what Ronnie said on the sleeve notes of their LP *'Igginbottom*:

''Igginbottom' are unique and completely original and although they love jazz music, and Coltrane in particular, I can't detect allegiance to any particular jazz musician in their work. They may well be the first group that has completely, naturally and unselfconsciously, evolved out of the ever-converging directions of good pop and jazz.

Their compositions (mainly by Allan Holdsworth) are fantastic and strangely moving, full of unexpected harmonic twists and difficult intervals, sung, again mostly by Holdsworth with amazingly precise intonation. These are not tunes to hum after a first or second or even a third hearing, but the more you listen the more you'll hear. And the standard of musicianship is phenomenally high by any standards. The interplay between the two solo guitarists gives the group a totally individual sound, rich with beautifully executed filigree runs and unusual voicings, completely free of clichés.

The bass guitar and drums complement each other and the front line excellently, coping with the changes in metre with rare expertise.

That four young men from Bradford who have been together for only a few months can produce music like this, performed with complete sincerity and lack of pretentiousness, is a little short of amazing. ''Igginbottom' are ready for you.

The point is—are you ready for ''Igginbottom?'

RONNIE SCOTT

After their first appearance at the club, 'Igginbottom were offered a residency upstairs. Queues formed every evening, and it was an honour not to have to join them, as Ronnie's minders always waved us past the crowd, through the front door and pay desk and into the darkness of the club that became a second, musical home to us. Years later, even Princess Diana queued outside, but that was through choice, as disguised in a black wig she enjoyed being incognito and was thrilled to be able to do what we mere commoners take for granted. Aren't human beings funny? Never satisfied with what we have, there I was, enjoying skipping the queue and a princess only too happy to join it, so she could feel normal. Wait a minute, I can legitimately say I have another royal claim, Princess Diana followed in my footsteps!

Having lived a sheltered life up until that point, I didn't realise that the club had another side that wasn't quite as friendly as I thought. It was a favourite haunt for members of the West End criminal underworld, many of whom kept guns inside their jackets. At any given moment, I was potentially seconds away from a London version of the shoot-out at the O.K. Corral, and there I would have been, still slurping my coke through a straw. I needn't have worried about any embarrassing slurping sounds, because under those circumstances the noise would have been drowned out by the sound of flying bullets. Sticky carpets, orange lampshades, condensation drenched walls, red table clothes with real candles, and the proximity of the audience to brilliant artistes remains my vivid, affectionate memory of the club. Oh, mustn't forget the peas with bits of lettuce and tiny onions—those small additions immediately transformed those pulses into cordon bleu cookery.

Goodness knows what Ronnie Scott's must have looked like during the day. Now, I've just surprised myself here saying that, but it just rolled of my tongue. The fact was, we visited the club on many occasions during the day, but there wasn't any daylight, so I obviously forgot for a moment, my memory mistaking the dark for night. Ronnie's looked just the same, except empty of people, apart from his team of staff that was short of a cleaner or two.

Ronnie, by his own admittance, had to watch his cash flow as best he could, so perhaps cleaning came low on his list of priorities and he was probably grateful there were no windows, the lack of light camouflaging an awful lot of dust, cobwebs, and grime. He wasn't in the business to make money, but simply because of his love of music and his accountant often despaired at the colour of the accounts, as they were for the most part, a perfect match to the table clothes.

Frith was the second street to house the club; it was originally in a rented basement in the heart of China Town on Gerrard Street. Ronnie loved to reminisce about those early days, when he and Pete King, his fellow musician, opened it was because they wanted to do something else apart from just playing in bands. They were happy because the club meant that they always had somewhere to play, New York clubs, many of which were also below pavement level, inspired them both, but for Ronnie it was his love of jazz, not making money, which was his driving force. Unique in London at the time, Ronnie Scott's was instantly popular and as it kept open 'til three in the morning, it was an ideal meeting place for not only music lovers, but cabbies and MPs, fresh from parliament, and word soon spread. I meant the MPs were fresh from parliament not the cabbies, though it's quite possible that the taxi drivers could have done a better job than the MPs.

Now, that's as political as I'll get, coincidentally, however, last night I was asking Mick to tell me more about Peter Frampton, as he and Peter always got on well. When Mick said that they spent a lot of time talking about politics, I jokingly said that if he'd enjoyed discussing politics that much, he'd perhaps chosen the wrong person when he picked me—Mick didn't contradict me. However, I can stick my own chest out because we'd only been married about a year when Mick received a telephone call from Peter's manager asking him if he'd be interested in joining Peter, playing bass. Peter had had a very successful career up to that point, first as guitarist in the Herd and then as a member of Humble Pie with Steve Marriot, but his time with Steve was about to come to an end and so his manager was testing the water as to which steps Peter would take next. I was relieved to hear Mick say thanks anyway, but as he'd recently got married he wanted to stay at home with me and he didn't think it would be conducive to married life. It's interesting to speculate how things might have turned out if he'd agreed, but I was relieved to hear his reply.

Ronnie's eyes used mist over as he described how once, when he was expecting the Bill Evans Trio to appear from America, that he thought that in order to do them justice he should get rid their old piano and hire a better one. After arriving at the club to deliver a grand piano, the hire company that owned it refused to leave it with them, saying that a) the steps near the entrance were too steep; b) they feared that drunken customers would spill drinks on it; and c) that women might drape themselves irreverently over it, so they could flirt with the world-class jazz pianist. Pete impolitely told the hire company's rep where to go, but the night was thankfully saved when Pete and Ronnie managed to borrow a piano from someone else. I can imagine their conversation 'Er, I hope you don't mind us asking, but we were wondering if you had a spare grand piano we could borrow tonight ...' No doubt that refusal from the hire company and similar other problems contributed to their decision to find somewhere bigger and they eventually moved to Soho. Opening night went well, even though the club wasn't properly finished or even safe. There weren't enough electrical sockets, so candles had to be placed on tables for light and the ceiling was covered in disconnected wires because they hadn't had time to fit the new ceiling lights. How the place didn't catch fire, with so many candles and tipsy, smoking customers, is anyone's guess. Ronnie proudly told Mick and me—in a manner that wouldn't have been out of place in a Monty Python sketch about four Yorkshire men who were attempting to outdo each other— that when Buddy Rich was introducing himself to the audience, he said that it was the first time he'd played in a condemned building. (The four Yorkshiremen were characters that became more and more extreme in their descriptions as to who was the most hard done by when they were boys. It concluded after one said he was so poor, they lived in a shoebox and even that was bettered by, 'That's nowt, we 'ad to lick road clean wit' our tongues' ...)

Ronnie also took inverted pride in the fact that, in true Bohemian style that suited the club well, the toilets were unisex. None of their patrons seemed to mind, perhaps the queue was a good gathering place for people to discuss the artistes or even find a new partner! At one point in the '70s, Ronnie's long-suffering accountant tried to persuade his clients that, because they were in such a financial mess because they were so far behind paying overdue taxes, they should call it a day. Ronnie turned to Pete to ask what he thought they should do, Pete simply followed his gut instinct, replying that they should carry on regardless, so they did. Despite its fame, the club never made any money, and Ronnie was spot on when he claimed that a wise businessman would never have taken the club on in the first place. By his own admission, he wasn't a businessman, simply someone who loved and lived for music. I remember being in Ronnie's inner sanctuary, and that statement of truth was easy to see. I was taken aback at its disarray because there were papers, overflowing ashtrays, and wine bottles everywhere. Ronnie was probably too busy with his master of ceremonies duties or popping over to the betting shop across the street, to bother about such minor things as a tidy office. It was a wonder that he could find the magnum of champagne that was in there somewhere, given to him by Albert Dimes on the clubs' inaugural night. Mr Dimes was an underworld enforcer, equivalent of a mafia godfather, who also happened to be a good friend of Ronnie's dad, as they used to go racing together. He gave Ronnie the champagne, with the instruction that it was only to be opened when the club was finally out of debt. I don't think it can ever have been opened, I wonder if it's still in the club somewhere, the label impossible to read because of the dust on the bottle, that is now a piece of Jazz history. If it is, those bubbles have been effervescing alongside music produced by some of the greatest jazz names ever, including Nina Simone, Ella Fitzgerald, Prince, Katie Melua, Jamie Cullum, and Jimmy Hendrix. Tragically Jimmy died within a couple of days of jamming at the club with his friend, former singer of the Animals Eric Burdon, who had a new band called War. Eric is quoted as saying that he'd asked Jimmy to play with them the night before he actually did, but Jimmy was so out of it, he wasn't capable and was staggering all over the place.

The star was exhausted, and had personal troubles, including a paternity suit against him, and he was attempting to break away from his manager. Although he wasn't in a good place, those who were close to him didn't think he was suicidal. It was initially reported that he choked on his own vomit, after taking barbiturates, but later there were many unanswered questions about what actually happened. There were rumours that he may even have been murdered, but the cause of his death remained inconclusive. It was so sad, particularly as he was only twenty-seven when he died. The Rock and Roll Hall of Fame describes Jimmy as 'arguably the greatest instrumentalist in the history of rock music'. Mick and I were distraught when we learnt that Ronnie died on 23 December 1996 and that there was lots of speculation that he may have taken his own life, but the verdict of the coroner was 'incautious overdose'. We liked Ronnie very much and were so grateful to him, he was a complex man and, sadly, prone to depression. At the time he died, he was upset because he was approaching seventy and devastated that he had to forget any hope of playing in his club at Christmas, or who knows, maybe ever again. Months of painful dental work resulting in loose implants made it impossible for him to play his tenor saxophone. His partner of almost ten years, Mary Hulin, had moved to America by that time, but they were still close and had been speaking on the phone shortly before he died. Although she knew Ronnie was down, she didn't feel he was suicidal as he was planning to go to bed after taking medication prescribed by his dentist. However, he'd also been drinking heavily, and the alcohol might have made him confused over how many tablets he was supposed to take. Tragically, it was their daughter, Rebecca, who discovered his body the next morning, when she went into his flat to check on him after they'd had an argument. Amazingly, she says that as she went up to his door, she felt a huge pressure on her chest, as if something was warning her not to go inside, it was almost as if Ronnie himself was trying to protect her from what she was about to discover. How terrible that discovery must have been for her.

On a much, much happier note, the Royal Albert Hall recently played host to *A Night at Ronnie Scott's: 60th Anniversary Gala*. It cost £2,000 for a box for eight people. My goodness if I'd had a crystal ball when I was with Mick listening to 'Igginbottom's Wrench rehearsing in the club, I would have seen that the very table and chairs we were sitting on would one day be reproduced, on the stage of that world-renowned venue, in front of an audience of over 5,000 people. I can't move on from my reminiscences about Ronnie before mentioning two of his favourite jokes that we heard so many times. Joke number one needs a slight explanation. When we went there, we were struck by the often unenthusiastic applause of the audience. When this happened, Ronnie loved to get on the stage and ask, 'What've you been drinking, concrete?' and the second one was 'I was dancing with a girl and she asked me if I liked Dickens and I said, I don't know I've never been to one'.

So now, I shall leave these affectionate memories of dear Ronnie; may he and Jimmy Hendrix both rest in peace.

16

A Terrifying Night Near Elstree Studio

When 'Igginbottom moved to London, Mick, Mo, and Morgan rented a beautiful, yet neglected house near Elstree studios for them, and it became their temporary home. One Sunday, Mick and I decided we would visit them but had no way of letting them know as there was no phone, so they weren't expecting us. Our taxi dropped us off at the end of the road, and as we approached the front of the house, we noticed Steve was by a leaded window, oblivious that we were approaching. We could hear music coming from a small record player next to him as he sat writing. Mick thought it would be funny to scare him and make him jump, so we crouched down and silently made our way towards the window where Steve was sitting. He was concentrating on his letter, so Mick seized the opportunity to slowly put his hand through the open window and lifted the arm of the record player away from the LP, just as Steve looked up. From where Steve was sitting, it looked as though a 'dismembered' arm was lifting the needle off the album, the shock must have been as tremendous as his screech, which left him white faced and trembling. It was cruel really, and I can empathise with how scared he must have felt, but it was also very funny, and we were given a warm welcome despite the prank. The boys were pleased to see two different faces and we settled down with cups of cup of tea, minus the milk as they'd run out.

Pleased with their new home, they showed us around the house and overgrown garden that must have been magnificent once. It contained lots of plants that were running wild around a pond covered in green weeds, and the statue in the middle of it, had long since given up its day job as a fountain. All the trees had such fat trunks that they must have been there for a century or more and were full of life as squirrels jumped from branch to branch and bees and insects buzzed as loudly as keeping themselves busy. As the sun started to go down over the Elizabethan-style building, Allan and Mick Skelly decided to walk to the local pub and treat themselves to a half pint of bitter. We turned down their offer to join them and stayed with Dave and Steve who was still recovering from his shock. The light quickly faded in the old house, and as we laughed again at Steve's expense, the four of us decided that it would be amusing to continue the 'horror' theme and play a trick on the other two when they got back. I didn't realise then just how unwise it is to dabble with Ouija boards and would never do it now as there are so many scary stories about what can happen, I'll tell you one I heard.

Two couples were staying in a reputedly haunted hotel. They decided to attempt to talk to spirits by using a glass and letters of the alphabet they'd written on scraps of paper. The glass moved, ignoring their question about the 'spirit's' name, and it hesitantly went towards the letters 'd ... e ... a ... d'. 'What happened?' was their next question and it gathered speed as it spelled out 'Killed myself'. 'Where?' they next asked. Answer 'In the bathroom'. Enough was enough, so feeling unsettled and not wishing to take it any further they decided to go down for dinner and forget about it. Feeling better after a relaxing meal and a few glasses of wine, they went back to their respective rooms and one of the girls decided to have a shower. Minutes later she was screaming, and her partner rushed into the bathroom to find out what on earth was going on. She was speechless and was pointing to a misted-up mirror where the words 'Help me' were plain to see. It turned out that a couple of weeks earlier, a guest had committed suicide in there, and had written the plea in lipstick on the mirror. The cleaners had failed to remove every trace of grease from her message, so when the room got steamed up, the words were still there. Not wishing to unsettle future guests, the hotel had kept the tragic event as secret as they could, and it was only through using their home made Ouija board that those two couples found out about it.

We came up with a plot, starting with pretending that we had contacted spirits. We found a drinking glass and wrote each letter of the alphabet on separate pieces of paper and arranged them on Steve's writing table, upturning the glass and scattering the letters as though they'd hurriedly been abandoned. We concocted a story saying that it had worked well, too well in fact, and when the glass had started moving, furiously pointing to letters that spelt out swear words, we were petrified and stopped after five, very dramatic minutes, convinced that we had unleashed an evil spirit. Next, like scheming, black witches, we went to the large bedroom that Allan and Mick S. shared, and armed with black sewing thread, we attached long lengths of it to a rocking chair, curtain rings that hung from a rickety curtain pole and a book in the bookshelf. We guided the threads under the door and hid the ends in the hallway, discreetly attaching them to small pieces of rolled up cardboard.

We couldn't wait for the two unsuspecting victims to return and when they did, we lit the fire in the inglenook and didn't say anything about scattered letters and horizontal glass, knowing that they were sure to notice them. When Mick S. eventually saw them, he was curious and insisted we told him what had happened. Steve went into great, convincing detail that made the hairs on the back of my head stand to attention, even though I knew it was all made up. The scene was set and as is often the case, one thing leads to another.

It's surprising how many tales of ghosts six people can come up with, and Allan was the winner hands down, obviously fascinated, yet hesitant about the subject. He began to enjoy scaring us with his tales, including one that involved the ashes of one of his ancestors that were kept on his grandmother's sideboard, the details of which I have forgotten, but I do remember how spooked out I felt as it was creepy and convincing. The grandfather clock started chiming eleven times and, as I was the only girl there, I offered to make some bedtime drinks and left the others chatting away as I made my way down the passageway towards the kitchen. It was a big house and the boys' voices faded into the distance behind me, as I walked towards the kitchen. I wasn't familiar with the old place and had to put my left hand on the wall in case I tripped as I couldn't see very well as the single bare lightbulb at the far end of the long hall and was dull and kept flickering. I was feeling jittery because of the conversation we'd just had and wasn't at all happy. I heard a buzzing noise and then the hall went black as the light gave up altogether. I slowly put my other hand on the wall to feel my way along it. Within seconds I had the shock of my life and was filled with sheer terror. I saw two huge, green, fluorescent, eyes staring at me through the blackness. Before you come to any wrong conclusions, no, I hadn't been passively smoking hash again, the only time 'Igginbottom were 'high' was when, as they admitted to us, they had been bored and climbed those tall, ancient trees outside, for no other reason than it gave them something to do. I thought it was the devil himself because the eyes were slits and I started screaming loudly and Mick later described it as 'the longest, most blood-curdling scream, you could imagine'. He said that they were all startled and sprang to their feet, but no one wanted to make a move and be the first to investigate as they were shocked to their already unnerved cores. Mick told me later that his legs felt paralysed, so he was momentarily unable to do anything, and his mind raced in an attempt to make sense of the situation. He was confused because he told himself that, although he thought that I was a good actress, I wasn't that good. His feet remained rooted to the spot, as were mine, on that broken-tiled floor that felt miles away from the comfort of another human being. Because the boys were so terrified, it took them several long seconds to come to my aid, but those seconds seemed like minutes and when they finally did, they found me trembling and just like the hotel guest in her bathroom, I too was speechless, and my index finger was pointing in the direction of my horror. It was a tiny lizard. In my highly aroused, nervous state, all I could see were the green eyes that I thought were huge, they stared back at me reflecting the tiny amount of light that there was. Its body was completely hidden because it blended into the background, I'd never seen one before and had no idea what it was and for a millisecond, it crossed my mind that we really had unleashed a demon. Relieved that I hadn't been attacked by dark forces, the boys went into the kitchen with me. No one admitted it, but nobody wanted to be left alone, even for a second. The stage was well and truly set for our practical joke and when it was finally time to go to bed, we all went up the well-worn stone steps together and split up into our own rooms. I could hear Allan and Mick S. chatting for a while, but nervous exhaustion helped them fall asleep in no time. Once the rest of us were sure they were asleep, judging by their beer-induced snores, we crept as quietly as we could to the outside of their half-open door and on the silent count of three, started pulling on the strings. It worked perfectly. The curtains started fluttering and the pole collapsed onto the rocking chair sending it into a slow squeaky motion as two drumsticks fell off onto the floor and they rolled noisily towards Allan's bed. Of course, the noise woke Allan and Mick S. up and they jumped out of their beds making a bee line for each other not knowing what to do. To their momentary relief, the chair stopped rocking and they agreed that the curtain rail had simply come unhinged and there was nothing to worry about, they'd fix it in the morning, so they got back into their beds again to continue sleeping.

How we four managed to stifle our giggles I will never know, but with like minds and a lot of gesticulation to shush, we waited until the snoring started again. Dave pulled his bit of string and the chair started rocking again, but this time he tugged much harder and its squeaky joints sounded like they were in agony. Mick S. shot out of bed followed by Allan and realising that there really was no logical explanation for the moving rocking chair other than concluding that the Ouija boards demon had joined them, they stood huddled together in their underpants with their arms around each other. Allan, his naturally bulging eyes now on stalks, was shaking for Britain and shouting in his Yorkshire accent that had gone up two octaves, 'Oh No, it's true, it's true, it's really true.' At that exact moment, a Pelican book with the title *Hitler: A Study in Tyranny*, written in large letters on its front, flew out of the bookcase and landed at their feet. By now, Mick, Steve, and Dave were on the floor hugging their stomachs in laughter with tears in their eyes while I was worrying that perhaps we had taken the joke too far, as our two helpless victims looked as though they were about to pass out. You couldn't make it up, but then again, we did, and it worked better than we could ever have imagined. From that moment on, belief in the supernatural was never quite the same for Allan and Mick S. and they vowed not to be taken in again, by anyone—never, ever.

I know that I have mentioned coincidences before, but I have another great one to include here. We hadn't seen Dave or Mick S. in over fifty years, until yesterday, the very day that I was writing this chapter. I am 'friends' on Facebook with Mick S. and Dave and we were able to arrange our get-together as Mick S. and his wife, Karen, are on holiday here, as they now live in Australia.

How on earth do you squeeze five people's stories of their past half a century into a couple of hours? It's not easy or possible, of course, but it was great to reminisce, though we all felt great sadness at Allan's recent death. For me, the '60s, because of this book, have been on my mind for months now, but Mick S. and Dave had hazier memories, though they soon came flooding back and it became hard for any of us to get a word in without rudely butting in on everyone else's sentences.

I asked if Mick S. or Dave had been at the Beatles concert when they played in Bradford and was fascinated to hear Dave say that he did try to get tickets, but they were sold out, so once the show had started, he and his friend made their way to stand in the street directly behind the Gaumont. They could hear every note played and they were crystal clear as the sound came straight through the wall of the building without bouncing off interior walls, people, and fabric. The two of them must have had the best audio experience of anyone that night because, as I know first-hand, inside it was impossible to hear anything other than screams.

I didn't realise at the time, but 'Igginbottom didn't always travel back home when they had their residency at Ronnie Scott's, and they often slept in the club. The round trip to their Elstree house would have cost more in petrol than they could afford, so Ronnie kindly said it was OK for them to bed down in the club. They didn't sleep the whole night, as most of it was gone by the time they shut their eyes, but they managed to get a few hours. Scary to think they were locked in and had to wait for someone to arrive the following morning to let them out. Their van was towed away one morning because with no way of getting out, they couldn't get to it in time to put coins in the meter.

Once, when they'd hardly eaten anything for two days, the owner of a nearby kebab takeaway took pity and gave them a huge kebab sandwich that they hungrily shared. Even though they could get to the bar and kitchen in the club, they'd all been being brought up with good, honest, standards and wouldn't have dreamt of stealing anything and were probably too embarrassed or polite to admit to Ronnie or Pete that they were beginning to literally starve. Mick S. remembers that they were also too timid to object when someone from a trio asked to practice using Dave's drum kit. Although he's not certain, Mick S. thinks they were the band America, as the drumming was identical to that on their later released hit, 'A Horse with No Name'. What he is certain about is the look of horror on Dave's face when he discovered that the repetitive, heavy use of his beloved bass drum had caused a large dent in its skin.

Mick S. reminded us of the time 'Iginbottom went to watch the Love Affair when they were playing in front of the mayor at a music festival called 'Oxfam Walk 69' held in Wembley Stadium. They were top of the bill that included Status Quo, Yes, Alan Price, Jimmy James & The Vagabonds, and Gun. Most of the kids present had walked to the concert to raise funds for the charity, and despite the fact that they must have been worn out, they still screamed as enthusiastically as ever. Much to 'Igginbottom's amusement, some of the fans even mistook them to be the Love Affair. They followed 'Igginbottom's slow moving, old, Ford Thames van and shook it almost beyond its capability, as Dave clumsily moved through the three-speed column gear change in a futile attempt to make an impossible, hasty exit. I wonder if, at that moment, Igginbottom were relieved or disappointed that they were mainly a jazz/blues band instead of a pop group and never had that experience ever again. Such times could be scary, as a tribal instinct seems to set in when girls literally forget everything, other than trying to get close to their perceived heroes.

My own dislike of motorways hadn't formed then, as on one occasion

'Igginbottom gave me a lift back to Bradford in that same van and I was more than happy to sit at the front next to Mick S, who was perched on top of the engine between Dave, who was driving as he was the only one who could and myself. Whenever Dave got tired during the 200-mile trip, Mick S. gallantly volunteered to give him a break by taking charge of the steering wheel. The veering of the overloaded vehicle didn't concern or scare me at all, any more than the fact that Steve and Allan were travelling in the back on a 1950s sofa that was precariously placed on top of their speaker cabinets. They say that if a rear passenger doesn't wear a seatbelt and there is a crash, then the force of their body as it is thrown forward would be equal to that of an elephant. Had it happened on our trip, the combined force of a sofa, bodies, and cabinets would have been the equivalent of a whole herd.

Although Dave says he only has a hazy recollection of his time in 'Igginbottom, he has never forgotten two occasions, and unsurprisingly both are about girls. While performing at Ronnie Scott's, 'Igginbottom used to visit a local corner street pub because drinks were cheaper there than in the club, and who should they bump into, but Pan's People. Dave confesses he instantly fell in love with Barbara 'Babs' Lord, who later went on to marry Robert Powell, best known for his title role in the film *Jesus of Nazareth*.

Reading that back, it almost sounds as though Babs fell in love with Dave, too, but sadly for him, that was not the case; however, I shall leave the sentence exactly how it is as I know that if Dave ever reads it, it will make him happy, and he can continue dreaming.

The second never to be forgotten memory for him was waking up first one morning at Elstree, and when he was waiting for the kettle to boil, he couldn't believe his eyes as he sleepily glanced towards the garden next door. He must have thought his Christmases had all come at once, as draped over and among the trees were several girls in various stages of undress. They were doing a photoshoot for an over-eighteens 'lads' magazine.

Selflessly, he ran upstairs and woke the others up and within seconds they were all hanging out of one of the none-too-safe ancient windows, clambering over one another, each trying to get the best view. Although at that time it was common practice to throw a bucket of water over family pets if they became over amorous, I don't think Steve, Mick S., Dave, or Allan would have appreciated their excitement being dampened in a similar way because if it had, they would no doubt have toppled into the slimy, cold pond that was immediately below.

17

No Minister

By the time 'Igginbottom were on the scene, my job at the tax office was history, I'd finished struggling with my 'Rs' in the estate agency and found myself working again for the government, but this time at the Ministry of Agriculture Fisheries and Food. Now, had I been assigned to the switchboard, I would have had less trouble than I did at Britton Brooke & Brown as I'm fine with 'As' and 'Fs', but it wasn't even a concern, as I was sent to one of their many, impersonal typing pools. My typing skills in those days were not great as I hadn't had much practice but that didn't seem to matter, as efficiency was a word they didn't seem to recognise, anything seemed to go. I was bewildered when I first went there, not knowing what to expect. I needn't have worried though, as I could hide my inadequate speeds because there were so many typists churning out sheet after sheet of strange figures and facts. It didn't matter how slowly I typed as long as the finished results were accurate, so I got through an awful lot of liquid paper. Incidentally, that very same liquid paper that I used had been invented by the mother of Mick Nesmith who was the singer and guitarist in the world famous Monkees. It's a pity I didn't know that at the time, because at least it would have given me something interesting to think about to relieve the monotony of that stuffy office.

I was in the 'Artificial Insemination of Cows' department. By that, I don't mean insemination took place there, and fortunately no one had to wear wellies or a plastic apron. We simply had to type details onto A4 paper and then place them into a tray situated next to our superior who, because she was a supervisor, sipped her tea out of a China mug; it was Tax Office hierarchy crockery rule, all over again.

It was a conveyer belt of, at least as far as I was concerned, the most boring statistics ever that helped the ministry to decide whether or not the numbers of cattle needed increasing or decreasing. I guess I could have easily got the numbers wrong and that might have made the difference between life or not for thousands of baby bovines. I had more power than I realised, it's a good job that I was ignorant, as I might not have slept so well for fear of depriving calves of their right to be born. I found the figures mind numbing and my eyes were constantly glazed over, and that's difficult when you're trying to type, but somehow I plodded through the statistics, along with the days I spent in that very high and mighty building. Who would have thought that little old me was working for 'the Ministry' sounded so grand, but I managed not to let it go to my head.

The Right Honourable Fred—that is, Fred Peart—was the minister at the time. I never saw him about, but then again, even if I had, I wouldn't have known because I didn't know what he looked like, just that he came from up north, from Workington, in fact, so we probably would have got on well.

One thing the civil service was good at was catering, so tea breaks and lunch were the highlights of the day, and despite the fact that the cheese scones were even better than my Nana's, you can see what a thrilling time I hadn't. I did hope that perhaps Harold Wilson, our then prime minister, who I did recognise, would pop in to sample one of those scones, so I could tell the customers in the pub; they would have been impressed, but he never did. Perhaps he preferred to stay home where he could work out how he could extract those last few remaining pennies in the pound from taxpayers. Mary, his wife, looked like a typical '60s housewife so she probably baked scones for him anyway, which were just as good as the ministry's.

I don't remember any chit-chat among us as we sat in a classroom-like room with an indifferent supervisor at the front, who really didn't even have to think as her job was to simply hand out the work from one basket and make sure the completed sheets landed safely in the other. She didn't need an eraser for anything, particularly not her brain cells as they must have shrivelled naturally years earlier through lack of use. The noise of all those typewriters was quite deafening, It was surprising that 'Health and Safety' didn't provide us with ear plugs, but I've just looked them up, and seeing as it didn't even exist until 1974, then of course they didn't.

The best part of the day was walking away from the building at night, and even though I hadn't a clue what I'd been typing, at least we kept the farmers busy. I would have much preferred to have been on their farms in the fresh air among their cows and bulls. Silly me, there wouldn't have been any bulls as it was artificial insemination, so I'd better rephrase that, I would have been quite happy among the cows—if not the syringes.

I said I would have preferred to have been on a farm and that is so true insomuch as whenever I did venture outside the capital, the sight of all the fields and countryside made me realise just how much I'd missed them, it really was like escaping. A place I would really have liked to escape to then was, of course, San Francisco, to be one of those people with flowers in their hair. I had to wait another twenty years before Mick and I did go, and when we did, it rained so heavily that my feet were drenched as the only footwear I took were sandals. Were those sandals a subconscious effort of mine to subliminally remind myself that at last we really were in the original city where hippies had hung out in their kaftans and macramé cardies adorned with beautiful beads? San Francisco seemed as inaccessible to my teenage self as the far side of the moon. While temping, the best I could do was simply daydream about it, in a futile attempt to stop myself falling fast asleep in the Ministry of ... Agriculture, ... Fisheries and ... snore.

18

Frankenstein's Mother-in-Law

How would you feel if you knew you were sleeping in a bedroom that once belonged to Frankenstein? OK, I'll admit it, that's a ridiculous question because, of course, the monster wasn't real, but hopefully it caught your curiosity and therefore attention. However, his creator, Mary Shelley, had possibly stayed in the same room in an ancient house called Elcot Park, as we did, as her mother-in-law had once owned the building.

We were there because the Love Affair were due to go on their tour of the UK, sponsored by Yardley cosmetics and the large house had only been open as hotel for a short while and had been exclusively rented by them because it had a large barn that was the perfect place for them to practice, far away from public ears. It had been empty for the previous ten years. As we walked through the front door, I sensed that the fabric of the grand house was seeped in mystery and misery. Each previous owner had their own story of course, and I suspected that for the most part, they were not happy ones.

Troubled energy, including Frankenstein's author's mother-in-law's, was left behind and felt as real as the furnishings. I learnt that misfortune, particularly heavy debt, was a common denominator. Jane Austen's novel *Lady Susan* was based upon the sadistic meanness of Elizabeth Raymond, the first owner of Elcot Park, who had it built as her dower house. Even the weather took its toll on Elcot Park as one stormy night the conservatory windows blew in and it was destroyed, but that, at least, I am glad to report, was not while we were there. Those few days when we were have remained etched on my memory ever since. I'm not sure if it's real or imagined, but I think that the group had stayed there previously. Mick can't remember, but it doesn't really matter, my point is that someone, I think it was Steve, told me that he had seen the ghost of a white lady in the middle of the night in his bedroom. I was, therefore, nervous even though it could have simply being him winding me up. The manager was a very efficient-looking person, smartly dressed in his suit and tie, but his housekeeper had a solemn face and wore a bedraggled uniform. They seemed in awe of the boys and very subservient, hardly daring to open their mouths to speak, and little more than a mumble came out of them when we introduced ourselves.

After they'd scurried away, we familiarised ourselves with the place and soon everyone began to feel at home and started to relax, well at least the boys did, I felt very tense, sensing something wasn't quite right. The furniture, which was once quite grand, was well worn but comfortable, apart from the odd lumpy spring. Mirrors placed in the most unlikely places had been dusted down along with the paintings of previous occupants, their eyes, very much like the Mona Lisa's, seemed to follow you. We were shown to the dining room for dinner and at last even I began to relax. I don't think that Egon Ronay would have approved but we were hungry and had a pleasant time, despite the blandness of the food, hastily plonked on plates, making it obvious that presentation wasn't the chef's forte. When in the early hours of the morning it was finally time for bed, I felt the butterflies start to flutter in my stomach as we made our way towards Frankenstein's—I mean, our—room.

It must have been the journey there or even nervous excitement wearing me out, but I was asleep in no time, and morning soon came, although to be precise morning had already arrived before going to bed, when the cooing of pigeons had taken over when the owls stopped hooting. When the boys went to the barn to rehearse, I was left alone to explore the place. It was a rather miserable day, the sky dark with clouds and a chilly breeze made me go back to our room to put something warmer on before venturing outside. I passed the manager in a corridor and was pleasantly surprised to see that he was wearing jodhpurs. We had a brief, polite chat as he swished the air with his riding crop in a manner more suitable to a fencing match. I had the feeling he was just making sure I realised how he was dressed, as if I could miss the riding hat, which was far too small for him. I had the distinct impression that the outfit wasn't really his. When he was satisfied that I had noticed, he suddenly remembered something he had to do and shot down the hall and I was left alone. I thought I'd go and find the stables because I hadn't had time to ask him where they were before he vanished. I felt happy that I could tell Mick the good news that the hotel had stables and thought we could enquire to see if we could go riding, whenever he had a spare couple of hours. It was silent in the grounds, except for the sound of the rain falling upon the leaves of the trees, at least the contrast was refreshing compared to the stuffy interior; the staff seemed to be having difficulty with the heating thermostat. The garden needed attention because the previous ten years of neglect had turned it into an unkempt, yet natural area. It made me think nature does know best, it was far more attractive than an area tamed to within an inch of its life. The lawns were more like meadows and were filled with buttercups and poppies that were doing their best to stay upright in the wind. I listened to see if I could hear the horses so that I could walk in the right direction, but it was silent apart from the group playing Hush in the distance. I imagined that the old barn must have been shaking in time and I was grateful to be some way away, my ears having a grateful rest for once.

'The stables must be at the back of the house,' I thought logically; of course, silly me, stables were always at the back. Inching my way along the overgrown path at the side, I eventually found myself by the back door. There was a long, wall nearby, but it gave no clue as to what was behind it. White hot pants were not the best choice of clothes for my exploration, but I'm quite good at self-preservation, and being in no rush, I managed to reach the wall with only a few bramble scratches and the odd nettle sting. Luckily, there were some dock leaves nearby, so I rubbed one on my legs, it lessened the itch, but I couldn't get rid of the green streaks it left behind. I'd only been out a matter of minutes and was already covered in sticky buds and my black-spotted shorts, for that's what they'd been downgraded to, were in urgent need of washing. Because some bright spark had imaginatively described mere shorts as 'hot pants', sales went through the roof when girls like me rushed to buy them, but at that moment mine felt anything but fashionable. I eventually reached the wall and found a wooden door and was surprised to find that it opened quite easily revealing nothing more than a long since abandoned garden and little else, certainly no stables, no horses. The area was scruffy, full of decomposing something or other, the smell was so awful that even birds kept away. The juiciness of any fresh vegetation had long since gone, the only thing that was still growing was the rust on a discarded garden fork. It was disappointing as I was looking forward to seeing another face, especially an equestrian one. By this time, I became uncomfortable on my own, so I decided to go back towards the house as I knew that the boys would be having a break soon. When I got there, I saw that the dining room where we had eaten our non-Egon Ronay approved meal was exactly as we had left it. All the plates, glasses, cutlery, and leftover food needed clearing, but they were left untouched, on the wine-stained tablecloth. I didn't think too much about it, as Mick came back from the barn, raving about 'Space Oddity', David Bowie's record they'd just been listening to. The others were still tired and went to their rooms. I told Mick about my search for the horses, and he also thought it would be great to stroke them and receive a nuzzle of their heads in return, so we went to look together.

Fifteen minutes later, we decided that the manager must go riding somewhere else, as there weren't any stables in the grounds, so we gave up our search. We decided to stay outside for a while away from the others and whilst we were sitting on a fallen log, I noticed that nearly every tree nearby had a bird hanging from it, suspended by string tied around their tiny necks. Mick assured me that it was not an unusual sight in the countryside, as it was an old custom to warn off other birds, but there was nothing to protect. I disapproved of those pitiful sights and spent the next hour feeling upset that someone could do such a thing, it just felt sinister. Fortunately, my mind was distracted when we later joined the boys for dinner and their high spirits made everything seem OK again. As usual things got out of hand towards the end of the evening when one piece of bread was thrown, then another and another resulting in a slight variation of a bun fight. Mr Manager heard the commotion and quickly appeared, as if from nowhere, now dressed in a waiter's uniform. He asked the boys to stop, but of course they ignored him, so he tried to prevent Mo from using a syphon to spray water over everyone by prizing it out of his hands, but he got wet through instead. Unbelievably, either through anger or in the spirit of joining in for fun, I'm not sure, he picked up a fire extinguisher, popped the seal off and squirted Mo with white foam, all the time keeping a dead pan face, but at least he had everyone else in convulsions of laughter. The more they laughed, the harder he pressed and the fiercer the flow. After much sliding about on a very slippery carpet, the foam won, and everyone turned in for the night.

Rehearsals started slightly later the next day, there was even time for breakfast in the 'breakfast room'. All seemed normal and unexceptional until, on the way to the barn, we noticed that the scene of the previous night's battle was exactly as we had left it. Cushions and bread were scattered everywhere, chairs upturned, and the red extinguisher and water syphon lying facing one another as if to start yet another duel.

This became the norm, that is, the un-cleared dishes, not the battle, and each meal was served in one of the many different rooms and then left un-cleared, and simply shut away from sight by closing the door. Normal people would have checked out, worried about hygiene or possibly getting food poisoning, but members of a pop group are not normal. We took it as just one other eccentricity in our extraordinary lives, and as long as we weren't asked to eat in an already used room, we were happy to have a constant change of scenery. My imagination made me sleep uneasily but apart from the curtains that wafted in a breeze that wasn't there, all seemed normal, that is until one night.

Mick was fast asleep as I lay there thinking, when the sound of someone fumbling with the outer doorknob to our room made him stir. By the time he opened his eyes, a woman's head was peering around the door and without saying a word, she just stared at us for several long seconds. Several seconds doesn't sound much I know, but as I learnt years later when Mick was racing cars, even a thousandth of a second can mean the difference between winning a race or not, and in those circumstances, a second is an exceptionally long time indeed. She then retreated by silently closing the door and we, as you do when you have just seen a ghost, went back to sleep. Well at least Mick did, I just clung onto him for comfort.

The following night I was determined to keep both my eyes open but of course I couldn't, and this time we were woken by an unearthly wailing noise, accompanied by what we learnt later must have been a wooden seat in a nearby cloakroom, being lifted and dropped onto porcelain toilet. The noise of the clattering wood had a beat that made it sound as though a frantic tribal dance was taking place. A silly thought went through my mind, perhaps whoever it was making such a racket had previously heard Mo's drumming and Steve's singing and was warming up in preparation of joining them in the barn the next day?—maybe. Had Mick thought it was a burglar, he would I'm sure have been out of that door instantly to sort them out, but no amount of nagging from me could persuade him to investigate a possible ghost.

The final day of practice arrived, and with nothing in particular to do, I had to find a way to occupy myself once more. As much as I liked to sit and listen to the Love Affair, it was good to do other things too and I was fascinated by the hotel and wanted to find out as much as I could about it, in the time left. I was sitting in the interesting library with a heavy leather-bound book when Mr Manager came jogging through the door.

The thick sweat band around his head made him look ridiculous as it had somehow managed to push all his wrinkles down next to his eyebrows giving him a slight hound dog look. There was no sweat that I could see, and his trainers were as pristine as the towel in his hand that looked as though it had been freshly unwrapped as there were distinctive creases on it where it had been folded. Why was I not surprised? Well, we'd quickly got used to his eccentric habit of changing his clothes several times a day. We'd accepted his quirky ways, without commenting on them, and the more we ignored them, the more desperate he became. He asked me if I would like a cup of tea and I accepted so he would leave me alone to finish glancing through the book. I decided, however, that when he got back, I would ask him more about the house's history and its ghost. Ten minutes later, he appeared with a silver tea tray for me, the gym towel now flung over his arm, in a waiter like fashion. I didn't get the chance to ask him, though, as he said he had to be somewhere else—no surprise there then. I found myself feeling relieved that he'd chosen to leave as he clearly wasn't of sound mind. Even though I really wanted to find out more about the building, I was also uneasy about what he might have done if he'd stayed as, after all, I was alone. I convinced myself not to be silly, that all was fine, and although he might be a bit unhinged, he really was harmless. I was glad for once to see the miserable housekeeper, who came in to clear my cup and saucer away. It didn't occur to me at first that it was unusual for someone in Elcot Park to take used crockery away, as that is what usually happens in a hotel. I'd momentarily forgotten that nothing had been cleared away since we arrived. Slightly disappointed in one respect that the manager had disappeared, and I'd missed my chance to pick his brains, I thought I'd ask her instead. She was surprisingly helpful, and I noticed a slight look of pleasure cross her face as she said that the house had a ghost and asked if I would like to see the ghost room. Not wanting to throw kindness back in her face, even though my instincts were telling me that it might not be a good idea, I said yes, thank you and naively followed her. We went up a second creaky staircase that I hadn't noticed before, and realised it was one that must once have been used by servants. She turned to me and said that the ghost room was her bedroom, and although I began to feel uncomfortable, I also didn't want to appear rude, so I continued behind her as my stomach began to turn cartwheels. When we got there, she pointed to the single bed and suggested that I should sit on it. The small room was sparsely furnished and there wasn't a chair, so I perched on the edge of the bed. Uninvited she sat next to me and was far too close for comfort. Sensing my nervous state, she offered me a cigarette. I accepted it, even though I hardly smoked, not realising how much my fingers were trembling until they clumsily snapped it as I attempted to take it out of the packet. It was at that precise moment that it dawned on me that far from being shy and withdrawn, she had lured me there and had obviously lied about it being the ghost room. The penny well and truly dropped as I fled her room. It must have been her head peeping around our bedroom door and also her voice that we heard wailing as she banged the toilet seat. She'd obviously sensed my fear as I walked through the door on that first day, and when she caught me alone she jumped at the opportunity to entice me into her bedroom. Maybe even all those oddly placed mirrors were two way ones and she'd been spying on me when I thought I was alone. We never found out if the manager needed psychological help or even if, as we later suspected, he was married to my female admirer. It didn't matter, no real harm had been done. Elcot Park is now a four-star hotel, owned by Accor, and it has been extended and modernised. I would love to go back for old time sake—after all, the housekeeper won't be there, but maybe the real ghost will and surely those dishes will have been cleared away by now, or will they?

19

Carnaby Street

In the '60s, the words of a well-loved Kink's song included 'Everywhere the Carnabetian army marches on, each one a dedicated follower of fashion'. Carnaby Street was world famous, and teenagers everywhere wished they could be there, alongside all the beautiful 'in' people. It's a stone's throw from the equally famous London Palladium and that Carnabetian army was real life theatre and the street itself their stage. It was possible to park down one side and it took a while for the council to realise that it would be safer to make it a pedestrian area, as thousands flocked to it every day. It was like a small back water compared to Regent Street and Oxford Street, so it was bursting at its seams. Carnaby Street became its own logo, it had a heart and felt like a market, full of small boutiques and shops with goods spilling over into the road or hung washing line fashion above their front doors.

Because cars took up quite a lot of space, visitors couldn't saunter along as now, and were squashed into much less space and had to be careful not to get run over. Most found their spirits rose when they looked at the shop fronts decorated with artwork of surreal images and patterns. It was so colourful and attractive that it was easy to feel happy there, even without the help of the many joints that were smoked openly. Pop music played everywhere along with the new sound, to the British public at least, of Indian sitars and tablas. Many people became interested in eastern philosophy and the guru Maharishi Mahesh Yogi, who became famous because of his contact with the Beatles when they became fascinated with transcendental meditation. The *bonhomie* between mods and spaced-out hippies, who loved everybody, made young people flock to Carnaby Street anxious to be where it's at. Whenever a city gent was there in his pin-striped suit and bowler hat, carrying his obligatory *Times* newspaper and umbrella, the contrast between him and those '60s followers of fashion couldn't have been greater.

Visitors went there not only for the shops and atmosphere, but because they also hoped to rub shoulders with pop stars, and they often could. The innovative Lord Kitchener's Valet boutique, for example, sold antique military uniforms as fashion items and it was frequented by the likes of Mick Jagger, Jimi Hendrix, and Eric Clapton.

It is said that Lord Kitchener's was a big influence on the Beatles and inspiration for the iconic cover of their *Sgt. Pepper's Lonely Hearts Club Band* album. Told that they needed to spend their earnings to avoid paying the government's unbelievably high tax rates, John, Paul, George, and Ringo were even persuaded to open a store known as the Apple Boutique. Unfortunately, it was only open for about eight months, not helped perhaps by its location that was away from Carnaby Street on a corner of Baker and Paddington Street. The outside was painted brightly because, as in the words of Paul, the intention was for it to be a beautiful place where beautiful people could buy beautiful things. Things started to go wrong immediately when the council objected to the outside artwork and it lost its cheeriness as a result, as it had to be repainted in an unattractive bland colour. Not every visitor to the Apple Boutique was as beautiful as Paul had hoped they would be, as there was a huge amount of pilfering. Taking people to court was not good for the Beatles image, of being full of love, peace, and forgiveness, so shoplifters got away with stealing thousands of pounds worth of stock and the business simply couldn't survive.

As Mick and I walked down Carnaby Street one day, we saw a stunning red velvet mini dress with gold braid trim on the hem and bell-shaped sleeves. It was wafting on a washing line above one of the boutiques and I was thrilled that he liked it too and bought it for me. It remains one of my all-time favourite dresses, I may still have it in the loft somewhere, but then maybe not, best not look though, as I would be disappointed if I couldn't find it. During this time, we decided to become vegetarians, so Cranks, just around the corner, became a regular haunt for us, it was very different to anything back at home in Bradford. Their delicious homemade soups, savouries, and puddings were accompanied by salads, whose combination of ingredients, so crisp and colourful, were a million miles away from the usual, boring, traditional tomato, cucumber, and limp lettuce salads that made people's appetites wilt too. The influence of their hand-thrown stoneware stayed with us, and Denby crockery, which was similar, was top of our wedding gift list. However, only a couple of our guests were familiar with such new-fangled crockery, and even though we were delighted with the jug and plate that we received, it was only when Mick and I celebrated our ruby wedding that we acquired a complete dinner set that I secretly collected via eBay so I could surprise him.

I could have eaten nothing but Cranks food forever. In fact, we have eaten it forever, though not exclusively, because one thing I still do have is an early recipe book of theirs. It hasn't gone brown with age, though, as it was brown already, in keeping with their earthy image. I thought I'd bought it at the time we are talking about, but I didn't, I've just checked, and I'm surprised to see that the date is way later: 1982. By the time we were eating at Cranks, they were in their second restaurant in Marshall Street. The first Cranks was opened in Carnaby Street in 1961 before it started swinging. Then it was just a quiet little street of cafés and small shops including a saddlery, chess set shop, ironmongers, and tailors that surprisingly only had to pay low rents. I'll leave Carnaby Street there for now, I know this is a small chapter but apt as, after all, Carnaby is a very small street.

20

Please Do *Not* Keep this Secret to Yourself

Please bear with me while I digress for just a few moments. This book, though quite squeaky clean, could have been written with a very different slant on it. However, a typical rock 'n roll version would not be conducive with my favourite role as children's author and narrator of audio bedtime stories.

There have been many banana skins along the path throughout this bedtime story project, but maybe, just maybe, the universe has been waiting for the right time before stopping sending them. I don't think there has ever been a more urgent need for assistance than now, when millions of children (and adults) throughout the world are feeling frightened, depressed, and anxious. My good news is that there is an enjoyable, easy way that can contribute greatly in helping to overcome many problems.

There are thousands of bedtime stories of course and also quite a few hypnotherapy audios for children, but the combination of bedtime story, hypnotherapy, powerful subliminal messages, and sound effects, make these downloads especially effective and possibly unique. I have drawn upon my experience during the past twenty years as a hypnotherapist who has had the privilege and joy of helping thousands of clients to write and narrate these gentle stories.

My mission is to get these hypnotic bedtime stories known throughout the world, so that they can comfort little ones and help them feel secure, happy, and confident enough to grow into caring, honest, responsible

adults. As future caretakers of our planet, they will then be able to make a positive, literal world of difference to this place that eight billion of us call home.

It occurred to me that many of the thousands of original Love Affair fans would now have grandchildren, and if I could reach those grandparents, they would get to know me *and* my mission. **It is the reason I wrote this book.**

The audio stories are gradually being made into apps and eventually I hope they will all be available on Apple App Store (iPhones) and Google Play Store (Android). At present any child, who for example, is being bullied, lacks confidence, has poor eating habits, or cannot sleep can be helped and comforted. Parents and carers can find the story they want by going to Apple App Store and typing SOS (short for Stories Overcome Stress) along with the title of the problem. Incidentally the beginning is the same on every children's story as children love repetition and familiarity relaxes them.

Here are the exact titles available now on iPhones (Apple). SOS Sleep Well, SOS Confidence, SOS Healthy Eating Child, SOS Separate Parents, SOS Child's Fear of the Dark, SOS Separation Child's Fear, SOS a Child's Being Bullied, SOS Good Manners, and SOS Your child's Bedwetting.

Coming soon: SOS Enjoy School, SOS Feeling Unwell, SOS Give up Dummy (also known as pacifier, comforter, or soother), SOS Morning Stress, SOS Car Journeys, SOS Feeling Insecure, SOS Feeling Left Out. (These titles may change slightly.)

Being 'hypnotised' is not being asleep, it is simply a form of relaxation, however, parents often tell me that their child and indeed they themselves often do fall asleep while listening to the apps and never reach the end, but that's OK as the subconscious mind never sleeps.

Hypnosis is perfectly natural, and children are very good at it. For example, when they are playing with toys, they go into their own imaginary world. Should someone call their name they often ignore them, not because they are being naughty but because they genuinely might not have heard as they are so focused on their toys, we often say they are in a trance (another word for hypnotised). Adults, when driving a car, can get from point A to B and not remember driving because they have been thinking of other things, that is also a form of hypnosis or trance! Hypnosis is sometimes described as 'magnified concentration'— such as when reading a book, painting, watching TV, etc., the list goes on and on and we all go into hypnosis several times each and every day. When driving and the conscious mind is focused on something else (as in daydreaming) we say we are doing the driving 'automatically' but what we are really doing is delegating the task to the subconscious.

We don't have to use our conscious mind to make our hair grow, make our heart beat, or our skin repair, those things seem to happen all by themselves (automatically), but again, that's because our subconscious mind is in charge. These are just a few examples of the millions of things that the subconscious can do—all at the same time—how magical is that?

When a child's subconscious hears the subliminal messages several times in the bedtime stories, such as 'everything is ok', or 'safe', 'sleepy', 'happy', the child then believes and becomes those things. The subconscious, although incredibly powerful, doesn't analyse (that's the job of the conscious mind) and absorbs like a big sponge those positive, subliminal messages so that they soon become fact.

Once a parent or carer agrees with all the subliminal messages after reading them (to make sure that they are acceptable to their child), and has listened to the app, then they can then let their child enjoy the relevant, charming bedtime story. I cannot begin to describe how much pleasure I have derived, knowing that already, children as far flung as Japan, Australia, and America etc., are now benefiting from these apps, simply by listening to them.

Before I leave this announcement for which I make no apology as this project is so important, there are adult titles available now in both Apple App Store and Google Play Store. They are SOS Lose Weight, SOS Stop Smoking, SOS Overcome Stress, SOS Happy Marriage, and coming soon SOS Sleep. Again, before listening it is important to read the subliminal messages first, to make sure they are appropriate.

Typically, as a wife, mother, and grandmother, I have got through piles and piles and piles of dirty washing that would be the size of a small mountain, but if you wanted to learn about my own dirty washing in the scandalous sense, hand on heart, by comparison, it wouldn't equate to even a quarter wash load. Of course, in general, many sixties 'pop stars' couldn't say that, but I don't want to be accused of telling tales anyway, children's author or not, besides my half a century of dirty washing is more than enough for anyone even though it's in a literal sense. On with my lily-whiteish version then.

Life on the road for the Love Affair was usually monotonous, covering thousands of miles, while they cramped together in one car. Everyone smoked to pass the time, so it was the usual practice for six people to be puffing away and, incredibly, the windows were usually kept closed. I find it difficult to believe now that it was even possible, but I know it was, as I travelled with them many times. How did we or indeed the driver manage to see through the fog, or even speak without coughing our guts up? How did we think we were so 'groovy' when our clothes were drenched in foul-smelling smoke? It wasn't unusual for the boys to be herded straight off stage into their car with their clothes completely drenched with sweat, before travelling to the next hotel, and, of course, lighting up, the stench of cigarettes and sweat mingling seamlessly. That was just another aspect of how unglamorous life on the road could be.

One of those cigarettes caused a great deal of trouble near Heathrow Airport when the group were travelling to catch a plane to Glasgow, which was notorious for tough audiences. The boys were not in the best frame of mind as they were all anxious about the forthcoming gig and the atmosphere in the car was tense. They were giving Pauline, Morgan's girlfriend, a lift to the airport where she worked and attempting to act as peacemaker, she thought she'd try and change the mood by handing her cigarettes around. Unfortunately, Steve's response was a grumpy one and included several expletives, and it was the catalyst to make Mick lose his temper, so he lunged at Steve. None of the boys were strangers to falling out, but thankfully not quite as literally as on this occasion. Mick and Steve didn't only fall out with each other, but out of the car when one of them caught a handle and the door flung open, propelling them out and onto the ground. They were determined to get the better of one another, after all it wasn't that long since Steve had been North London Schoolboy Boxing Champion and Mick had experienced his feral days as a ragamuffin street fighter. They continued to wrestle beside the road, not a wise thing to do, especially when unknown to them, they were being observed by the occupants of the police car that had been behind them since the argument first broke out. Seconds later, they were being cautioned and told to follow the police to the cells at the airport. There they remained, for several hours, before John and Sid were summoned thinking they would have to bail them out, but fortunately the boys were let off with a caution. Sid was a clever businessman and because they were valuable to him, he looked after them well and they were often treated like royalty, so much so, that just like the queen, they didn't have to carry cash as Sid and his accountants were usually there to settle their bills.

Mick has a fond memory of the days before the group made it, when he and Steve went to Sid's house to ask for a sub on their wages. It didn't occur to either of them that ten to midnight was not a considerate time for or them to make an unexpected house call. Disappointed that no one was answering the door, they were just about to leave, when it slowly and carefully creaked open and their reluctant, yet curious, sleepy manager whose tired eyes could hardly focus, stood there in his dressing gown and enquired through clenched teeth, 'Yes?' Realising that Sid must have been asleep, and their timing wasn't great, they explained why they were there. Too weary to object, Sid nodded his head. Mick and Steve resigned themselves to a few more chilling minutes waiting on the doorstep, while he retrieved the requested money from somewhere inside. They were both aghast, however, when they didn't have to as Sid simply put his hand in his dressing gown pocket and pulled out a thick wad of notes and peeled a substantial number from the top. Mick has often wondered why anyone would keep such a stash in their dressing gown, presumably it wasn't simply to pay the paper boy or milk man, even though prices in London were pretty steep.

Despite their arrest at Heathrow, they made it to Glasgow just in time, though what happened there must have made Rex think it was anything but fortunate that they managed to catch their flight. He wished that they'd remained locked up for longer and it wasn't anything to do with his fear of flying—the stage was in a topless cage. It was about 15 feet from the floor, and a safe distance away from the audience. The Love Affair were therefore behind steel bars for the second time in hours, because the organisers thought the set up was a good precaution in stopping over enthusiastic fans from reaching their idols. Boyfriends of the fans often got jealous, and they were safely kept away from the boys—just as well, because the majority enjoyed a good fight and could have no doubt taught even Steve and Mick a thing or two.

The teenage magazines of the time often ran question and answer pages including super intelligent queries such as what Mo's favourite colour? Or Morgan's preference in breakfast cereals? As a result, most fans knew which aftershave Rex liked. The cage was no barrier to bottles of Brut, coins, and goodness knows what else that were hurled over the top. One bottle was thrown with such force that, as it gained momentum, it became a powerful missile that hit Rex on the head and he was urgently pulled off the stage by the bouncers, bleeding profusely. The others soldiered on, and no doubt nervous tension caused them to be highly amused at poor Rex's mishap, which under different circumstances would have been anything but funny. No different to the times when snow or extreme traffic jams often brings people together and strangers become friends in adversity, that extreme experience made Steve and Mick forget their own battle earlier that day, as they bonded once more, to face one of their toughest audiences ever. In contrast, Steve and Mick did have many enjoyable times together, for example, one memorable day was when they staying next to Lake Zurich in Switzerland. They both thought it would be great to swim in the icy water, it was no surprise to them, however, that the others chickened out. Undeterred, the two action men donned their swimming gear and swam to a platform that was quite a distance from the shore. Shocked at just how far out the wooden structure was, they shivered violently, gathering enough courage for their return both wishing that they hadn't been so gung-ho. It's quite possible that, while they were resting before having to swim such a long way back to the safety of a shore with no lifeguards, they would have preferred the danger they'd faced in Scotland to the predicament they found themselves in at that moment. At least in Glasgow they were on dry land with zero risk of drowning. Pals in peril, they encouraged and supported each other on the almost impossible swim back, and as a result, they managed to make it to the lake's shore. Poor Sid would have had a fit had he seen the danger his boys were in. That night they were so proud of themselves and each other that they stayed in the hotel bar, long after everyone else had gone to bed, to celebrate their safe return.

Their competitive streaks coupled with the adrenaline that was still surging through their bodies found an ideal outlet when two German guys challenged them to a drinking competition. Never ones to give in, they tried to keep pace, drinking beer followed by schnapps, but their tiny frames were no match for their beefy challengers. Steve's body had finally succumbed to the enormous amounts of alcohol, their gruelling schedule as well as their earlier swim, and he collapsed in a semi-comatose heap. Mick staggered upstairs; it wasn't an easy task either as he had to carry Steve up them too. For once, it would have been impossible for Steve to inevitably win any singing competition, as his diction was slurred and his voice inaudible as he tried to thank Mick for the piggyback ride back to his room. Just as Mick was heading back after dropping Steve at his door, and was looking forward to slumping into bed himself, he could hear Steve attempting to whisper but his naturally powerful voice increased in volume and sounded quite desperate as he called down the corridor, 'Mick, Mick'. Anxious to make sure he was OK, Mick zig-zagged back, the amount of alcohol he'd imbibed made it difficult for his eyes to focus on anything. Steve, far from in need of assistance, had somehow brightened up considerably and wanted to party some more—with a king-sized joint. He managed to persuade Mick to join him for further couple of hours that they spent in fits of laughter, until dawn broke, a sign they'd better get some sleep. They'd sobered up enough by that time to realise that they didn't realise what or where they were heading that day. It didn't matter because even though the group was often squashed together like sardines in a car that was smokier than many a kipper, and fists did occasionally fly, they were all more than grateful to go along for the ride.

21

Anyone Can Disappear for a Grand

The Love Affair were at an after-gig party held in a mansion on the outskirts of Edinburgh when Mick learnt that life was not quite as valuable as he once thought. After the show, they'd been herded straight from stage towards the gothic country pile, and as they hadn't even had a shower, Mick felt neither comfortable nor sociable. When he walked through the door he was immediately greeted by an Irish wolfhound and made friends with him, pleased in the knowledge that he wouldn't be asking scores of questions or trying to persuade him to drink more than he wanted. Mick found the grey, long-bodied and legged animal the most interesting character at the gathering, and his own dishevelled appearance matched his new canine friend well, as his usually shiny hair was just as unkempt, and they had instant rapport. Mick had never seen a dog the size of a small donkey before, and knowing him, during that initial greeting, he would have held out his hand in act of friendship. I have lost count of the number of times I've seen him do this whenever he meets a dog, and I'm always afraid that the dog would not recognise the gesture as being peaceful and bite him. Touch wood, it hasn't happened yet under those circumstances, but he was once bitten badly when he was taking a rescue Alsatian on a walk and it bit through his hand, narrowly missing an artery—the scars are still there.

The wolfhound was a guard dog, and although the other guests chose to stay well clear, Mick spent his time getting to know him and the dog then followed him from room to room for the rest of the night. Mick often prefers animals to humans, particularly dogs and cats, and as he is not a party person, he was happy to have just a dog for company. Their cosy twosome was interrupted by a burly, muscle-bound character who took the opportunity to chat to Mick who had settled on the bottom step of the large sweeping staircase. Once the small talk was quickly out of the way, it became obvious that he was touting for business. Without giving even the slightest hint that he needed reassurance Mick was told in a big brotherly way, 'Don't worry mate, if anyone ever gives you any trouble, here's my number, you just let me know, you'll never have any trouble from them again. It doesn't matter who they are, anyone can disappear for a grand.' It just shows how deceptive appearances are, because Mick was so angelic looking then, Mr Muscles must have thought he couldn't say 'boo' to a goose, but he couldn't have been more wrong. By the time I met Mick, he'd had more fights than he could count (though usually not of his own making) and knew how to look after himself, though in fairness he and his friends almost viewed fighting as something of a hobby and weren't usually serious. Even so, Mick was taken aback at the brazen way the stranger was trading his 'wares'. It was an eye-opening experience to be approached by the likes of someone, who up until that moment he had only seen at the pictures. It began to dawn on Mick that he really was learning fast that, in certain circles, disputes were sorted out not by fists, where the participants would often shake hands and make up afterwards, but true Mafia style.

A grand doesn't sound such a lot now, but then it was a lot of money, £15 a week or £750 a year was considered a good wage. The stranger didn't hang around as he had lots of 'business' cards in his pocket that he was anxious to distribute among the other potential punters at the party.

Surprised by what he had just been told, Mick looked at 'wolf' and began to wonder if the host of the party had chosen him as a guard dog, and not one to necessarily deal with burglars only, but possibly potential assassins.

When the party was finally over, Mick was pleased to be leaving, especially as the host had made two Aston Martin DB6s available to take the group back to their hotel. It was the early hours, dawn was fast approaching, and Edinburgh was deserted, just as well, as the drivers of the two cars, decided to race down Princess Street as fast as their accelerators would allow. Red traffic lights were no deterrent to the determination of each of them to win and were completely ignored. Mick was thrilled by the excitement, all thoughts forgotten now of how easy it was for anyone with money to make someone disappear. I can't help but think how grateful he must have been that Madge couldn't witness that night, as not only had he been mixing with hit men, but he was also a passenger in a car that was playing Russian roulette not only with the traffic lights but his life.

22

Hanging Out With The Who

The group usually travelled to Europe by plane, but not always; happily for Mick, as he loves boats, one occasion when it was decided that they would go by sea was his twenty-first birthday. He's not even sure where they sailed from, but he told me that he thinks it was Hull across to Gothenburg. Sadly, for many, but not me, P&O Ferries stopped that route a few years ago. As he was recounting this, it occurred to me that Gothenburg was where Batman lived, I know he's not real, but even so, Mick has put me right and says Bruce Wayne was from Gotham City. Had it been my birthday, and I was told that I was to spend it on a ship, it wouldn't be a treat unless there was a 100 per cent guarantee that there would be a calm sea, and of course that's not possible. For Mick, the rougher the sea the better, he'd choose to be up on deck, loving being battered and bounced about, and I would be wishing I were somewhere else. I can't think of many things much worse than being on a boat in a storm, it takes on nightmarish proportions for me. Even though his twenty-first was such a landmark birthday, for once, I was pleased that I wouldn't be joining him on that trip, especially as it was winter.

After the equipment and vehicles were safely loaded on board, they made their way to the bar, and it was decided that in no way would the boys let Mick see the day out without downing twenty-one drinks. That would have been fine had the drinks been non-alcoholic, but of course they weren't, and Mick's tipple was vodka and orange. The birthday boy was not fazed in the least and more than ready for the challenge, thinking it would be a remarkable story to tell his grandchildren. Onlookers packed into the bar as word had got around that the Love Affair were also passengers, and as it was the bass player's twenty-first, a wager was in force. Even the captain popped in a couple of times to see what all the fuss was about and judging by the delight of his passengers, he and Mick weren't the only ones with a tale to tell their grandchildren.

Determination is such a large part of Mick's make up that it should have been his middle name, and although I am very proud of him for that, I must confess that there were occasions such as this one when I wished that he had been more mouse-like instead. However, it's fortunate he wasn't, otherwise if his full name of Michael had been Mickie instead of Mick, and the others would then have no doubt jumped at the chance to nickname him Mickie Mouse—instead of plain Jacko. It was a long crossing and that steady pace resulted in him achieving the goal and winning the bet. Although he managed to stagger to his cabin, he didn't remember getting to it, but there would have been willing volunteers to steer him in the right direction. A drunken stupor was instantly upon him, but so, unfortunately, was something else, in the form of a misinformed, male member of the ship's crew. This was shortly before the rainbow flag became the symbol of the LGBT community, and the intruder had imaginatively used his own initiative to flag up his sexuality by wearing large, plastic, daisy earrings and that's fair enough but what he did next wasn't. Despite the drinks, Mick was conscious enough to be aware of the uninvited guests burly shoulders pushing under his top bunk bedcovers, and he intuitively kneed their owner in the face. The unwelcome visitor recoiled backwards and landed in a heap on the lower bunk opposite, and then despite his flowery adornments, he was not the pretty sight he was trying to be because blood was gushing from his nose. Further explanation as to Mick's sexual orientation wasn't needed, and the unfortunate man managed to escape into the bowels of the ship almost as fast as Mick could shout 'F*** O**'.

Mick tried to get back to sleep but the intrusion coupled with the excitement of his birthday made it impossible, so as naked as he was at his breech birth (he's continued to land on his feet ever since, by the way), he staggered out of his cabin onto the top deck wrapped in only a blanket. He can still recall seeing huge icebergs and feeling the freezing temperature biting into his flesh as he shivered uncontrollably, despite his unconventional cloak.

He looked up at the clear, star-studded sky and even in his inebriated state, he says he felt in awe of the brilliance of those stars and vividness of the sky unpolluted by city lights. He certainly was living a charmed life, and any less blessed person could easily have tumbled overboard into the water and no one would have known until the next day. However, Mick didn't end up in the sea, unlike one of the group's dressing rooms in Lyme Regis that was perched precariously close to the water's edge.

That tiny building was a nightclub belonging to a promoter whose gig at a different venue he owned was cancelled at the last minute due to circumstances beyond their control. Understandably, the promoter was disappointed, but unfortunately also very annoyed, so much so that he threatened the Love Affair with legal action. To placate him, Sid agreed that they would play at his club in Lyme Regis, not realising just how unsuitable and dangerous it would turn out to be. By the time the group appeared, they were famous, and the promoter couldn't believe his good fortune. From the outside it's difficult to imagine how hundreds of young fans managed to squeeze in there, and typical of the time, most of them were chain smoking. How it didn't burn down, let alone how any other catastrophe didn't occur, is beyond me. Mick had often recounted how they had once thrown a dressing room into the sea out of sheer boredom and frustration and Miss Prim and Proper me never approved. It wasn't until many years later when I saw the tiny building for myself that I began to understand the circumstances that led up to their act of vandalism. For once, I thought that greedy promoter got what he deserved, as he'd put many people's lives at risk. Safety was of no concern to him, only profit I'm afraid. The time of our much later visit to Lyme Regis was not long after the Bradford fire, where fifty-six football supporters perished. Dad, Brian, and my mum's brother Leslie were there, but miraculously wishing to avoid the crowds, they left the grounds minutes before the tragedy. With that still fresh in my mind, it made me shudder as, staring at the then-almost dilapidated building, I listened again to Mick's recollection of waiting to go onstage that night.

Milking the situation for all he could, the promoter, oblivious to any danger he was putting people in, kept the audience waiting for over an hour before allowing the boys on stage. His logic was that the more fans there were, the more drinks would be sold, particularly as the temperature was so high, due to the number of people squashed together. Anxious to make a name for himself, the promoter had invited the chief constable and local MP who found themselves huddled together in the wings. Even if the duty-bound VIPs had wanted to escape, they couldn't, due to the increasingly frustrated expectant crowd of bodies pressed against the stage and exits. Backstage, the atmosphere was just as bad, if not worse, as that where the impatient audience were, particularly as the group didn't want to be there in the first place. They were unable to physically walk away from the dangerous situation, as they were penned in, but even if they had been able to escape, another legal threat was out of the question, so they simply had to grin and bear it, the best way they could. Feeling trapped, they couldn't even pace up and down to relieve their tensions because they were in such a tiny room. It was inevitable that something was going to give in this pressure cooker—I mean, shoe box. Although it is no longer the case, the tide then reached the part of the building where the dressing room was situated. The waves smashed against the walls as if in agreement with the mood inside, and as they did so, Mick tried to open the window for some fresh air. It had not been open for years, and the rotten wood disintegrated with the sheer force needed to free it, and the crumbling frame fell into the sea. It was a light bulb moment and almost in unison, the boys, who really didn't care one jot what the consequences would be, had the same idea. Wouldn't it be a laugh and relieve the monotony to follow through with other bits of the room?

An hour is a long time, and I can confirm quite long enough for the entire contents to be hurled out through the windowless gap, before landing in a gratifying splash into the salty water. When the room was eventually empty, not satisfied with that, they decided that the toilet and wash basin were next and promptly tugged at the sanitary ware until it too exited in the same way. Mick assures me that all that remained were a few of the wooden floorboards. They did go on stage and play, but for Mick, the rest is blurred; he has no idea what happened as a result, and as usual, it was Sid's job to sort out the mess, theirs was simply to appear, wherever and whenever they were told.

On the outside looking in, it might have looked as though they had a carefree existence and got away with most things, and that was true, but it was also one where individually the boys had no control. Their management made decisions on their behalf, and they had to go along with them. Although royalties from records were very welcome, they earned the most money from appearing in concerts and gigs and that involved constant touring and extensive travel throughout Europe. That sounds wonderful, but in truth, they saw very little of each country as they couldn't venture anywhere alone. To keep them going throughout relentless schedules, they were handed uppers to keep them awake and downers to help them sleep. One hotel room looked very much like another and most hotels then, didn't have the variety of differently furnished rooms as now, and they were uniformly monotonous. Lots of groups were notorious for trashing them, but I have got to say that despite the one-off complete destruction the Love Affair caused in Lyme Regis, as a general rule, none of them were anyway near as badly behaved as their fellow musician, Keith Moon of The Who, whose antics they often witnessed first-hand.

Keith was a law unto himself, and enjoyed every minute of his destructive reputation, in truth he was a likeable person who might have felt pangs of guilt in different circumstances but as money was no object and everything he broke was always replaced or paid for by The Who, he didn't see any problem. In fact, he no doubt justified the trail of devastation he left behind by thinking it provided work and therefore an income for the people who had to clear up after him, so in his mind at least, he thought he was being helpful. Just as the Love Affair benefited from appearing in court after climbing Eros, Keith and the rest of The Who also knew that there was no such thing as bad publicity. All publicity shone a light on them and kept them in that spotlight and every time they dismantled anything, wrecked a guitar, tore down scenery, or threw objects out of windows, it was also putting more money into the coffers of 'Team Who' and fans were left wanting more. The start of the destruction was a happy accident when an over exuberant Pete Townshend accidentally damaged his Rickenbacker guitar on a low ceiling while they were on stage, and to save face, he pretended he meant to do it and followed through by destroying it completely. The audience went wild he'd stumbled across a unique way to work their audiences into a frenzy. Keith loved it and, not to be outdone, from that day on, he frequently destroyed his drum kits whenever he could; I don't know how many instruments were ruined in total, but it's reported that in 1967 Pete wrecked over fifty guitars (but not all at once of course). Keith's behaviour became increasingly extreme and second nature to him and with no financial conscience to worry about, he flung much larger and heavier things than mere toys out of his pram. It wasn't to gain publicity either, it became something to do—because he could. Once, when The Who had just left their hotel, Keith told their driver to turn around because he had forgotten something. It was only when he was getting out of the car to go back into the foyer that he shouted, 'I've forgotten to throw the TV out of the window.'

Mick remembers being in a television studio in Germany with The Who, and it was usual practice to line up the positions of where members of the groups would be standing so that the cameras could get the best angled shots. On that particular day, the producer was taking so long and was so pernickety that everyone was feeling beyond frustrated. It was always a chore at the best of times, and although John Entwistle, who usually kept fairly still whilst performing anyway, occupied himself by quietly strumming his unplugged bass guitar, Roger Daltrey, Pete Townshend, and of course Keith found that their patience was running out and the more that that they were told to 'Be quiet!' the more dispirited they became. Eventually having had enough, Keith completely ignored the demands and increased the volume of his drumming until it was at its maximum and, not satisfied with that, annihilated his drum kit. The Love Affair were due to sort out their positions after The Who and as they waited their turn, Mick watched the whole scenario with admiration. Keith's antics might have delayed The Who, but they hastened his time there and the Love Affair were able to get back to the comfort of their hotel earlier than planned. The Who stayed in the same hotel, and as the two groups relaxed together in the bar, the drink flowed as freely as ever, but at one point of the evening the usual buzz became almost subdued, and Rex realised why—Keith was nowhere to be seen or heard. I say heard, because it was not unusual for Keith to entertain himself by blowing up various bits of hotels with his home-made bombs, especially the toilets, that he learnt exploded in a particularly, at least to him, satisfying way, whenever he tipped a mixture of weed killer and sugar into them.

Rex was similar to Keith as he also loved to be what could be best and kindly described as impish, though he was nowhere near as bad as the drummer, and as a consequence Rex looked up to him, seeking inspiration for his own pranks and often copied Keith. Rex asked Roger where 'Mooney' was and learnt that he'd gone to his room, and when Rex announced that he thought it would be a laugh to disturb the mad boy, he was wisely advised against it, that is if he wanted to continue living. Meanwhile Mo was quietly watching and listening to the conversation and was cringing at Rex's suggestion because the last time he and Rex had gone into Keith's room, a radio had started buzzing and they couldn't make it stop. Rather than doing what most sensible people would have done, and phone reception for help, Mooney took the matter into his own hands by picking it up and lurching it out of what he considered to be his own version of a waste bin—the open bedroom window, regardless of who or what was below. Rex must have momentarily forgotten that experience, either that or because he was possibly high on whatever, he couldn't resist the urge bubbling up inside him to follow through with his intention. He found even more Dutch courage when Mick volunteered to be his accomplice. Mick was so chilled out that the 'Hail fellow, well met' mood he was in meant that he couldn't envisage that anything other than peace and love would emit from Keith when he saw them. How wrong he was. Rex and Mick only had one problem: they needed the key to get into Keith's room. However, they found it easy to persuade the young receptionist in charge of guests room keys, that it was in safe in their hands, particularly because she was in awe of the hotels famous guests and didn't have the courage to argue. Once close to Mooney's door, the pair of them became rather reticent to be the one to use the key. After raucous giggles and failed attempts to keep quiet, they decided that they would do it together, after counting to three. The key was too small to be handled by two pairs of hands, and consequently Mick found that it was his that finally unlocked the door. The light was on, despite the fact that Keith was tucked up in the pristine sheets, snoring loudly, completely oblivious that he had two uninvited visitors. Mick was amazed by Rex's courage (perhaps I should say stupidity), when he put his mouth as close as possible to Keith's ear and shouted 'MOONEY' in a voice that was almost as loud as one of Keith's explosions. For several seconds, there was no response; had any normal person being lying there, they would have shot out of bed in an instant, but whatever Keith had earlier imbibed caused a delayed reaction until first one and then the other eye opened—they had the look of the devil in them. Keith jumped up and straight onto the top of the adjacent wardrobe, bounced back onto the now crumpled bed and off again towards the silent TV that he picked up and hurled through the closed window sending shards of glass in its wake. With that, Keith's demeanour instantly changed from a madman's to that of an angel and he got back into bed without saying a word or even acknowledging Rex and Mick and promptly went back to sleep.

The two intruders couldn't believe what they had just witnessed (not surprising as parts do sound like a repetition of Freddie the frog), perhaps they were dreaming, perhaps Keith had been dreaming too and was acting it out, who knows? However, they did now believe Roger's warning. Keith Moon appeared to have super strength by throwing an extremely heavy TV at, and through, a window and could just have easily thrown one or even both of them out as well, as their combined weight was only slightly more than the national average for one person.

Although they, along with the rest of the music industry, knew of Mooney's reputation and Rex had been there when a small radio had been disposed of in an unusual way, it was nothing compared to this, and to actually witness it up close and personal was shocking, even to them. They were relieved because they knew that not only was the look of the devil in Keith's eyes real, had they not also had the luck of the devil themselves, then they could so easily have been out of that window along with the TV.

23

A Tragic Encounter

Sheila thought that it would be good fun to share a flat with other people and because she was more knowledgeable than me, she knew that it wouldn't be difficult, because there were companies who specialised in bringing people together called share-a-flat agencies. We moved north of London to live in a flat with two male actors, near attractively named Swiss Cottage. That sounds rather interesting, but I'm afraid it wasn't. Still, under Sheila's wing and grateful to be there, I simply went along with her wishes to move in with others, even though I would have been quite happy to have remained put, but at the same time looked forward to a new phase of my life. It turned out to be temporary, very temporary, as we only stayed for a month because we hardly saw the two thespians, if at all, so much for having more company. I don't recall much about it other than pride of place on top of the fireplace was a vase filled with peacock feathers. Those feathers with their beautiful emerald green, gold, and blue patterns resembling eyes certainly entranced me. I especially liked Peter Sarstedt's single 'Where do you go to my lovely' and never got bored of playing it over and over, possibly to the annoyance to our very temporary flat mates, but there were never any complaints or shouts to turn it down. Living away from home as a teenager certainly had its advantages. Despite their tolerance, we moved out because they weren't sociable and that had been the whole point of moving in with them in the first place. The agency found us another flat in a house nearby, where we became the new flatmates of a girl called Rita who was living on the top floor. This time, instead of being in the space below stairs like Earl's Court, we were high up under the attractive, red-tiled roof where domestic staff would once have lived. The living room window looked out towards the Post Office Tower, such proximity tricked me into believing we were living in central London, but in reality it was quite a distance. It was fine at first, Mick especially loved the place, but he could hardly ever stay over as only Rita had a double room and Sheila and I still had to share ours. It was the sort of house that Mick and I dreamt about having one day.

My journey to work was also pleasant, London buses ferried me to and fro as I daydreamed on the top deck, happy with my unusual dual life. Nowadays, girlfriends of well-known groups often have to say goodbye to any privacy they might previously have had, as their lives become an open book too, but it wasn't like that then, and I'm grateful for that. Keeping such a low profile for the sake of the Love Affair's fans— correction, no profile at all—also protected me. Living in a goldfish bowl is hard and not as sparkly as first appears, and just like water, life in the public eye can quickly get cloudy as you can't put a price of privacy.

Whenever the other girls in the flat went back home to see their parents, I at least had the place to myself and spent many hours listening to my latest favourite music; it's a good job that for the most part I was happy alone, as Mick was away so much. Peter Sarstedt was by now gathering dust in a corner alongside several of my eastern philosophy books—that weren't, but he didn't seem to mind. The Beatles' double *White Album* became my nightly entertainment. (Amazingly this is now much sought after and one, owned by Ringo, was sold for thousands of pounds recently!) I tried to work out the meaning of the words, most of it going over my head, not surprising as the 'the fab four' were heavily into transcendental meditation and drugs and I wasn't. The distinctive, plain white cover with only their name printed on it was produced as a complete contrast to their previous eye catching LP— *Sgt. Peppers' Lonely Heart Clubs Band*. Little did I, or anyone else, know that when they were making it, John, Paul, George, and Ringo were going through turbulent times in their relationship, resulting in Ringo leaving for a short time. Up until then, their wives and girlfriends had been banned from attending recordings, but John insisted that Yoko was there, and the others didn't like it, and although it wasn't intentional I'm sure, as all she was doing was supporting her husband, she contributed towards their final split.

My days appreciating our 'penthouse' flat was during the summer of love and Woodstock, and as I adored the concept of Flower Power and the song 'All You Need Is Love' that was and still is one of my all-time favourites, I just want the world to be calm and everyone in it loving towards each other. It never entered my head that, at the tender age of seventeen and fending for myself in London, things could have gone badly wrong or been dangerous, but I guess I've always had a sense of self-preservation that's kept me safe, that and my pink-tinted glasses of course. I do sometimes wish that I had not been quite so Victorian and let my hair down more, but it meant that I never came to harm and was happily oblivious to the darker side of life the capital. Ignorance certainly is bliss, because we were so wrapped up in our own immediate lives that just over a year earlier, we were both totally unaware and unconcerned about a pandemic that was spreading throughout the world called Hong Kong Flu. It killed over a million people and although the boys went to Germany a lot, nobody spoke about it, even though in Berlin there were so many dead that their bodies were stored in subway tunnels.

One thing that didn't escape my notice once I did move to London was the number of homeless people living on the streets. They didn't have the cute appearance I'd seen illustrated in children's books, of tramps (as homeless people were once called) carrying a red and white knotted handkerchief on a stick, containing all their worldly possessions, but were heartbreakingly in genuine need of love and affection. Although there were soup kitchens then, I don't think that there was as much help for them as there is now.

Mick has two long lasting memories, one sad, the other tragic. The first one was when one of the roadies introduced him to an all-night takeaway food van parked on the Thames Embankment. It was in the early hours of the morning and not feeling in the best of spirits or health after weeks of exhaustive touring, his despondency soon changed as he realised that he was surely one of the luckiest young men in the UK.

A middle-aged lady hurried towards them, she was oblivious Mick was in a pop group and therefore she wasn't another fan anxious to get an autograph. She was a very hungry, shivery human being in filthy clothes and bare feet, the dirt that clung on to them caked in blood. That night, at least, thanks to Mick and his roadie, she and her fellow rough sleepers had more food and drink given to them than they could possibly eat. We don't know what became of her, of course, but I like to think that, like Cinderella, she had a happy future. His second tragic encounter was while walking along Wardour Street in winter, after leaving the Marquee, when it was bitterly cold. Mick noticed a person sleeping in a doorway, at least he thought the man was asleep, until he went up to him to see if he was OK and discovered that he was covered in ice and his eyes were closed, not because he was asleep, but because he was dead. So, so sad, time to move on to something else, my next and final home in London, Heathrow. No, not the airport, but the Great West Road, it was where Morgan's girlfriend, Pauline, lived with her mum, dad, and sister and she very kindly could see I was missing a family environment and her generous mum agreed to let me become an extended part of theirs.

As I just said, I wasn't living in the airport, but it felt as though I was, as the noise from planes taking off and landing was deafening. When you sat in the garden on the other side of their triple glazing, you could see clearly the faces of people on the Boeing 747s as they peered through their little round windows; I'd no idea they were such monsters, I mean the planes of course, not the passengers. I could have waved and done my bit for British tourism helping new visitors to feel instantly welcome but didn't. I was so self-conscious and lacking in confidence then that to wave at a stranger felt embarrassing and awkward, even one that was up in the sky.

The first time I went into Pauline's garden, a jet was taking off, and I ducked for cover, shocked at just how near the top of my head it was. It's amazing how quickly you get used to things, though, and before long I hardly noticed the noise. Come to think of it, I've been blaming my diminishing ability to hear on the earphones I used while hypnotising clients for the first ten years after starting, I don't use them anymore as a safety precaution, but maybe those jet engines were as much to blame, along with Mick's amps and, later, racing car engines. *C'est la vie*!

My surrogate mum was wonderful and treated me exactly as she did her two daughters and I loved living there as it was a real home. She also took over from Sheila in giving me shelter under her wing and very good at it she was too. I have always been and always will be grateful to Sheila for making my first few months in London so much easier than it might have been had I never met her.

Not only had I left Sheila behind, I had to find a new job, so my temporary 'mum' helped in that department too. She was a silver service waitress and suggested that Pauline and I could join her at a forthcoming wedding and, not to worry, as we could cheat and, instead of silver service, we could use a beginner's joined-up fork and spoon that made it much easier to keep food securely held between them.

However, when we got there, the serving cutlery for novices was missing and we had to use the real thing. Happily, for me, the guests were kind and didn't voice their dismay when every other person became aware that their inexperienced waitress lacked not only spatial awareness but couldn't get the hang of how to correctly hold a spoon and fork together and ended up putting almost as much food in their laps as on their plate. Fortunately, they did have napkins to protect their lovely wedding clothes. I must have lost several ounces of weight due to anxiety as I hid behind the kitchen screens, waiting for the oh-so-important *Maître d'* to give us the nod when it was time to clear away. I was afraid that it would be me who would drop a stack of plates, sending them crashing to the floor with a sound only a few decibels quieter than those jumbo jets. There's usually someone in a catering setting that does that, and I just didn't want it to be me, because whoever is responsible for dropping the plates usually gets stared at or even applauded as they become the centre of attention, for all the wrong reasons. Although I did get paid, I wasn't surprised when Pauline's mum never asked for my help again.

My next Hounslow job was selling ice cream in the local park with Pauline. I thought that a group of boys sitting on a wall behind us were simply being friendly, until realisation dawned that it was nothing of the sort, so we quickly moved on. They'd been making the most of our miniskirts' failures to protect our modesty, and every time we had to reach down into the freezer, they had a clear view of our knickers.

24

The Love Affair Were Not Easy on Scott Walker

Whenever he was playing in the Love Affair, Mick learnt for himself that the description of the girls' fainting that I experienced when I went to see the Beatles was so true. On one occasion, when Mick typically had to step over a mass of unconscious bodies to get to their dressing room, a pretty West Indian girl, who weighed far more than he did, jumped up from among them and gave him the biggest bear hug ever, shouting 'Mick I loves yer, I loves yer Honey' causing him to almost pass out and join the horizontal heap himself. It was the same every night when Scott Walker and the Love Affair were on tour together. One night when they appeared at the venue in Bradford where the Beatles had played, history was repeated and girls were piled up in the wings, but this time it was Mick stepping over them, not the fab four. Mick asked his mum if she would drive us down to that gig at the Gaumont theatre in her white and grey Austin Cambridge. Having only recently passed her test, she was understandably nervous, but she agreed, thinking it would at least be a good chance to show off her new driving skills. As we approached the theatre, we had underestimated the number of fans that would be outside—it was thousands. At first, none of them suspected that Madge's ordinary but rather large car for her contained the bass player of the group they were queuing to see. It was fine until one eagle-eyed girl spotted Mick and threw herself against the car, calling his name and blowing his cover. The next moment another joined her, then another, and another, several climbed onto our roof, and it began to buckle, and

I was frightened that it would collapse completely beneath their weight. Luckily for us, there is a cobbled narrow street, a throwback to Old English packhorse days, which runs behind the building. Recognising that we were now in trouble, Mick instructed Madge to go that way, so we could escape the throng. Our newly qualified chauffeur did an amazing right-angle turn and sped down it far faster than the mandatory 5 mph. My brain felt as though it was rattling against my skull as the car bounced over the cobbles, and one by one, the girls were shaken off. Poor Madge, even an experienced driver would have been traumatised in that situation. We thought we were safe when we saw the minders at the stage door, but sensing it was too dangerous to get us out, they told us to keep going. Madge had no option other than to drive back home again, where, shaking uncontrollably, she downed a large brandy to calm her nerves— even though she didn't drink.

Mick rang the roadies to ask them to come and fetch us but, efficient as ever, they were already pulling up outside the door to take us back, but Madge was so traumatised she went to lie down, fell asleep, and the combination of nervous exhaustion and brandy made her miss her youngest son's moment of glory in our hometown.

We found it increasingly difficult to walk around Bradford without Mick being recognised but even more so after that appearance. One busy Saturday afternoon, for example, when we were in Woods music shop, we had to make a quick exit before the six girls that recognised him became 600. It was around that time that the group stayed at the Adelphi Hotel in Liverpool, because they were on tour with Scott Walker, and Scott's manager, Maurice King, phoned Sid saying, 'Ma boy can't sleep.' He was complaining that the Love Affair were in a room above Scott's and making so much noise that his charge was angry. That accusation amused them, so instead of complying, they filled several large laundry bags with water. It took all five of them to carry each giant, jelly-like missile to the window and launch them out and down onto the courtyard below which was thankfully deserted, otherwise someone could have been killed. The boys were high and full of mischief and didn't even consider that they could injure someone. The noise as the bags exploded was, according to Mick, absolutely deafening. Satisfied that they had got their own back on Scott for complaining, they went to bed, leaving the former Walker Brother to further toss and turn with fury. Poor Scott, the boys were totally oblivious of the fact that apparently he'd suffered frequent nightmares ever since he was born in Hamilton, Ohio, and it's quite likely that, as a result, his nightly quest for peaceful sleep was traumatic for him at the best of times. No wonder he gave the group a wide berth and was aloof with them, keeping himself very much to himself, a rather wise man I think. Gene Pitney behaved the same way when they later did a tour with him, he was also serious and quiet, I don't know the reasons why, but at least he didn't suffer the from the groups boyish pranks like Scott did.

25

Shoulder to Shoulder With Steve Marriot

I think most people are familiar, because of the book of the same name, that *Men are from Mars Women from Venus*, and it became apparent when Mick enthusiastically asked if I'd included here the snippet about the time he went down to breakfast with Mo and Rex while staying in a hotel in Dublin. I'm sure that my expression told him that I hadn't as I didn't find it particularly funny, but I'll pop it in here anyway, just to keep him happy and me out of trouble. They'd been awake all night, smoking, drinking, and generally messing about, and to continue their pranks, they decided to dress up before going down for their Sugar Puffs (sorry boys, but I couldn't resist, as I seriously think the following antics are more suitable to little boys).

Rex slicked back his hair and made some fangs out of paper pretending to be Dracula, while Mo wrapped a sheet around his waist to resemble a skirt after stuffing two small cushions down the front of his T-shirt. My ever so sophisticated fiancé, who has a rather serious attitude a lot of the time, borrowed a cushion to make a none-too-convincing massive stomach for himself. Hilarious or not? What do you think? Even I have to smile, though, when Mick's shoulders always shake as he tells me the next bit. Little did they realise that the table next to theirs was taken by five ladies wearing habits and coifs, each secured by a wimple, with veils at the back. Unfortunately, though, their outfits were not fancy dress as they really were nuns.

I do, however, like hearing about the Love Affair's return journey from Ireland when, after landing at Manchester airport, they had to catch a train back to London. They were escorted by several roadies who had not only been put in charge of the boys, but the takings of the previous numerous gigs, most of which were paid for in cash. To ease the monotony of their journey, Steve, Mick, Rex, Morgan, and Mo decided to play cards, and much to their minders' dismay, they grabbed the money bags and placed countless quantities of £10, £20, and £50 notes in the middle of the table before dividing the haul into individual stakes. 'I'll raise you by two hundred' said Mo, Mick's replied 'Ok' and getting really into the joke he threw £1,000 into the middle. Bearing in mind that the average week's wage at the time was about £10, the four stuffy businessmen seated opposite them in the first-class compartment kept rubbing their bulging eyes to make sure they weren't dreaming. They couldn't stop their jaws dropping so that they almost touched their corpulent chests. The prank then escalated as usual. First Mo set fire to a £50 note and lit a cigarette with it, and Rex pretended to suddenly acquire a cold, and blew his nose incredibly loudly, nothing terribly shocking with that, of course, except his paper handkerchief was decorated with an image of the queen and worth £20.

Back to that open air concert in Constance that I mentioned at the beginning of Chapter 1. Imagine that you are in Mick's shoes, standing on an outdoor stage. There is a pleasant lull in the proceedings, and you are comfortably and calmly looking at a sea of happy multi-national people. You are in a gorgeous valley that is surrounded by mountains and the audience stretches as far into the distance as you can see. They are in a party mood, and you realise that the clouds of marihuana smoke that hover lightly above their heads is responsible for your dreamy yet elated feelings. The atmosphere is more electrifying than any you have ever experienced, before or since.

The sun is tired and is sinking lazily and gratefully down towards the earth, it's had a busy day, and is now bowing out gracefully, unable to support its own weight as it disappears beneath the horizon. Beautiful people are dressed in multi-coloured, bright clothes, the flowers in their hair sway in a pleasant breeze. Everything seems so magical, and you feel as though you're wrapped in a soft cashmere blanket of love as the sky turns from perfect blue to the deepest of gentle pink. Time seems to stand still, and you can hear nothing for a whole millisecond that seems like an hour. The distinctive zing made by a Zippo lighter, brings your hearing back to your awareness. The lighter is held high in the air by the swaying hand of a young man, who is near to you, just below the stage, and the golden flame pulls your gaze towards so all you can do is stare at the mesmerising centre. There, you stay a moment, forgetting where you are, and then in another instant, you are back behind your eyes that now see the multitude of twinkling lights. Thousands of them stretch far into the distance, as one person then another, copies the original 'torch' bearer.

Excitement surges through your body and you experience euphoria as the elation of one of the largest crowds to ever gather at a music festival causes not only you, but everyone present, to bathe in a shared cocoon of bliss.

Multiply that imagined feeling you were experiencing just now by a hundred and you can get some idea of the near orgasmic feeling (his words, not mine) that Mick said he experienced when the Love Affair actually played there.

Not since he'd first heard the Gershwin-like chords, played by the string section, in the Beatles' 'I am the Walrus' had Mick experienced such a musical highlight. I know I have perhaps gone overboard on the description here, but I need to paint a picture as clear as I can to emphasis the ridiculousness of what I'm about to tell you.

After—I can't say final curtain had fallen, as they were outside, so this will just have to suffice instead—the last note of the evening had been played, the artistes were gathered together in a huge marquee that acted as everyone's dressing area. Still sweating profusely, Mick needed to ground himself, so he found a quiet corner, behind a table piled high with food and drink and closed his eyes, his heart still beating loudly in his chest and his thoughts swimming in happiness. It wasn't until he felt a tug on his arm that he came back to the moment and the unreality of reality. Steve Marriot had felt the same need as Mick to collapse somewhere, as he too was exhausted and was slumped next to him. The owner of one of the best voices in the business urgently needed to soothe his parched vocal cords, which had just belted out hits, including my favourites 'All or Nothing', 'Little Tin Soldier', and 'Itchycoo Park'. Sensing Marriot's urgency, Mick intuitively handed him the champagne bottle he'd been drinking out of.

Mick must, I think, have recovered just enough to pinch himself to make sure he wasn't really dreaming, as there he was, shoulder to shoulder with one of our early teenage idols. If it had been me, I think I would have been struck dumb at that point, but then I wasn't a member of a group that at the time was equally as famous as the Small Faces, but Mick was. He was simply talking to a fellow musician, but nevertheless he must surely have been inwardly thinking he was at the pinnacle of his musical career, nothing could get any better than this.

Congratulating each other on such an amazing night, Steve commented, 'Wow, that was a blast' and without thinking Mick looked him straight in the eye, and in his flat-vowelled, though increasingly London sounding, Yorkshire way, that was sincerely meant, he said, 'Yea, we must do it again some time.'

The ridiculous, funny irony of what Mick had just said as casually as if he was suggesting they should meet up again, after having had a pint in a pub, had them both bent double in raucous fits of laughter that bonded them in such a way that the usual rivalry between their two respective groups to reach the top of the British charts was momentarily forgotten.

That battle to remain on top of their game and be seen by as many fans as possible continued with their constant life on the move, travelling to every corner of Europe that they could possibly reach. Apart from a few gulps of fresh air, snatched between being ferried to various venues and hotels, they never had time to explore anywhere, and one city was very much like the next.

It's often the tiniest of details that stand out now, thankfully acting as pointers to where they were, otherwise most of what is contained in Mick's memory would make every day seem the same. Each week and month blurred into one, and unlike the film starring Bill Murray & Andie MacDowell that was purely fantasy, their days were real life 'Groundhog days'.

26

My Girlfriend's Not My Girlfriend

The group was so frantically busy that, to quote the Beatles, even 'eight days a week' would not have been enough to give Mick and me the time we needed for personal rest or play. Even though I was glad that I'd taken the initial step to leave the comfort of home, or more precisely a pub, Yorkshire was where the four other most important people in my life, at that time, were. As the hours that I could spend with Mick became ever more spasmodic, I began to yearn to be back with them. My adoptive Hounslow family were kind, but they'd inadvertently made me more conscious than ever that I had my own family, and as I was still only eighteen, the home sickness I felt grew to such an extent that I decided to leave. I packed my belongings into a suitcase and headed back to be with my parents, Brian, and Nana. I wasn't prepared, however, for how difficult it was at first, as in my absence, my friends had either gone to university or had boyfriends; as a result, I didn't have anyone my own age I could socialise with. It felt strange and I hadn't a clue how things would work out, other than knowing that Mick and I would get married eventually, but meanwhile, I had to readjust and carve out a temporary life until we could. It wasn't easy as Mum and Dad were totally involved in their pub business and Brian was newly married to Jenny.

My Nana did have time, of course, but as she was nearly ninety, the age difference meant that she wasn't exactly ideal to spend girly nights out with, although I'm sure she would have willingly done so, if only her lovely wrinkly face had matched her young heart.

The second week I was back at the pub, I must have looked miserable because Marilyn, the ladies' football team centre forward, asked me if I would like to go to Batley Variety Club with her to cheer me up. I'd had my fill of watching the Clampetts from *The Beverly Hillbillies* with Nana, so I jumped at the chance of going out to a club even though it wasn't exactly my 'scene'. I thought it would, at least, be a change from having to watch yet another episode, along with *Crossroads*, both of which were my Nana's favourite programmes, but at least both were funny especially *Crossroads* and their wobbly scenery that shook every time a door closed.

The night was fine, it was good to be out once more, and as the evening ended, I appreciated Marilyn's kindness and also for giving me a lift home. Her car approached the pub and because last orders had already been called and it was closed, I started looking for my keys. I was surprised when she drove straight past.

'Thought you'd like to have a coffee at my place.' she explained, sensing my enquiring look of confusion. I thanked her, but secretly thought that, given the choice, I'd have preferred to go straight home. I'd never been to her flat and the sight of a dozen stone steps leading to her front door made me feel even more tired, but purely out of politeness I followed her up them and two further flights inside before flopping down on her settee while she went to put the kettle on. We chatted for a while but realising that Marilyn was getting her 'second wind' as my Nana would say and I wasn't, I decided to give her a hint by getting up to leave and fortunately she got up too, but as I got to her door she pinned me against it and was surprised when I pushed her away and asked her what she thought she was doing. I don't know who was the most embarrassed, her or me when she realised that she had made a big mistake, and it dawned on me, that although I was engaged, I must have been giving out the wrong messages without realising it. It never occurred to me that there had been any alternative reason for her invite to the club, other than just being nice. Curious to know how she could make such an assumption, I managed to calm the situation down by asking her lots of questions, especially why, as I was engaged, did she think that I was the least bit interested in her?

She gave me two reasons, the first being that I always looked her in the eye when talking to her and the second was that I referred to Sheila as 'my girlfriend'. It just went to show how, in her opinion, I'd literally been giving her 'the eye', and secretly flirting with her by telling her I had a girlfriend as well as a fiancé. Although I knew Marilyn was rather masculine in her manner, she also had a 'Sugar Daddy', so I never dreamt that she would be attracted to me, and I was apologetic that I'd actually been leading her on without meaning to.

I explained that I called Sheila 'my girlfriend' because she addressed me the same way and I simply thought it was a 'southern thing'. I learnt quite a lot that evening, as looking back on my time in Earl's Court, I realised that perhaps Sheila had also viewed me as a genuine potential girlfriend too, even though I hadn't a clue. I was, after all, wearing an engagement ring and I thought that it was blatantly obvious that I wasn't gay not realising that you could be 'bi'. We all learn somehow and by looking Marilyn in the eyes, mine were truly opened, and I'm just grateful that both my female suitors were perfect 'gentlemen' and left me alone when they learnt the truth.

The next morning, after visiting Batley, my mind was completely distracted when I received a letter confirming that I'd been the successful applicant at an interview I'd attended a week earlier. The job, as trainee junior reporter at our local *Shipley Times & Express* weekly newspaper, was perfect for me, as it was anything but a nine to five job. With hindsight, I can't help but think that the editor had given me the job because he was impressed, not particularly with me, but with my fiancé and thought that I'd bring some fresh air and interest into the Dickensian office with its antique typewriters and desks that had been there from the end of the nineteenth century. I liked the set-up immediately, the office was tiny, musty, full of intrigue, and nobody dared ever go upstairs as the floorboards up there were so old and frail that they couldn't support any weight. Goodness only knows what was lurking there as no one knew when a person had last gone up those forbidden steps.

I'm afraid my imagination ran away with me on my first day when I learnt that the adjoining shop made prosthetic limbs. It flashed through my mind that perhaps that was why there was such a mystery about the uninhabited floor. Maybe, in a style not dissimilar to Sweeney Todd, the floor above us might just possibly house a collection of human arms and legs, put there by the professionals next door who were only pretending that the lifelike limbs they sold were false as they silently scurried back and forth through a secret opening they'd made. That idea was too silly and horrific to dwell on I know, but I didn't ask for that thought to enter my head, so let's quickly move on before I give you nightmares.

The unsociable hours of the job, where you had to drop everything to attend an incident that could turn out to be scoop, suited me down to the ground. I hadn't much to drop, the vacancy for a clubbing friend was still unfilled, and I had nothing else to occupy me as Mick was so far away, apart from our letters and phone calls.

I did say to attend a scoop, but to be honest there weren't that many in a small town and it would be years in the future before it and surrounding areas became the focus of nationwide attention when the Yorkshire Ripper was finally caught, and we learnt that he worked in Shipley and lived just up the road from our office. Week after week, the paper followed the same format it had for decades and relied on reporters attending court and visiting local police and fire stations. Writing the names of as many people as possible who were present at bazaars and jumble sales was my job, so that they would buy the paper because they were in it. I absolutely loved it and often got distracted reading yellowing old papers to copy exerts for the '25' and '50 years ago today' features. I think the press was much better received then than today after so much negative publicity has been thrown at them, and when people realised you were from the paper they bent over backwards to be helpful. My colleagues and I were definitely on a par with Fleet Street paparazzi in one particular area, we were regulars in all the nearby pubs and seemed to spend every lunchtime in one or the other, usually with the excuse that we were keeping our eyes and ears open for news.

My first solo assignment was to visit a blazing church, perched upon a hill near the centre of the town. It was only my second week there, and without any guidance at all as to what I should do, I remember standing alone with my reporter's notebook in hand, as scores of firemen did their best to save it. Sadly, they couldn't, as it was so badly damaged; it had to be pulled down. To describe the church was difficult as I couldn't really see it properly, as it shimmered behind the flames. I just know that I intuitively felt sad, so much so that it must have affected my brain and I didn't even attempt to write anything on those expectant lined pages as I simply didn't know where to begin.

Amazingly, my editor never said anything, and I wasn't in trouble, but that was the trouble, he never ever said anything—ever—to help me progress in any which way. Surely, he must have at least thought I had at a tiny bit of potential mustn't he? But apart from saying I had to learn shorthand and that the training course would be sometime in the near future, he never showed me how to do anything or taught me anything, I was simply left to my own stumbling devices.

Mr Shearer, possibly for devilment, asked me to cover a cricket match the next weekend. He must have known that I didn't know one end of a cricket bat from another, had never watched a match, didn't have a clue what was going on, or knew any cricket terminology apart from 'leg before wicket'—whatever that was. I was bewildered as to the meaning of the numbers displayed on the scoreboard below the clock, whose hands hardly seemed to move, and once again my metal spiral-bound notebook, of which I was immensely proud, because it helped me look the part at least, waited in eager anticipation of being written upon, and this time, I was determined not to disappoint.

Goodness knows what Mr S. thought when I'd typed up my report, he probably took it to his local that night so he and his fellow drinkers could have a good laugh, but what could a greener than the grass the cricketers were playing on girl do, apart from make something up? I described the weather, the relaxed atmosphere of the crowd and even how impressed I was at the sharp creases down the centre of the pristine, white trousers the cricketers wore, but not a word about the game itself, but how could I? It was a bit like asking a parrot to read out the evening news eloquently and logically. It was impossible. Apart from his own amusement, perhaps 'he in charge' had a slightly warped sense of humour too, as I had to endure two whole days, and not any old days, but Saturday and Sunday, watching grown men run up and down with a stick and playing ball. It's a good job that the editor didn't publish my attempt at a report, otherwise had any of the players, after anxiously waiting for exciting column inches about their brilliant game, read it, they would certainly have thrown in the towel—or is that boxing? Mr S. seemed to have had as much time to spare as cricketers and was completely unhurried or unfazed about my hopeless attempts, but my presence there must have served some purpose for him and it certainly did from my point of view, as even though Mick and I were not together, at least *The Times* occupied me for most of the time until we could be.

I did try to learn shorthand, and although I know it sounds like an excuse, I'm afraid my choice of teacher was unfortunate and the chances of me getting anywhere with it were virtually nil. Mr Beaumont was a true gent and I liked him tremendously, but I think he was born a couple of centuries before I was, and I have never met anyone so pleasantly pedantic before or since. Even though I'm not sure if it's even possible to make Pitman's exciting, I know for certain it's possible to make it the most boring subject ever, particularly when he went into the nth degree in a deadly serious, though kind, monotone voice. My visits had to double up as accountancy time too, as Dad was getting increasingly worried about his books and Mr B. simply tied him up in knots whenever he tried to explain the pub's financial situation. I, in turn, beginning to worry about Dad's health as the stress was getting to him, was trying to de-mystify the figures. Needless to say, I ended up just as confused and my visits became hopeless on both counts and, reluctant though I was, I stopped visiting our dear friend and I never saw him again.

27

An American Dream Shattered

The Love Affair were one of the first groups to have huge backing, when Yardley sponsored them to promote a new range of make-up they'd brought out called the 'Love Mist' range, aimed at teenagers. It was quite gruelling as they played at around thirty Top Rank ballrooms up and down the country, but it was a great honour and a great success. No expense was spared by Yardley who, knowing that most girls were not much older than typical pantomime audiences, made the promotional materials for the tour exceptionally pretty, in keeping with their new products. Every foyer displayed the makeup that was lovely. The boys would have been forgiven for feeling as though they were in pantomime themselves, as they had to wear pastel satin shirts, they weren't thrilled, but it was a small price to pay to be on such a lucrative tour and even Steve agreed, as long as it wasn't the pink one, that dubious honour was given to Mick.

With so much 'love' around due to the Love Affair, Love Mist, and 'Everlasting Love', the swooning fans were encouraged to believe that their dreams of stepping into my and the other girlfriend's shoes might just come true, and also because in any write up about the group, each member was always described as being single. It was little wonder that every gig was utter chaos, and it took many bouncers all their strength to control the girls that were crammed together on the dance floors. It was disturbing to see that every night, several genuinely, unconscious girls, were flung to the side of the stage like rag dolls in order to stop them getting crushed.

The tour was a sell-out, each ballroom packed to capacity and the screaming so loud that even the best amplifying stacks available at the time weren't powerful enough to allow the group to be heard. It wasn't just the girls whose physical welfare were threatened, as I have previously mentioned, the boys were often at the receiving end too. In the middle of the troubles in Ireland, they were doing a month's tour and were used to very enthusiastic audiences but on one occasion there were a disproportionate number of young men watching and they were getting very jealous of the attention that the boys were getting. The longer the gig went on, the more jealous they became, not helped because the insults that they were shouting were drowned out by the music so they started throwing coins in frustration. The boys more or less tolerated this behaviour in the hope that they would win the rowdy crowd over, but as the minutes ticked by, the coins came through thicker and faster and were beginning to sting and hurt, depending upon which part of their bodies they bounced off.

The stage became awash with coins, and to the boys' disbelief and amusement, one of their part-time roadies, hired for the tour, began scurrying around the floor on his hands and knees so he could put them into his hat, he must have thought it beat winning pennies at a fair because they were raining down on him faster than he could scoop them up. At first, Mick and Steve, who were at the front as usual, thought it was funny, but their mocking facial expressions and laughter enraged the men even more and the raining coins turned into a torrential storm. Enough was enough for Mick and Steve so they grabbed the hat and fistfuls of coins and threw them all back. Talk about light the blue touch paper, the audience started to climb onto the stage but were kept at bay by minders and bouncers, culminating in the promotor shutting off the stage lights and beckoning the Love Affair to exit the stage. This made things even worse, and a riot broke out in the hall and the boys had to be rescued by a combination of their own minders, venue bouncers, the police, and eventually even the army. It was a night to remember but for all the wrong reasons and the deflated roadie didn't even get to keep the money, or his hat as it was stolen.

Over the five years that the Love Affair were together, they did many tours and individual gigs of Scotland. The Scottish audiences were great fans and really enthusiastic, but sometimes they could also be very frightening. One night they were appearing at an ice rink with a revolving stage at one end, things got out of hand when the group having finished their hour-and-a-half set were unable to get off it as it was under siege from hundreds of female fans and the boys had to be protected on the stage by a ring of roadies, minders, and bouncers. A make-shift tunnel of crash barriers was hastily erected leading from the stage to the exit doors. The idea was that on a given signal, the boys would literally run the gauntlet, jumping off the stage, running along the gap between the barriers and bouncers, and escaping out of the building. The group jumped off the stage with no trouble, but the barricade didn't last more than five seconds and was overwhelmed by the crowd. It was getting very serious as the group members were having clothes torn, hair pulled, skin scratched, and some girls were so into the moment and out of control that even burly bouncers struggled to grab them off. Mick got trapped with his back up against the barrier, several girls were pulling on his shirt and the collar just got tighter and tighter, the fans didn't realise that they were strangling him, all they could think of was getting a trophy bit of Mick. Unable to shout or cry for help, he began to choke; the pain was so awful that he momentarily lost consciousness as the next thing he remembered was being under a warm shower in the dressing rooms surrounded by concerned staff with blood running off the many scratches and wealds on his face. Several minutes and a couple of shots of whiskey later, Mick recovered enough to join the rest of the group as they were herded through the exit doors and onto a waiting coach and were safe at last.

The ice rink gig wasn't the only place where Mick was rendered unconscious; the other time, at Boston Gliderdrome, left no scars but could have been fatal. It was due to a very nasty electric shock that was caused by him grabbing a metal microphone stand and holding his metal stringed guitar with the other hand, thereby completing an electrical circuit that must have been a fault in several thousand watts of amplification, while he was sweating profusely.

The high voltage went through Mick, and he thought that someone was squeezing him tightly before hitting him on the head with a cricket bat. After losing consciousness, he woke up in A&E but happily he was OK. On the way home, his long hair refused to lie flat, and he looked like a cross between Ken Dodd and Einstein. Mo was with him and showing an endearing and unusual amount of concern at Mick's 'Ken Dodd-like' hair, said, 'You look funny Mick, would you like a cigarette?' and without thinking, Mick who'd successfully stopped smoking several months earlier, took one, resuming the habit that lasted for another twenty years.

When the group were on *The Ken Dodd* show at Granada, Manchester, they spent a memorable afternoon with him as Ken chatted away constantly telling jokes and admitted that he also used to be a pop star and had fifteen girls banging on his hotel room door but had to let them out eventually! How I wished I could have met him. I am full of admiration of the fact that far from simply not forgetting his roots, he actually lived among them all of his life. He was born, bred, and died in the same house in Liverpool. I suspect he was so focused on touring that he had little time left for such a 'menial' task as moving. When he was happy in Knotty Ash, his birthplace, he used to say, 'why bother?'—what a wise man he was. Ken was a prolific performer and must have had millions of people in stitches throughout his long career, and I suspect would not remember specific details or nights, just as Mick didn't during the much shorter public life of the group. Ken was as a firm favourite of the royal family and given a knighthood. I hope, in return, he paid better attention whenever he appeared before various HRHs than Mick did when the Love Affair were presented to Princess Margaret. It was a popular, royal event, televised and watched by millions, but Mick can't remember what the show was!

I suppose I should remember better too, but at least I have the excuse that it wasn't me who was on the stage at the Royal Variety, Royal Command, or Royal whatever performance—but they were. It was a last-minute thing, I have tried to clear the mystery up but can't find the group's name mentioned in any list of performers, but if they stood in for someone else and it was a quick switch, then that would explain why I can't find them listed. However, it was at the London Palladium, and as was customary after a show watched by a member of the royal family, the royal representative went backstage to meet the entertainers. The princess slowly made her way down the line of performers and presented each one with a certificate in beautiful copperplate writing containing her signature at the bottom. The next bit, unsurprisingly, Mick does remember because he swears that when she shook his hand, she squeezed it, unlike the rather limp fingers she offered to everyone else and held his gaze far longer too. Perhaps it wasn't all in his imagination, though, as it was only shortly after that that she found her toy boy in the form of Roddy Llewelyn, who was seventeen years younger than her, but that was when her marriage had broken up and her confidence in shatters. Of course, if Mick hadn't lost that souvenir, there would be no mystery as regards what the occasion was as I would have framed it and proudly hung it on the wall.

Whenever the boys were playing within reasonable driving distance of the pub, there were plenty of volunteers to take me there, especially David or Mick's cousin, Bevan, who was so proud of Mick that he spent many hours visiting the bar, where he was popular due to his encyclopaedic knowledge of everything 'Love Affair.'

Bevan is a loveable character, incredibly bright, yet happy to play the clown and downplay his intelligence, whenever it suits him. He loved the fact that because he was Mick's cousin it brought him lots of attention and because he also owned a lovely, soft top, XK 140 Jaguar and wore an impressive looking sheepskin coat, some of the locals even thought he was the Love Affair's manager. Just in case you are a car enthusiast, for a change, it is Bevan as opposed to Mick who has educated me further on that beautiful car. That model was made between 1952 and 1955 and then replaced with the XK150. The numbers 140 and 150 indicated the car's top speed. Bevan says he never had it above 120. The problem, he says, was stopping at speed on normal roads, because the brakes, made before they had discs, were not up to the job and it was a major problem, but he never told me that when I was a blissfully ignorant passenger. Bevan went to so many gigs that he knew the members of the group well, and so he good humouredly never objected whenever he became the focus of their teasing. Mick and I were once amazed when he bet us that he could fit into Mick's skinny velvet jeans and a super slim fitting frilly shirt. Feeling certain that in no way would Bevan be able to get into his clothes, Mick handed them to Bevan who thirty seconds later proved him wrong. That ever-present sheepskin coat had made Bevan look at least two stone heavier than he really was. The stage clothes may have been a perfect fit, but something about Bevan's thick glasses and smug 'there I told you so' expression made him temporarily look like a cross between Austin Powers and the late, great Eric Morecambe in drag, so any secret dream that he might have had of becoming a sixth member of the group, was instantly shattered when he realised we couldn't stop laughing, but he took it in good spirit, as always.

Yardley wasn't the only major company that wanted to sponsor the group, as following the success of the 'Love Mist' tour, Geest wanted to jump on the banana wagon so to speak and do the same, but next time in America.

America had fallen in love with British groups after the Beatles had made such a great impression there, playing to thousands upon thousands of new fans. It was the start of 'the British musical invasion' and the 'Fab Four' paved the way for all other top groups from our shores. It was a complete turnaround, as so many musicians here had been first influenced by music from across the pond. Geest recognised that the popularity of the Love Affair could be duplicated many times over on such a huge continent, and saw a golden, commercial opportunity to make a further fortune for themselves, and consequently the group. Hilary 'Gussy' Geest, heiress to the existing family fortune, took the opportunity to watch them while they were playing at The Lyceum in London. I should imagine that being young herself, she would have looked forward to seeing them perform, before confirming that her family were making the right business decision. However, luck wouldn't have it, as unfortunately that night was even more frantic than usual, and due to the over exuberance of those present, the venue suffered a great deal of damage. Unsurprisingly, the family changed their mind immediately, as they naturally didn't want to risk the same thing happening on any tour that they backed. All hopes of the Love Affair making a name for themselves in America were dashed. Fame and financially-wise, it really was disastrous for the group. It would have been such a huge opportunity, as they would most probably have made it and, in doing so, would have been paid equally as well, as the profits from bananas that were huge. That is, the profits were huge, not the bananas. Gussy's family obviously thought they had had a narrow escape from making a disastrous decision, though I like to think that it would have gone well.

I read recently that Jimmy Savile was chaperoning Gussy at times throughout the '60s, I don't know if that's true or not, but if it is, it was at a time when he was one of the nation's favourite people, loved and admired because of the millions of pounds he raised for charity. I imagine that anyone then would have felt proud to have him as a friend because of that. This was many years before the truth came out about him, of course. If he really was a friend of Gussy's, then perhaps JS was subliminally hinting at his success in mixing with such an affluent family as Geest, when he once wore a suit decorated in bananas while presenting *Top of the Pops*. Mick never liked JS as he felt, like many people, that he was not the person he pretended to be, and Mick says that the first time he met him, despite the bleached blond hair, he could sense a darkness surrounding him. Hindsight is a wonderful thing they say, but we all tend to go along with mass opinion and because Jimmy Savile was incredibly popular in his heyday, so many people thought he could literally do no wrong. Unknown to Savile's fans, he was even viewed with suspicion by the police, who were hunting for the Yorkshire Ripper, as he lived in Leeds and apparently befriended prostitutes from the area where Peter Sutcliffe struck. I was taken in by him after reading an autobiography he wrote many years ago where he described keeping the clothes that had belonged to his mother, who he referred to as 'the Duchess', just as she'd left them as a sort of shrine to her. I thought it was a touching gesture, especially as he had them all dry cleaned annually, to keep them in pristine condition. I found his book fascinating without realising why, but I must have been reading between the lines, not realising that my intuition was telling me there was something much deeper to him than he was letting on. His IQ was apparently so high that he was in the top 1 per cent of the most intelligent people in Mensa—at least he said he was. How different that real side of him was compared to the one he presented to everyone, when he regularly parked in his Rolls-Royce at the welcoming little café on the moors next to the Cow & Calf in Ilkley. There he would be the life and soul of the party just as long as all the attention was focused on him, but the moment it wasn't, he switched off and was very different.

Shortly before JS died and thousands of people lined the streets of Leeds to catch a glimpse of his gold-coloured American coffin, I saw him sitting near the entrance of Dick Hudson's, a well-known pub in Eldwick near Ilkley Moor. He was with a young man and out of respect for his privacy, which I mistakenly thought he would appreciate, I resisted the temptation to say hello and chat about old times. Again, he must have wanted to be seen and acknowledged by everyone, and just as a vampire needs blood to survive, he needed to be constantly at the centre of attention, wherever he was. It makes me shudder to think that I had to walk within inches of him to get to the door and, by doing so, passed through one of the most disturbing auras imaginable. Just as it's said that you can't always see wood for trees, perhaps had everyone looked a little closer at the end his surname there was a real clue, it would have jumped out that he was truly … vile.

Soon after the Yardley 'Love Mist' tour ended and the Geest family disastrously changed their mind about the American tour, the group released 'One Road'. Although it made No. 16 in the charts, the boys had got used to their records being in the Top 10 and viewed it as a flop. Fortunately, things improved with its follow-up, 'Bringing On Back the Good Times' that made it—just—to No. 9.

Steve was getting restless by this time and began thinking about which direction he should take. The boys were still young and the disappointment that they felt after having their hopes raised that they would be given the dream opportunity to make it in America and then cancelled was shattering. The atmosphere within the group began to change. Steve's frustration with how things were turning out were affecting him badly, and only he really knows the difficult emotions that he was going through, it was getting intolerable for him and he wanted to break free. Steve, along with the others, had given his all to the group, and mentally and physically, things were finally taking their toll. One night while on tour in Ireland, Mick, through necessity, was asked to stand in for Steve at the last minute, and although Mick may have known the words of all their hits inside out and upside down, to be suddenly thrust before such a huge crowd and without warning was a massive ask and shock by any standard. He really had no choice, either do it or they could have a riot on their hands. Mick knew that his singing wasn't in the same league as Steve's and was filled with trepidation. There wasn't time to transpose all the numbers into a different musical key that would suit his range and make it easier for him. Fortunately, Mick knew through experience that the noise of the screams coupled with the volume of the instruments meant that nobody would really be able to hear him anyway. Worried and missing Steve, they bounced onto the stage to a standing ovation, and much to their huge surprise and relief, the gig was a success.

Things went from bad to worse, however, when their next single 'Baby I Know' struggled to get into the Top 40, and Steve had had enough, he finally walked out—he needed time and space to rethink his musical career and John Cokell soon followed to continue managing him. Steve's absence meant that Sid had a huge problem on his hands and needed help so he could sort things out, but he didn't have to look far, as the Love Affair's fan club was run by a lovely lady who was married to Ken Street, an extremely experienced old hand in the business. Ken had been in showbiz virtually all his life and was the lead guitarist for Emile Ford and the Checkmates, whose record 'What Do You Want to Make Those Eyes at Me For?' was the UK's first No. 1 hit of the '60s. Interestingly, in 1962, Emile, at the height of his career, topped the bill at a show in New Brighton and was supported by the Beatles. That No. 1 is still etched into my memory, mainly because of the 'shoo wap bee do bee doo wap' bits.

Steve had to be replaced, but rather than recognising that one solution was already under his nose, following the success of the night when Mick stood in for Steve, Sid didn't do what he perhaps should have done and make Mick the lead singer.

Alternatively, had I been Sid, I think I would also have tried to recruit an already established singer such as Andy Fairweather Low of Amen Corner as Amen Corner and the Love Affair played many gigs together and he would have fitted in well—had he wanted to, of course! Andy wasn't approached, however, and went on to have a long and successful career, often playing alongside the likes of Eric Clapton,

Why, Sid could even have approached Phillip Goodhand Tate, who'd already written three of the Love Affair's hits, he was a good-looking singer, musician, and, of course, songwriter. When Mick and I met up with him a couple of years ago, he told us the story he must have told so many times as it is so unusual and proves that lady luck definitely exists. When the Love Affair were trying to find their ideal song while they were signed up to Decca, Sid and John did what they always did when searching for something—they placed an ad in *Melody Maker*. It read 'Hit group requires hit songs'. He saw the ad and sent them a demo called 'Gone Are the Songs of Yesterday'. As he didn't hear anything, he more or less forgot about it, and it was only when 'Everlasting Love' was at No. 1 that he learnt that his composition was on the 'B' side, and it earned him a small fortune in royalties. Of course, I'm not Sid and he had other ideas, and after much research, he decided that the man for the job was Gus Eadon. I think that Sid was mainly impressed with him because he was a multi-instrumentalist. He played the harmonica, guitar, trumpet, flute, keyboards, and drums. Gus, although a nice guy, seemed ancient compared to the others, even though he was probably only about five years older, but in percentage terms that was approximately 25 per cent, so it was a lot. I felt that the management had made a mistake in not changing Mick's role to that of lead singer, and although Gus was a showman, he had an impossibly hard act to follow. Gus, though not unattractive, wasn't in the same league as Steve, and was so hairy that he looked as though he could have kept even a quick barber busy for a whole day. Although the rest of the boys liked Gus, who moulded himself on Ian Anderson, front man of Jethro Tull, they weren't convinced that he was the right choice for their new renamed group, L.A. Maybe before he finally chose Gus, Sid should have invested in a few rehearsals, changing the key signature of all the group's songs to see how they got on with Mick doing the vocals, but Sid wasn't having that. It wasn't until about eighteen months later after the demise of L.A. that Sid realised that the huge hole left by Steve should have perhaps been filled by Mick after all. Mick went on to form a group called Calvary with Steve Robinson and a drummer Steve knew called Howard. They recorded songs on a cassette tape that Mick had written, while huddled together in the small attic in Mum and Dad's pub. It was surprising how good they were, considering the very unprofessional setting and they decided to post them to Sid in London. The songs were called 'Better Way', 'New Day', and 'Dierdre'. When Sid responded with a phone call, the boys were excited when he told them that he liked the songs very much, and if they wanted to, he would arrange for them to re-record them at EMI's central London. Howard, Steve, and Mick decided there was nothing to be lost, and it would be great to hear the songs professionally recorded.

The date at EMI was fixed, it was agreed that they'd spend no more than a day, but apart from that, they could take as long as they wanted to get down as many complete tracks as they could. They had to be in the studio at 9 a.m. and decided to travel down to London in Howard's van. Thinking they could turn the trip into a bit of an adventure, they decided not to do the obvious and book into a hotel, but to stop off and sleep on Hampstead Heath. It was only about an hour's drive away from the studio and they'd save themselves quite a bit of money at the same time. It wasn't the best night's sleep they'd ever had, but they managed to arrive bright and early, helped by the invigorating dip they'd earlier enjoyed in Hampstead Heath pond. The session went well, not just musically but because the vibe in the studio was good and they put down all three titles—recording drums, bass, and lead guitars with Steve overdubbing his usual impressive guitar solo pieces. Mick did the main vocals, which were double tracked to give extra depth, and Steve did the harmonies. Mick thought it felt great to be singing his own compositions in a key that was comfortable for him with simple funky arrangements that he'd put together with Steve. Elated, they made the journey back north that evening, where they would have to wait to hear from Sid.

When their anxious wait was over, Sid phoned and said, 'Mick there's really good news, I would like to manage you, EMI would like to sign you to their label and would like you to start work on your first album as soon as possible. I'll get the paperwork and meeting organised—when can you get back down to London? Oh! there's only one small hitch, but it's no big deal, EMI don't like the name Calvary, they want you to be called the Love Affair'. Mick replied, 'I can't believe what you are saying about the name, I'm not happy about that, but it's not just my decision, let me talk it over with Steve and Howard, but in particular with Pat'.

Mick phoned Sid the next day and told him that everyone felt it was wrong to use the Love Affair name and a deflated Sid replied, 'That's how it's got to be.' Mick thanked him for his involvement and said that they wouldn't be taking it any further.

Back to when the Love Affair renamed themselves L.A. The boys began rehearsing and writing new material in preparation of their new album 'New Day'. They had a brilliant music launch at the Revolution Club in London. The club was packed with people from record companies, newspapers, and television, and their live performance of 'Speak of Peace

Sing of Joy', 'That's My Home', and 'Ge's Whiz' went down a storm. Despite their previous reservations, after that reception, Mick, Mo, Rex, and Morgan felt reborn, re-energised, and with Gus's new blood among them, absolutely raring to go.

Mick still remembers to this day how, after that exciting night, he stepped out of the Revolution into the street and saw the most beautiful car he had ever seen, it was a bright orange Lamborghini Miura, and it sparked his lifelong passion for cars.

They released 'Speak of Peace Sing of Joy', a track on their album, as a single and were delighted to be on *Top of the Pops* once more, it was then followed by 'Lincoln County', another song by Phillip Goodhand Tate, and were kept busy doing radio and television appearances including *The Old Grey Whistle Test*. I never appreciated it at the time, but when I listen to 'Lincoln County' now, it is much better than I thought it was back then, but I think I was so biased towards Steve that it clouded my opinion. However, at the beginning of the new start with L.A. and with renewed optimism, the group settled into life with Gus, and although the screaming had gone, they began to enjoy the change, playing in colleges and much smaller, intimate venues in the UK, along with an extensive tour of Scandinavia. It was while they were in Sweden that Mick received a phone call in his hotel room to say that the promotors and local television people wanted to do an interview with him and would it be OK to meet in twenty minutes and chat while having breakfast. Not overly pleased to be disturbed at such an early hour, he nevertheless felt better when, after pulling back the curtains, he saw they were staying in a beautiful place, and it was a bright sunny day. After a quick bath, he pulled on his jeans, T-shirt and turquoise leather jacket and made his way down to the lobby where they were waiting for him. As they introduced themselves, Mick noticed that they were looking a little uncomfortable and possibly shocked, but all became clear when they gathered enough courage to ask him, without appearing rude, if he thought it would perhaps be wise to put something on over his jacket. There had been a slight misunderstanding, and although Mick thought that they'd be having breakfast in the hotel, it was their intention to take him to a café ten minutes' walk away. They were trying to say that, as it was cold outside, he should wrap up warmly. Whether out of bravado or simply because he didn't have anything warmer to wear, Mick isn't sure now, but because the sun was blazing, he said it's OK he'd go as he was. A look of anxiety and disbelief crossed their faces, but too polite to say anything else and having possibly heard about 'mad dogs and Englishmen' that went out in the midday sun, maybe they thought that this particular Englishman was foolhardy enough to ignore their climate too, and knew what he was doing, so off they started. The revolving doors swallowed them, but a millisecond later they were propelled outside. Mick recalls that he was now the one to be surprised, as the shock to his body was similar to when he and Steve jumped into the cold water at Lake Zurich, but even greater. Never one to give in, Mick didn't say anything about his discomfort and the little group strode out into the beautiful morning air, continuing with polite introductions and conversation. Within three minutes, Mick began to shake uncontrollably, and after three point five minutes, his teeth were chattering so loudly that he feared that they'd become so frozenly brittle that they might even shatter. His new companions realised the seriousness of the situation and even though they'd only just met, took Mick by the arm, swung him around, and marched him back to the hotel all the time huddling as close to him as possible whilst walking. It dawned on them that even though their interviewee was 'famous', he was only human too, and did not possess superpowers beyond their own. Mick hadn't known the danger of going outside without a coat in the Swedish winter and had therefore put himself in danger of hyperthermia or worse. It was minus 40 degrees Celsius!

28

Our Wedding

Unfortunately, chinks began to show during those times Mick was playing with L.A., and after the initial euphoria following the night at the Revolution, he gradually got more disillusioned with the direction they started to go. Those feelings of frustration culminated when he did his last ever recording with them of an Italian song called 'Wake Me I Am Dreaming', he thought it had no connection at all to either the Love Affair's sound or L.A.'s, he describes it as being a nothing track. And he hated it. Mick was feeling less content by the day, so we began to seriously concentrate on our plans for finally setting up home in Yorkshire. I scoured the newspaper adverts for a house and within a couple of days, I spotted a tiny square-inch ad for a newly-renovated, four-bedroomed cottage in Little London, Leeds. Mick was due one of his trips back home and we arranged to view it, and it was perfect for us; we didn't have to look any further. The weaver's cottage was three stories high and would look pretty on any chocolate box as it really did have roses around the door. Most importantly, it had been completely redecorated and had a new bathroom—I almost said kitchen, but in truth the kitchen area had a new sink but little else as everything else was freestanding. I was so excited; the years of waiting were over.

I had our future to look forward to, my mind was completely taken over by knowing that we were so close to realising our dream of being married at long last, however, there was one more hurdle to get over and that was the wedding itself. I refer to our wedding as a hurdle, because that is how I viewed it, I dreaded the fuss and although I'd dreamt of a fairy-tale wedding dress since being little, my actual dress was awful. Mum had a customer who owned a wedding gown shop and she arranged for us to look at her stock. I was disappointed to find that she didn't have that much choice and the dresses she did have were meant for brides quite a few years older than my then-nineteen-year-old self. We were reduced by elimination, to finding one that might be vaguely suitable.

I think that, unfortunately, Mum's priorities were confused, and she felt obliged that we chose one, instead of thinking that perhaps what was more important was that the bride had the loveliest dress possible. Mum was kindly paying for the dress, so I felt obliged to please her and her friend, so we settled for the best of a bad lot, and I didn't even like it, so much so that once we left the shop, I never saw it again until half an hour before our wedding, when I put it on. That may sound incredible, but shortly before we were to tie the knot, I think I had a mini-breakdown of sorts, as one day I couldn't stop crying after Mum raised her voice slightly. My tears were disproportionate, as all Mum had done was to raise her voice to show that she wasn't best pleased that I'd spilt some makeup on a dressing table, after all she was probably feeling stressed herself as a future 'mother of the bride'. My concerned Nana realised that my unstoppable tears meant that something was wrong and the culmination of unobvious, but real stress of the past few years and forthcoming wedding had hit me all at once, so she insisted that I saw a doctor. The tranquilisers I was given may have helped my nerves, but they also rendered me zombie-like and unable to make rational choices or decisions to do with the wedding. I was simply carried along with everyone else's desires, so much so that my new, legally-drugged self, felt detached; I was in a constant dreamlike state, as my emotions and logic almost disappeared after taking the very first tablet.

There was no hen night, just a huge fuss the eve of our wedding, to make sure that visiting relatives could be accommodated in the living quarters of the pub. I tried to get an early night and a good night's sleep, but it was impossible due to the noise of the taproom below. The fact that I was sharing my bed with my cousin, Olivia, who I hadn't seen in years, didn't help much either. Under different circumstances, it would have been great to catch up with her life and of course, she had no choice other than to sleep where she was told, but I couldn't wait to fast forward the time to when Mick and I would be alone, permanently, at last.

Mick meanwhile was enjoying his stag night; of course, I don't know much about it as I naturally wasn't there. However, I do know that Brian got very drunk, and because he was walking home alone from wherever they'd been, he really wasn't that aware of what he was doing or where he was. Apparently, he sat on a low Yorkshire stone wall for a rest and in his drunken state fell backwards and was covered in mud, but not just mud, as he found himself prostrate in a field where pigs were kept. When I listened with amazement that it really did happen and wasn't written into the storyline of a television sitcom, I was just grateful that it was Brian and not Mick we were talking about.

On the morning of our wedding, without any prior experimentation, my hair was put up with scores of uncomfortable hair grips, by a hairdresser I'd never met before. As if that weren't bad enough, a short unflattering, sticky out, net veil (I'd always imagined I'd have a long, floaty, romantic one with a diamond tiara) was attached with an awful headdress of oversized silk flowers that had been forced upon me with a that'll do attitude by Mum's wedding shop friend. Half an hour before the ceremony started, I stood in the bedroom alone, as the bridesmaids made their own way to church, directly from their homes. I remember opening the box containing the dress, hoping that the alterations that had included sewing a bustle beneath the skirt, intended to make the style at least appear 'younger', were OK. It doesn't bare thinking about, but had there been a fault, or the wrong dress put in the box, I've no idea what I would have done, walked down the aisle in my jeans perhaps? I put the dress on for the first time since seeing it in the shop and decided it looked a little bare around the neckline, so remembering I'd bought a tin necklace the previous week, I quickly popped it on, with less thought than I'd usually have given in deciding what I'd wear on a night out, and that was that. If someone had been with me, they'd have probably advised me not to wear it, but the only other person in the building was my Dad and he obviously hadn't a clue as he told me I looked lovely, but I thought his giveaway nervous little cough I knew of old confirmed otherwise.

We walked outside and got into the waiting car as the pub customers crowded around to wish me luck. The church was just around the corner—at least that was my choice, not because I went there, but because I discovered it doing my rounds for the newspaper. It had a lovely feel about it, and when you went inside, the sudden peace and holy atmosphere beyond the vestibule made you feel as though you'd walked into a different dimension; it was one of the nicest parts of our wedding. My bridesmaids, Kathy(who was my best friend during my last year at school) and Jenny, were waiting on the tiny patch of grass outside the church, and I thought they looked lovely as their dresses were pretty, pastel, and empire-lined and, for Jenny, ideal because she was expecting Vanessa, our niece.

Even in my numbed-down state, as we approached the church, the enormity of the commitment I was about to make made me think that if it wasn't for the guests waiting inside, I would have turned around and fled back home. It was no reflection, of course, on my feelings for Mick, just I guess that I was so young, I'd only been twenty for just over a week and I'd never been the centre of attention before—ever, in my whole life. It was truly daunting. Too late, of course, so inside we went and when I saw Mick I was stunned, he looked so smart in a dark suit with a pink satin tie and matching carnation buttonhole, but his face, it was whiter than white. He had also felt overwhelmed when he got to the church and couldn't face going in straight away and asked the chauffeur to drive around the block to calm his nerves. Thank goodness for the other friendly face waiting for me at the altar, it belonged to the vicar who I knew well because he was a regular in the pub and jolly and reassuring. The ceremony was a haze and even though no video was taken of it, it didn't matter really, as we just wanted to be married, and everything else about the day was something we had to do so that we could. The reception was held in a handsome, Italianate-style Victorian Villa, one of many that were built for mill owners when Bradford was the world centre of the woollen industry. I remember very little about it other than we had tinned grapefruit with a bottled cherry on the top (minus the bottle of course) for starters.

David was not only the best man, but a bread delivery one too, and he handed me a French stick thinking it was extremely funny. I can still feel the embarrassment when he did, and my face instantly went the same deep red as a half-eaten cherry that was on the side of a nearby plate. Having got the reception out of the way, we felt it was two down and one to go, first the ceremony then the meal followed by drinks in the pub. We cadged a lift back to the pub with one of the guests and went into the smoke room, not exactly the ideal place to sit in a white wedding dress! Mick and I became instantly more at ease as the juke box was on and we felt we were back where we belonged—among the sound of the hits of the day. I couldn't wait to get out of that dress, so I slipped upstairs and changed into one I'd bought specially for the evening, which, at least, was pretty short, fashionable, and sheer, and I felt comfortable at last. That is until the Valium I'd taken that morning started to object to the sparkling wine I'd drunk during the toast, and I had to make a dash to the toilet just in time to say goodbye to my wedding breakfast. When I went back down again, the party could have been for any occasion as there was no longer an obvious bride in sight and I could mingle almost anonymously with the drinkers who appeared to forget why they were there. However, at least they were having a good time, you could tell by the ash trays that were beginning to overflow. Not only that, Morgan decided to liven things up a bit, much to everyone's delight, by playing the old upright piano. He instantly transformed into a typical pub pianist (think Les Dawson, minus the mistakes) and everyone gathered around him for a good old sing song. I was surprised by the number of oldies Morgan knew, or perhaps he was just improvising and the longer he played, the louder the singing, clapping, and cheering. After two hours of Honky Tonk and several pints of scotch and coke, he was well and truly done in and was just about to stop but couldn't because my Uncle Wilf wouldn't let him. He'd never come across anyone quite like or as insistent as Wilf who was a complete teddy bear really, but he had the voice of a grisly one. Unless they knew better, his voice alone would have made even an all-in wrestler run for cover—it was naturally loud, gruff, and demanding. Although he was a sheep in wolf's clothing, he was never one to be over empathetic ('that were wife's job'), Wilf knew what he liked and he liked Morgan's playing, thinking it was the best thing since his first sip of Barnsley Bitter. He kept insisting that Morgan played on—with his 'Come on luv, can thee play …'—and because he could, Morgan did, for another whole hour; he must have been exhausted when he made his way back to London the following day, having left every last ounce of his energy with my dear old uncle, because he'd sapped it all. By this time Mick and I felt it would be a good time to make a discreet retreat, so once we were sure that our guests were happy and fresh enough not to miss us, we escaped by taxi to our cottage. We were alone at last, well almost that is, apart from Merlin, who was my wedding gift to Mick.

Mick had always wanted a dog since his pet Timmy, who we refer to as a scruffy dog, because he had long unkempt hair, mysteriously disappeared when Mick was a child. I must have done something right at the newspaper as Mr Shearer's dog had recently had a litter of gorgeous Labrador puppies, he let me have Merlin at a greatly discounted price and it was a really kind gesture. While we were taking our vows, Merlin had been chomping his way through our newly laid vinyl kitchen floor and lower leg of a chair my Nana had been sitting on for over sixty years. She wasn't still on it that night, of course, she was back at the pub on her favourite bar stool, downing neat whisky with the best of them.

Mick lit the fire and we sat side by side in front of the blazing coal as he uncorked a bottle of champagne. We were relieved, as at last we were not only alone, but married—it was such a romantic moment. Not wanting our wedding day to end, we stayed in front of the fire until the embers died down, naturally wondering where life would take us. Merlin, by that time, had got impatient in the dining room and started to whine so I went to let him out. He looked sheepish and I realised why, when I saw that he'd knocked over a box with all of the Love Affair's singles in it and they were scattered on the floor. He'd been chewing them, and they were covered in drool and deep scratches, making every label almost illegible. I couldn't help thinking that Merlin's handywork was rather symbolic in that our long years of waiting to be together were finally gone, just like the writing on those records.

That was the first evening of our new life as man and wife, it was over fifty years ago and when we celebrated our golden wedding anniversary, Mick rewrote the words of his favourite composition and dedicated them to me , not the blues this time, but an uplifting ear worm of a song called, 'Christmas Dreams'. Looking to the future once more, my now, no-longer-'secret' mission, will hopefully achieve its goal in contributing towards helping children everywhere to be confident and caring. As future caretakers of this world, they will then be able to make sure it is loving and wonderful, just like the happy marriage that Mick and I have been so very fortunate enough to share, best described perhaps, as our very own 'Everlasting Love'.

CHRISTMAS DREAMS

Written, Sung, and Recorded by Mick Jackson 2021

Christmas dreams
That fill my head with such magic schemes
It seems clear to me
That you and I were just meant to be
You see ... (Repeat)

Looking now into your eyes
It is clear that we should be together
It is really no surprise
Our Christmases will surely last forever

Christmas Dreams etc.,

Looking back throughout the years
Each Christmas brings us ever even closer
Sharing all our hopes and fears
Our love is like a winter roller coaster ...

Christmas Dreams etc.

APPENDIX

The Love Affair's Discography

1967 February:	'She Smiled Sweetly'/ 'Satisfaction Guaranteed'	Decca F12558
1967 December:	'Everlasting Love'/ 'Gone Are the Songs of Yesterday'	CBS 3125
1968 April:	'Rainbow Valley'/'Someone Like Me'	CBS 3366
1968 August:	'A Day Without Love'/'I'm Happy'	CBS 3674
1969 February	'One Road'/'Let Me Know'	CBS 3994
1969 July:	'Bringing On Back the Good Times'/ 'Another Day'	CBS 4300
1969 October:	'Baby I Know'/ 'Accept Me for What I Am'	CBS 4631
1970 February:	'Lincoln County'/'Sea of Tranquillity'	CBS 4780
1970 May:	'Speak of Peace, Sing of Joy'/'Brings My Whole World Tumbling Down'	CBS 5017
1971 February:	'Wake Me I Am Dreaming'/ 'That's My Home'	Parlophone R5887

Albums

| 1968 December: | *The Everlasting Love Affair* | CBS 63416 |
| 1971 September: | *New Day—LA* | CBS 64109 |

There have been numerous compilation albums mixing together various 'A' and 'B' sides and album tracks, for example *Love Affair Everlasting Hits*, *Love Affair: The Best of the Good Times*, and *Love Affair No Strings*.

Mick Jackson's Discography

1969	'Out of Confusion/'Igginbottom' LP	SML105 Remastered Cherry Red Records Ltd www.cherryred.co.uk

Albums

2015	*69 ... one more time* 'A Better Way/Black Cat' 'Sixth Form Love Sick Blues' 'Win, Don't Crash/Deirdre' 'One Road' plus '69 One More Time'	www.69onemoretime.com iTunes/Facebook/ Spotify/YouTube
2016	*69 ... Live In Concert* 'Another Way to Die/6th Form Love Sick Blues' 'Watcha Gonna Do/Black Cat/Better Way' 'Voodoo Chile/Summertime Blues/Tobacco Road' 'Black Coffee/I Don't Need No Doctor' 'Bad to the Bone/Heartbreak Hotel'	www.69music.co.uk iTunes/Facebook/ Spotify/YouTube

EP

2018	*69 New ... Everlasting Love* 'Everlasting Love/Sunlight Dreams' 'Mr. Pocket/Speak of Peace'	www.69music.co.uk iTunes/Facebook/ Spotify/YouTube

Singles

2018	'New Everlasting Love' By 69	www.69music.co.uk iTunes/Facebook/ Spotify/YouTube
2021	'Christmas Dreams' The Mick Jackson Band	Bacon Empire Publishing iTunes/Facebook/ Spotify/YouTube

69 are …	Mick Jackson—bass guitar, lead vocals
	Dave Johnson—lead guitar, backing vocals
	Al Harnby—drums
The Mick Jackson Band are …	Mick Jackson—bass guitar, lead vocals
	Dave Johnson—lead guitar-backing vocals
	Mo Bacon—drums

Patricia Jackson's Discography

Audio Bedtime Stories (2021)

Available now in Apple App Store (iPhone):-
For your child:-

SOS Sleep Well
SOS Healthy Eating child
SOS Separation child's Fear
SOS Separate Parents
SOS Your Child's Bedwetting

SOS Confidence
SOS child's Fear Of The Dark
SOS child Being Bullied
SOS child Good Manners

Coming soon in Apple App Store (iPhone) (Titles may change slightly)
For your child:-

SOS Enjoy School
SOS Separate Parents
SOS Feeling Unwell
SOS Morning Stress

SOS Give Up Dummy (Pacifier)
SOS Car Travel
SOS Feeling Insecure
SOS Feeling left out

It is intended that all the child SOS audio apps will be available soon in Google Play Store (Android)

Stories Overcome Stress—Audio downloads for adults
Available now in Apple App Store (iPhone) and Google Play Store (Android)

SOS Lose Weight
SOS Overcome Stress

SOS Stop Smoking
SOS Happy Marriage (iPhone)

SOS Sleep Well (effective for grown-ups who don't mind listening to a child's audio)

Coming soon for grown-ups in Apple App Store (iPhone) and Google Play Store (Android)

SOS Sleep

Audio Book—Written & Narrated by Patricia

2022	*Everlasting Love and Love Affair*	A pop idol's life and secret 'rock' romance in the swinging 60s Audible.co.uk